African Social Movement Learning

International Issues in Adult Education

Series Editor

Peter Mayo (*University of Malta, Msida, Malta*)

Editorial Advisory Board

Stephen Brookfield (*University of St Thomas, Minnesota, USA*)
Waguida El Bakary (*American University in Cairo, Egypt*)
Budd L. Hall (*University of Victoria, BC, Canada*)
Astrid von Kotze (*University of Western Cape, South Africa*)
Alberto Melo (*University of the Algarve, Portugal*)
Lidia Puigvert-Mallart (*CREA-University of Barcelona, Spain*)
Daniel Schugurensky (*Arizona State University, USA*)
Joyce Stalker (*University of Waikato, Hamilton, New Zealand/Aotearoa*)
Juha Suoranta (*University of Tampere, Finland*)

VOLUME 29

The titles published in this series are listed at *brill.com/adul*

African Social Movement Learning

The Case of the Ada Songor Salt Movement

By

Jonathan Langdon

BRILL
SENSE

LEIDEN | BOSTON

Cover illustration: Artwork by Moses Adjei

All chapters in this book have undergone peer review.

The Library of Congress Cataloging-in-Publication Data is available online at http://catalog.loc.gov

ISSN 2352-2372
ISBN 978-90-04-42206-3 (paperback)
ISBN 978-90-04-42207-0 (hardback)
ISBN 978-90-04-42208-7 (e-book)

Copyright 2020 by Koninklijke Brill NV, Leiden, The Netherlands.
Koninklijke Brill NV incorporates the imprints Brill, Brill Hes & De Graaf, Brill Nijhoff, Brill Rodopi, Brill Sense, Hotei Publishing, mentis Verlag, Verlag Ferdinand Schöningh and Wilhelm Fink Verlag.
All rights reserved. No part of this publication may be reproduced, translated, stored in a retrieval system, or transmitted in any form or by any means, electronic, mechanical, photocopying, recording or otherwise, without prior written permission from the publisher.
Authorization to photocopy items for internal or personal use is granted by Koninklijke Brill NV provided that the appropriate fees are paid directly to The Copyright Clearance Center, 222 Rosewood Drive, Suite 910, Danvers, MA 01923, USA. Fees are subject to change.

This book is printed on acid-free paper and produced in a sustainable manner.

Salt for Life (artwork by Moses Adjei)

CONTENTS

Foreword *Anne Harley*	ix
Acknowledgements	xiii
List of Illustrations	xv
Chapter 1: Introduction	1
Historical Legitimacy of Africa as a Unit of Analysis	1
Social Movement and Social Movement Learning Studies	1
Social Movement Learning in Ghana – A Gathering of Voices	3
A History of Movements Defending Communal Access	6
Moving with the Ada Movement	7
Structure of the Book	13
Chapter 2: African Social Movements and Learning	17
Social Movement Studies and Subaltern Movements	19
Social Movement Learning and Critical Adult Education	21
1st Wave: African Liberation Movements	27
From the 2nd Wave of Democratization to the 3rd Wave of Contemporary Struggles	31
2nd Wave: African Democracy Movements	32
3rd Wave: Protest Movements in Contemporary Times	34
Moving from Africa to Ada	38
Chapter 3: Ada Movement Knowledge Production, Questioning National Development	41
National Development and Neoliberalism as Topographies of Power	42
The Adas, a Salt People from the Start	44
Ada Songor Focus of British Colonial Divide and Rule Tactics in Area	47
Ghana Emerges from the Gold Coast Colony, but the Post Independence State Promotes the National over the Local	49
Adas Dispossessed, Fight back through Legal, Political and Physical Means	51
A New Dispossession on the Horizon Means New Tactics Are Needed	64
Resisting the National Development and Neoliberal Narrative	72

CONTENTS

Chapter 4: Stories and Restorying as Social Movement Learning — 77
    Literacy of Struggle — 78
    Challenging How the Root Causes of Struggle Are Framed — 80
    The Thumbless Hand, the Chameleon, and the Dog — 84
    Challenging Male Dominance through Rooted Restorying — 97
    The Struggle of the Songor Salt People Book Project — 100
    Restorying Struggle as Learning — 108

Chapter 5: The Pedagogy of Creative Dissent: Using Creativity to Broaden and Deepen Social Movement Learning — 111
    Introduction — 111
    Creative Dissent and Pedagogy — 112
    Creativity, Learning and Democratizing Knowledge — 120
    Overlapping Registers of "Spreading" Learning and Creativity — 136

Chapter 6: Conclusion — 139
    African Subaltern Movements Thinking and Acting on Their Future — 140
    African Subaltern Social Movements Producing Potential — 143
    Creativity and Non-Violent Activism — 146
    Where the Movement Is Headed Now, or the Latest Area of Learning — 148
    Learning in, through and to Struggle — 149

Appendix A: Timeline of Events Surrounding Songor — 153

References — 159

Index — 165

FOREWORD

Since I first encountered Jonathan Langdon's writing about the struggle in Ada, Ghana, a number of years ago, I have considered his work to be some of the most important in the growing field of social movement learning. *African Social Movements and Learning: The Case of the Ada Songor Salt Movement* is a further significant contribution.

The book tells the story of a particular struggle, in a particular context – that of a movement defending communal access to the Songor, West Africa's largest salt yielding lagoon and the livelihood of over 60 000 people. Over a period of decades, the lagoon has been subjected to a sustained process of neoliberal-inspired 'development,' exacerbated by the discovery of oil in Ghana in 2008 since salt is a crucial additive in petrochemical processes. State-led granting of concessions to private companies, the proposed removal of communities living around the Songor, and the steady, insidious enclosure of the commons of the lagoon through 'atsiakpo' (small private salt pans created on the edges of the lagoon by local and national elites), have all been contested by a movement that has shifted and morphed over time.

Whilst the book focuses on this particular struggle, rooted in a particular context, Langdon situates this within broader social movement learning theory, particularly the learning of subaltern social movements (SSMs) in an African context. In this, he draws on the intellectual work he and I have done together with activists involved in SSMs on this continent (Harley et al., forthcoming). We argue that SSMs display a number of characteristics, including that they are:

- Rooted in grassroots organising, and remain accountable to that over time. Because of this, they are always fluid and shifting, responding to the burning issues and analysis of their members.
- Integrally connected to people's livelihoods and being (i.e. including the social, creative and emotional work of being human).
- Connected to a strong sense of identity, but an identity which is not absolute but porous – i.e. one rooted in the singularity and temporality of experience, but which goes beyond this, beyond identitarian politics.
- Non-partisan, in the sense of beyond political parties, but nevertheless fundamentally political.
- Ontological spaces of learning – i.e. it is in their very nature to think their experience and their politics.

Langdon uses this theoretical framing to consider the Songor struggle. He also situates it within the waves of social movement protest across the African continent over time, from the national liberation movements of the 1940s to 1960s, to the

FOREWORD

redemocratisation movements of the 1980s and 1990s, the mass protests which have characterised the last decade. Thus, the struggle for the Songor is situated both theoretically and historically.

Langdon argues that we should use three lenses in thinking about social movement learning – we need to consider learning *in* struggle (a relatively long-term process); learning *through* struggle (in which heightened moments of engagement can reveal important insights); and learning *to* struggle. Each of these lenses is employed in considering the case of the Ada salt movement. Whilst, as he discusses in detail, members of the movement have learned in and through the struggle, and in the process, learned to struggle more effectively, critically we can also learn from the case of the Ada salt movement. One essential learning is that organic, grassroots, subaltern movements have the greatest capacity to resist neoliberal globalisation. This is precisely because they emerge in struggles that cut across livelihoods and identities, thus resisting both stultifying identitarian politics and narrow self-interest. A second learning is the necessity of remaining dialogue-based, ensuring that processes and thinking are collectively owned, rather than the domain of a small group that knows what is best for all. This allows subaltern movements to reinvent themselves as their context (and hence their struggle) shifts.

The thinking of African SSMs such as the Songor Salt Movement is also profoundly important in helping us think an emancipatory politics; a point which is made by Michael Neocosmos in his recent award-winning book, *Thinking Freedom in Africa: Toward a theory of emancipatory politics.* Neocosmos seeks to answer the question, "How can we begin to think human emancipation in Africa today?" He constructs a careful argument, in which he identifies essential elements of an emancipatory politics, using as a point of departure that everyone thinks (although not always). Politics, he stresses, is about thought; and to be emancipatory, it must be collective, and it must be related to our doing – it must be practical. In other words, "politics is a collective thought practice." Emancipatory politics is also always universal, although it always emanates from a particular place. It is dialectic; and it is excessive. By this, Neocosmos means that emancipatory politics transcends the particular, it goes beyond the expressive (identity, difference, interest). Neocosmos considers a number of examples of emancipatory sequences from the African continent and diaspora over a period of centuries. He warns that emancipatory political thought is ultimately fragile, and hard to sustain.

The Ada story, as this book shows, is a complex one; and it is presented here with all its contradictions. Neocosmos says that "whereas academics may be able to detach themselves from a political practice, activists cannot fully avoid the contradictions between subjectivities as expressions of place and their excess: their 'expressions of place' because all rebellion is socially located, and 'excessive thought' because it sometimes consciously outstrips its location. It is only through gradually resolving these contradictions on a continuous basis that a process of politicisation and emancipation can be sustained" (2016, p. xxv).

FOREWORD

It is in relation to this that the struggle for the Songor, and this book, is so important. One of the book's most important, and original, contributions is the bringing together of social movement learning and storying. Langdon argues that it is through a process of restorying that the Ada movement produces knowledge – revisiting stories, and editing them based on their learning *in* and *through* the struggle. He shows how the movement does this, in a collective, dialogic process. The story of the Ada salt movement, and its process of restorying, reveals the collective, ongoing thinking of the movement, as it shifts over time. The story is a story about the nature of this thinking, about the broadening of the idea of who can think, and how good that thinking is – how, in particular, the thinking of women comes to be both acknowledged, and increasingly pivotal, in the collective thinking of the movement. The struggle is rooted in a particular place, in a particular time, related to people's lived experiences and livelihoods; and yet it is, in Neocosmos' terms, excessive – it goes beyond identity, difference, interest, in the movement's absolute insistence on 'Songor for all.' The origin stories, and the restorying of these and development of new stories, reveals how this process happens. Perhaps most critically, in terms of emancipatory politics, the Ada salt struggle continues as an emancipatory project; possibly because the process of restorying is precisely the process of gradually resolving the contradictions between expressions of place and excessive thought.

Ben Okri, in *A way of being free*, says "Homo fabula: we are storytelling beings," and "we are part human, part stories." On an ontological level, then, storying and restorying is part of the continuous process of becoming. Okri also says, "stories are always a form of resistance," and "politics is the art of the possible; creativity is the art of the impossible." By looking at the process of storying in the learning and knowledge creation of the Ada Songor salt movement, Jonathan Langdon provides us not only with a rich account of learning in and through struggle, but also a space from which we can learn *to* struggle in profoundly emancipatory ways.

Anne Harley
Pietermaritzburg, South Africa

ACKNOWLEDGEMENTS

This work is the product of many people's efforts. It is first and foremost the product of the effort of those at the forefront of the struggle in Ada, Ghana to return the Songor to its rightful place as the foundation of livelihood for all in Ada: the Yihi Katsɛmɛ, the Ada Songor Advocacy Forum, the Ada Salt Cooperative, and others. It is also the result of the solidarity and support of community broadcasters at Radio Ada, who have carried the voice, analysis and struggle of the marginalized in the Ada area since the station went on the air in 1998.

It comes from the efforts of the many research assistants who have worked on this research over the last 10 years, within the Ada movements, within Radio Ada, and undergraduate and graduate students coming from St. Francis Xavier University in Canada, as well as other Canadian universities. It is also the result of the many colleagues in the social movement learning and critical development studies communities, such as Anne Harley who wrote the foreword to the book, who have encouraged this work over the years.

It was also made possible through the ongoing support by Canada's Social Science and Humanities Research Council (SSHRC) through the provision of a Standard Research Grant and an Insight Grant for this work.

Finally, I must acknowledge my family, including my mother and father-in-law who helped start Radio Ada, for their inspiration and support in this work. In this sense, this work is the product and result of many hands, and credit goes to all of them for helping me "outdoor" this text. That said, however, ultimately any limitations of the text are carried by me alone.

ILLUSTRATIONS

FIGURES

1.1.	ASAF meeting in Radio Ada's open air studio (photo credit: Nii Obodai)	11
1.2.	Woman winning salt the communal way (photo credit: Nyani Quarmyne)	12
1.3.	Atsiakpo individual salt pans in the Songor (photo credit: Nyani Quarmyne)	12
3.1.	Map of Songor (from ASAF, 2016)	42
3.2.	Memorial Statue of Margaret Kuwornu (photo credit: Nyani Quarmyne)	57
3.3.	Ada Songor Advocacy Forum members, including Akpetiyo Lawer, third from right, Mary Akuteye, first on right, and Jane Ocansey, second from left (photo credit: Nii Obodai)	69
3.4.	Women marching in 2012 Asafotufiami demonstration	71
3.5.	Yihi Katsɛmɛ Manifesto, 2016	74
4.1.	The Story of the Songor Lagoon Tapestry, by women's leadership in ASAF (photo credit: Nii Obodai)	91
4.2.	Jane Ocansey shares the women's Songor Tapestry story with a group of Ada children (photo credit: Leah Jackson)	92
4.3.	Woman in Toflokpo shares her thoughts on book draft while Radio Ada producer captures her statement for later broadcast (photo credit: Rachel Garbary)	104
5.1.	Yihi Katsɛmɛ demonstrating in Sege (photo credit: Noah Dameh)	121
5.2.	Dance Drama advertisement (photo credit: Liliona Quarmyne)	124
5.3.	Leaf/stick/stone analysis, done at Radio Ada (photo credit: Jonathan Langdon)	134
5.4.	Leaf/stick/stone analysis, done at one of the Songor communities (photo credit: Erica Ofoe)	135

TABLE

2.1.	African movements	19

CHAPTER 1

INTRODUCTION

HISTORICAL LEGITIMACY OF AFRICA AS A UNIT OF ANALYSIS

I seek neither to set the African experience apart as exceptional and exotic nor to absorb it in a broad corpus of theory as routine and banal. For both, it seems to me, are different ways of dismissing it. In contrast, I try to underline the specificity of the African experience, or at least a slice of it. This is not an argument against comparative study but against those who would dehistoricize phenomena by lifting them from context, whether in the name of abstract universalism or of an intimate particularism, only to make sense of them by analogy. In contrast, my endeavour is to establish the historical legitimacy of Africa as a unit of analysis. (Mamdani, 1996, p. 13)

Social movements in Africa are understudied. Studies of learning in these movements, or of the knowledge these movements generate, are even more scant (Hall & Turay, 2005). This book provides one effort to address this gap. And yet, as important as it is to speak to this gap, the way in which this gap is addressed is of equal if not perhaps greater importance. As Mamdani's (1996) note makes clear, this is especially true in the context of research on African phenomena. It can and has been argued (Rodney, 1973; Ferguson, 2006) that European colonialism's impact was greatest upon this continent. As such it is crucial that African phenomena are studied not through Eurocentric lenses, but on their own terms. This concern frames this book's contribution, presenting first, African social movements and their learning as important units of analysis, and then providing a rich case study of the learning and knowledge production of a particular African movement defending the artisanal communal salt production of the Songor Lagoon, located in Ada, Ghana. This book does not argue that the Ada case study speaks for all social movement learning in Africa. Rather, it is on its own terms, through its own analysis, a rich example of an African phenomenon – one example that will hopefully draw out others.

SOCIAL MOVEMENT AND SOCIAL MOVEMENT LEARNING STUDIES

In the chapter that follows this introduction, social movements and social movement learning in the African context are discussed in greater detail. Nonetheless, these terms need to be introduced here. The use of the term 'social movements' is both new and long-established in sociology. Marxist theorists, like Luxemburg

CHAPTER 1

and Gramsci (1971), looked at movement dynamics in order to articulate how revolutionary change might emerge. In contrast to this, more status quo sociologists of the past looked at social movements with suspicion, describing their potential to lead to mob rule (e.g. LeBon, 1896). In the African context, movement analysis was first popularly used to analyze independence and anti-colonial movements (e.g. Fanon, 1968; Nkrumah, 1973; Cabral, 1979). However, while acknowledging the importance of this early work, social movements have been very much taking on a new valence in recent decades, with the rise of new social movements in Europe and North America, as well as anarchist thinking, that has deeply influenced such contemporary global movements as the Occupy phenomenon (Hall, 2012). Climate change and its global impacts have facilitated the emergence of transnational social movements on an unprecedented scale (Kluttz & Walter, 2018). Many scholars have seen such movements as contesting the globalization of capitalist penetrations through a globalization from below (McNally, 2006). Other scholars have noted a difference between contemporary social movements, where some movements argue for social inclusion and challenge inequalities, while other movements insist on social exclusionary ends through various forms of fundamentalism (cf. McMichael, 2009). Still other scholars have worried about the potential dominance of Eurocentric co-optation of global movements to serve colonial ends (e.g. Choudry, 2010). The exploitation of First Nations and Indigenous peoples' voices is a perfect example of this (Tuck & Yang, 2012). Echoing this concern for co-optation, as well drawing on post-colonial subaltern studies theories (e.g. Guha, 1983; Spivak, 1989), a number of scholar-activists have called for movement embedded research that resists and contests Euro-american dominance in social movement theorizing (Kapoor & Choudry, 2010; Kapoor, 2008; English & Mayo, 2012).

This call for movement articulations of their own theories and realities is forcefully made in social movement learning discussions. Much like social movement theory, social movement learning (SML) has also been accused of Euro-american dominance (Kapoor, 2008). As an extension of critical adult education, SML focuses on learning from and learning in social movements (Holst, 2002). SML first began to be used as a concept with the emergence of new social movements, and an analysis of how their presence provoked learning in broader society and opened up the potential for shifts in social norms (Welton, 1993; Holford, 1995). At the same time, critical adult education has a long connection to worker and labour movements and their learning (Hall & Turray, 2006). SML analysis in this area focused on learning from social action and attempts to shift unequal material social relations (Foley, 1999). As recently as 2005, there have been calls for SML studies that look at the African context to examine how movements across the continent learn, as well as empirical studies that move away from simply theorizing SML (Hall & Turray, 2006). Both of these calls informed this current work, and it was also deeply influenced by those critiquing existing Euro-american dominated SML literature that places movements in theoretical boxes, rather than seeing them as the makers of their own theory, their own analytical tools (Choudry, 2010; Kapoor & Choudry, 2010; Kane, 2001;

INTRODUCTION

Harley, 2012). From this position emerges the focus of this current book to share a movement articulated analysis of social movement learning in an African case study context – that of the Songor Lagoon in Ada, Ghana.

SOCIAL MOVEMENT LEARNING IN GHANA – A GATHERING OF VOICES

Beginnings matter (Chamberlin, 2003). Before elaborating the structure of this book, I want to honour and foreground a number of the voices of those who frame the analysis that follows. While I cannot bring them all in here, it is important to acknowledge these colleagues and other activists in Ghana whose knowledge, experience, and analysis forms the basis of my understanding of social movement activism and learning in Ghana. This understanding, and the way in which it emerged, provides an important background to the Ada study. While I have published and presented with many of these colleagues, this text represents my own gathering of these learnings – therefore any mistakes must be considered my own.

Alhassan Adams, a long time Ghanaian anti-water-privatization organizer, has described movements such as the one in Ada as "organic, or unbranded" (Langdon, 2009). By this he means the movement is rooted in and emerges naturally from people's defence of their livelihood and their cultural identities, but has not become a permanent fixture, an institution with a brand name. Adams made this observation during the participatory analysis stage of a study I conducted in 2008 on social movement learning in Ghana since the country's return to democracy in 1992. During this same participatory analysis session, held in Tamale in Ghana's Northern Region, Adams, Coleman Agyeyomah, Tanko Ibrahim, Gifty Djah, Kofi Larweh, and myself all agreed that it is such unbranded movements that have the greatest capacity to contest globalization and its impacts in Ghana, as they are not only rooted in people's livelihoods and identities, but are also not institutionalized or captured by a static leadership. In other words, we concluded such movements are dialogue-based as opposed to strategy-based – their power comes from the groundswell of collective voices, and the process of learning through action that emerges. As will be seen in the pages that follow, the Ada movement has changed names several times, based on the nature and leadership of the struggle at a given time.

Given how this study set up the research discussed in this current book, a bit more should be said about it. The six people mentioned above formed a participatory research (PR) group that analysed 22 interviews of Ghanaian social movement activist educators, and looked specifically at social movement learning in the period since Ghana's return to democracy in 1992. That said, one of the first changes made to the study by the PR group was to focus on the period in the lead up to re-democratization, as much of the learning in the democratic era had antecedent connections to this previous period (Langdon, 2009). In addition to exploring learning from unbranded, or organic movements, such as the one in Ada, we also looked at other Ghanaian movements – the Women's Movement, the People with Disability Movement, the Anti-mining Movement, and the Democratization Movement itself. As part of the

CHAPTER 1

focus on the pre-democratization period, we included the socialist movements of the later 1970s and early 1980s.

Three key ideas from this study emerged that frame the point of departure of this book, and form the basis of a Ghanaian-framed typological approach to movement learning analysis. These three key ideas form the basis of the logic of this current study, as the work with the Ada movement is a direct extension of this PR group's work, and of the analysis it produced. The first of these ideas was shared at the outset of this section, namely that it is unbranded and organic movements such as the Ada movement that have the greatest capacity to resist neoliberal globalization in Ghana (Langdon, 2010). This is because they are rooted in people's livelihoods and identities (blurring the line between material and identity-based movement theories). They also tend to resist becoming institutionalized, and dominated by a core leadership that decides on the strategy without consultation of the larger movement (Langdon, 2009). Hence they remain dialogue-based, reinventing themselves as the challenges they face change. This distinction between dialogue-based and strategic-based is the second main learning of the PR group. These two typologies emerged from the PR group's analysis of how movements continue to learn and adapt through dialogue, or become static and strategic in nature, where only a core few have the know-how to determine what is the best course of action. Strategic movements are likely more effective at making policy change, but also run the risk of alienating support on the ground. Dialogue-based movements are effective at keeping momentum alive, and ensuring movement processes and thinking are collectively owned, but may not be able to react immediately to unfolding events as quick decisions are not easily collectively-made. These typologies are constantly in flux, and are not in themselves rigid frames. They rather represent heuristic devices for discerning differences in outcomes and methods of Ghanaian movements over time. Finally, this study articulated a third idea that began with an engagement with Foley's (1999) concept of "learning in struggle" – discussed more fully in the next chapter. While a useful lens through which to look at movement learning as something dynamic, something in motion, our PR group did not feel Foley's concept had enough nuance to capture the different ways in which this learning in movements was happening. As such, the PR group described learning *in* struggle as a long-term process of learning through social action. To this they added the process of learning *through* struggle – the incidental learning that came from heightened moments of engagement, such as at a demonstration or through a specific campaign. This type of learning often reveals people's true intentions as the tension of conflict makes them pick sides and take action. It also reveals who is an adversary and who is an ally – what Michael Newman (1994) calls "defining the enemy." Finally, the group articulated a third learning lens, learning *to* struggle, where movement theorizing and internal pedagogy on teaching how to struggle can be explored. The overall framework of this study, as well as these three lenses in particular have since been used by others analysing Ghanaian social movement learning (cf. Anyidoho & Gariba, 2016).

INTRODUCTION

It was during the course of this study that I first met with activists who have been working on Ada Songor issues for a long time, and this was my entry point for the work that follows. As will be discussed further in a moment, the Ada Songor is West Africa's largest salt yielding lagoon, and has been the site of artisanal communal salt production for hundreds of years. Kofi Larweh, former coordinator of the local community radio station, Radio Ada, described the situation this artisanal production was facing to the participatory research group in Tamale, and organized a series of meetings for us to go deeper into the situation. These meetings led to an invitation for our group to work with these activists on the Songor cause. Radio Ada was both the host and facilitator of this conversation, and ended up playing a leading role in mediating the participatory action research process that emerged from these first conversations in 2008.

This study wasn't, however, my first visit to Ghana, nor to the Songor Lagoon. After spending a number of years of my childhood in East Africa, I have spent much of my adult life living in Ghana and working on Ghanaian social and political issues. It was in 2004, in the lead up to the 2004 national election, that I visited Ada and the Songor in my role as research officer for the Tamale-based Institute for Policy Alternatives. At the time, the Institute was conducting a community-based participatory evaluation of government services called "Community Voices" (Gariba & Langdon, 2005). During this first time in the Songor Lagoon area, the power of community radio to hold local governance to account became clear to me, as was the willingness of Songor community members to speak out on issues. In this sense I have become aware of and engaged in Songor work gradually since 2004. In 2010 I secured a small grant to open up a space to put together a collective research proposal and then in 2011 begin a three-year study of social movement learning in the Songor. This three-year grant led to an additional five-year grant continuing and deepening the research. The details of this interlinked research emergence process are shared below, but it is the participation and mutually-owned nature of this process that has led Kofi Larweh and I to label this research approach as "moving with the movement" (2015).

Thus over the past nine years movement activist colleagues, Radio Ada members and myself have been engaged in a participatory research case study of movement learning in Ada. Before turning to introduce the Ada context, as well as share the methodology of this work, it is worth spending a moment further emphasising why a case study of the Ada salt movements is important. Adams, in our Tamale discussions, noted the relevance of the Ada case for many activists in Ghana. Agyeyomah echoed this when he described how crucial it was to focus on movements defending livelihoods in the face of globalized expropriation. From a critical perspective, the issue of voice in the way in which resources come to be managed, or mismanaged, is a crucial one – who wins, who loses, who bears the costs, who reaps the rewards, and whose voice is heard above all others. This book aims to capture the dynamics of this dilemma around the Songor, the issue of voice in decision-making, and the way in

CHAPTER 1

which people organize themselves to exert some control over what is happening with this precious salt resource. The central variable in this dynamic, though, is learning, especially learning through social action and struggle. This is not a static tale, but rather a tale of people on the move, of efforts of accumulation by dispossession, and efforts to resist this accumulation and rather counter it with collective and communal management strategies. The case of the struggle for the Songor also helps this study present an African social movement case in a rural context – something hardly found in the literature. It also represents a rare feature in that the movement, and some of its learning and knowledge production has been documented in the past. These reasons make it a crucial contribution to social movement learning studies, and especially to social movement learning studies in Africa.

A HISTORY OF MOVEMENTS DEFENDING COMMUNAL ACCESS

In a recent publication on Ghana's salt industry, the Third World Network-Africa (TWN-A) (2017) notes the importance of the Songor Lagoon to Ghana's salt production, and also notes the overwhelming presence, as well as potential of artisanal salt miners in the sector. Despite this potential, the Government of Ghana focus in the sector is on large scale mining companies, echoing its approach in other sectors of the minerals economy, such as gold. The TWN-A study documents how tensions between large scale and artisanal salt miners in the Keta Lagoon, near Ada, led to demonstrations in 2017, and to state violence in response. At least one person was killed by police gunfire. At a forum at Sogakope, in May 2018, the current realities of Keta brought back bitter memories to the Ada movement members present, as they recollected when similar tensions between artisanal salt winners (as they are called in the Songor) and companies led to killing of Margaret (Maggie) Kuwornu, an innocent pregnant woman, by a stray police bullet on May 17th, 1985. Similar stories of tension and state sanctioned violence against artisanal miners are pervasive in other mineral sectors, such as gold (Hilson, 2012). The activism and organizing of the Ada movements has meant the Songor does not currently face the same situation as Keta, but this prospect remains on the horizon. Ada's history of struggle, and current organizing, is all that keeps it at bay. This book shares this history, the current effort, and the learning that has led to this current situation.

The Songor Lagoon is situated along the Gulf of Guinea, near the Volta Estuary. The Lagoon has been the site of solar evaporation artisanal communal salt production for over 400 years. Ada salt is well known throughout West Africa, with a reputation going back to the salt routes that preceded the slave trade (Amate, 1999). Salt winning is a crucial part of the livelihood of the roughly 60,000 people living in the 45 contiguous communities that surround the Lagoon, along with fishing and farming (Dangme East District Assembly, 2012). The Ada identity is intrinsically tied to salt production and to the Lagoon, so much so that being able to speak the language, Dangme, is equated to eating salt. (Langdon & Larweh, 2017). For women in Ada, the importance of the salt Lagoon is even more pronounced, as it has been

INTRODUCTION

the historic source of economic independence, and a source of household financial security (ASAF, 2016).

The different iterations of the social movement that has emerged in the Ada area to defend communal access to the Lagoon began when the natural flooding pattern of the Volta Estuary was interrupted by the building of the Volta Hydroelectric Dam in 1965 (Government of Ghana, 1986). After this, the Lagoon suffered several years without salt formation. With no help forthcoming from the state to contend with this challenge, some local traditional authorities allowed companies to gain concessions in the Lagoon, which one of the companies promptly turned into an almost total control of the resource – dispossessing local artisanal salt winners in the process. A period of legal activism ensued. After a revolutionary change in government in 1981, a people's movement emerged, which in Ada then turned into a cooperative of salt winners. The use of state agents (police, military) to exert one company's claim against this cooperative resulted in Maggie's death. Her death led to a commission of inquiry that saw the artisanal salt winners as an important element in the salt industry that should not be prevented from winning salt (Government of Ghana, 1986). A Master Plan was drawn up to balance small and large scale use of the Lagoon (Government of Ghana, 1991), and a law, PNDC 287, was enacted to legislate this plan (Government of Ghana, 1992).

After this victory, the Adas waited and waited for the Plan to be implemented, but democratic government after democratic government came and went without putting it into action. As the years passed, this neglect gave unscrupulous interests within and outside Ada an opening to create individual salt pans, undermining the artisanal communal winning process. Called Atsiakpo, these salt pans represented a new threat to the livelihood of many Adas, especially women living around the Lagoon.

With this threat another Ada movement emerged. The Ada Songor Advocacy Forum (ASAF) built on the sporadic activism of the 1990s and 2000s, and in collaboration with Radio Ada developed a concerted strategy to both stop Atsiakpo, and prevent secret Government plans to undermine PNDC Law 287. As the years progressed, though, the women within ASAF began to feel they bore the brunt of the livelihood impact, and the brunt of the activism actions. As such, they began moving towards establishing their own association within this movement, finally forming the Ada Songor Salt Women's Association, better known as Yihi Katsɛmɛ (Brave Women), in 2015. This book shares the story and the learning of these three dynamic iterations of struggle for the Songor Lagoon to remain a resource all can benefit from: (1) the 1980s struggle against company take-over; (2) the emergence of ASAF tackling government and local elite accumulation by dispossession; and (3) the rise of Yihi Katsɛmɛ, and women's leadership in tackling exclusion in the lagoon.

MOVING WITH THE ADA MOVEMENT

In studying these movement iterations and their learning, the research shared in the pages that follow used a methodology that "moved with the movement" (Langdon &

CHAPTER 1

Larweh, 2015). This was possible because the research was grounded in participatory action research approaches. Participatory and collaborative research approaches in general, and PAR in particular, have been identified as being important and synergistic methods for studying social movement learning (SML) (Hall & Turray, 2006). Yet, the way these approaches are framed and, ultimately, constituted has deep implications on the nature of the collaboration: whether, for instance, it replicates extractive forms of research that mine movements for data, or parallels and reinforces movement processes and deepens movement reflections, leading to what Foley describes as a "complex ... basis for future strategies" (1999, p. 143). Key to this process of framing and constituting participatory research is the research design process. As Kane (2001) and Choudry and Kapoor (2009) note, it is the way research relationships are formed, and the way these relationships are embedded in movement-articulations that determine whether the research is positioned to be a synergistic addition to movement processes or an extractive process that serves only academic purposes.

Hall (2005) has written a reflective piece on the history of participatory action research and its connection with adult education. Similarly, Fals-Borda (2006) has written a reflective history of PAR and its connection with an anti-Eurocentric desire to stop the studying of exotized "others," and rather generate spaces of mutual meaning-making. And yet, Fals-Borda (2006) notes how participatory action research (PAR) – a term he coined – has become institutionalized in thousands of research bodies with very little acknowledgement of the Southern origin of the term. A similar point is made by Chambers (1993), in acknowledging that much of his work on participatory processes was inspired by Freire (1972) and other Southern thinkers. Fals-Borda further expresses a worry much more forcefully articulated by Jordan (2003) that PAR is being co-opted away from its desire to make research mutually constituted and owned by communities/groups/movements and researchers. Jordan (2003) notes how this co-optation, exemplified by the World Bank's adoption of the term, runs the risk of turning participatory action research processes designed to help marginalized communities gain better control over their own definition of reality, into a mere stabilizing process of "inclusion" without any substantive changes in power dynamics. Vincent (2012) has shown how this stabilizing version of participation is often used by those external to communities to construct apolitical decision-making groups that undermine histories of struggle – further evidence of the importance of working from within locally constituted movements.

Focusing on research with such movements, then, Hall and Turray (2006) reveal how integral participatory action research processes have been, and continue to be, for movement research in adult education circles. This stream of research, known as social movement learning (SML), has a strong tradition of PAR and, yet, as Walter (2007) has pointed out, the majority of these studies are dominated by Euro-american dichotomies drawn between Old Social Movement (Marxist and labour movements) and New Social Movement (identity-based movements, such as the LGBTQ2SIS+ movement) theories of organizing (cf. Finger, 1989; Holford, 1995; Holst, 2002). Speaking to this potential, Choudry and Kapoor (2010) have

INTRODUCTION

argued that participatory research, and PAR in particular, must be owned by the movements at the centre of social movement learning studies, rather than being used by academics – especially in the North – carrying out studies ultimately more concerned with extracting information than in responding to movement needs and priorities. Choudry and Kapoor (2009) note that the relationships that frame such research, along with the way in which the research is conceived (i.e. is it owned by the movement from the outset) is critical to avoid this type of extractive relationship. This echoes Fine (2007) and Fine et al. (2004) who have expanded on the importance of mutually-defined and owned participatory processes and goals, especially in contexts of struggle. These points in many ways echo some of the early proponents of PAR (e.g. McTaggart, 1991) who saw a deep ownership of the whole research process being the definition of participation, not a thin version that was either more concerned with academic outcomes, or in stabilizing participants through co-opted processes. Common to these early proponents was the idea of collective design.

This logic very much informed the framing of the study at the centre of this book. In fact, the collective framing of the design process led it to become a site of movement knowledge-generation and action. In this sense, the very design of the PAR became part of an emerging space of democratic knowledge production. The act of debating the design democratized knowledge about the context. Through movement meetings to design the research, more and more people came to know more and more about their resource struggle from each other, even as the radio station also took the lead in broadening this knowledge base through programs disseminating these discussions. The issue of whose knowledge counts also came into this, as women especially, and younger people who had generally been excluded from any planning processes in the past, devoured the emergent knowledge, and added their own voices and direct knowledge to the research design process. In fact, as the examples from the research shared below show, this open space not only facilitated the flourishing of a women's analysis and agenda, but also encouraged it to become the central analysis of the movement.

A crucial way that knowledge production within the movement has taken shape is through the generation of collective narratives of the struggle. This research has used the restorying of these narratives over time, and through reinterpretation of these stories by different elements within the movement as a dynamic way of documenting learning within the movement. Mattingly (1991) has established the importance of telling stories and believes that putting experience into narrative form can contribute to meaning-making processes and make participants aware of the every-day on deeper levels. Clandinin and Connelly (1991, 2000) and Karpiak (2000) suggest the telling and retelling of stories contributes to personal reflections and growth. This telling and retelling of stories has been linked to the narrative inquiry concept of restorying (Fitzclarence & Hickey, 2001; Mulholland & Wallace, 2003; Randall, 1996; Kenyon & Randall, 1997). Randall (1996) sees "restorying as the central process of transformative learning" (Rossiter, 2002, p. 4). In analyzing Randall's contribution, Rossiter (2002) notes that when individuals "externalize their own

CHAPTER 1

stories they are better able to locate and assess their own stories within the larger familial or cultural context" (p. 4). Restorying has been used to deepen learning around the story of individuals, but as Mulholland and Wallace (2003) note, there are many types of stories that can be restoried, including those that emerge from collectives such as movements. As will be shared in the chapters ahead, the use of story not only enabled a dynamic way of documenting movement learning, it also became an important component of movement strategy.

To give a picture of this research from a methodological point of view, the participatory action research design process took place in 2010, after initial conversations held in 2008 where the PR group was invited by Kofi Larweh and other members of the Ada movement to add Ada's story to the study of broader Ghanaian social movement learning (Langdon, 2009). This initial conversation led to a further invitation by movement members mentioned above to explore questions of learning in the movement, as well as emerging challenges, in a longer participatory action study. Thus, four meetings were held over the course of Ghana's 2010 wet season (June, July, and August) – the period when no salt could be collected and therefore the best time to discuss Songor issues. Each of the meetings was attended by 30 to 40 members of the movement (with roughly half coming from communities around the Songor Lagoon and half from the capital of the district). These meetings were entirely in Dangme (the Ada language) and were open-ended, with discussions of the research proposal quickly becoming only a minor part of the focus. Indicative of the democratic knowledge space that was central to this research, these four meetings became preoccupied not with what a future research process might look like, but rather with what were the multiple understandings people had of the issues confronting the Songor. Thus, the central question of the design process, "what themes and processes should frame a potential longer-term study of movement learning in the Ada movement?" was reconfigured to the question, "how do we achieve a similar and collectively determined understanding of what our struggle is today and how best to tackle it?" As an illustration of the way the process was movement owned from the outset, members of the movement leadership and Radio Ada opened the very first meeting not by stating why they had all gathered together, but rather by asking each person to share how they had come to be involved in the Songor struggle. This provoked lengthy discussions as to what the major problems facing the lagoon were, and what routes there might be to solve them – all embedded in people's mutual recognition of their knowledge and commitment to the cause. At another of these meetings, the third, virtually the entire time was spent discussing what people thought they were pushing for, and who should decide this. Though this was a discussion that has never entirely been resolved, as the movement maintains a crucial democratic internal tension, the consensus that day was that the movement should focus on defending communal access to the lagoon, and that this was something all Adas, not just those who live around the Songor have a stake in – and can therefore help defend. Though it was unbranded at first, it was later named Ada Songor Advocacy Forum (ASAF).

INTRODUCTION

Figure 1.1. ASAF meeting in Radio Ada's open air studio (photo credit: Nii Obodai)

These meetings were held in the open-air studio of the local community radio station, Radio Ada, and as such anyone passing could listen in. In the nine years of the PAR process that followed, this openness, and the fact that the participatory process began by mutually educating each other on how people understood the Songor context, made the actions of the movement, as well as the research that moved with it consistently able to preempt accusations that it was pushing a secret agenda. This was in stark contrast to the way local and national elite operated – a point that surfaced again and again as the reason ASAF and Radio Ada, and now the Yihi Katsɛmɛ should be trusted. In these eight years, every wet season would see a series of these open-ended reflective and mutual-education oriented meetings come about, both at the open air studio and in several of the Songor-surrounding communities. Focus groups of older men, older women, young men, young women, girls and boys would generate broad-based discussions of challenges facing the resource, and then would debate these views back in plenary. In all, it is our estimate that these participatory movement discussions on Songor issues engaged with roughly 8700 people over the last eight years (7200 people in community discussions, and 1500 at the open-air studio meetings). This is alongside the listening audience who would tune into the programs on the Songor that Radio Ada generated from these discussions and phone in with comments. Over the course of the nine years, through this open process, the research has been able to document the transformation of relationships and leadership within the movement, especially as the women within

CHAPTER 1

the movement began to assert their voices and lead the movement – becoming the Yihi Katsεmε (Brave Women). Capturing this dynamic process, driven by learning within the movement, underscores how this research "moved with the movement."

Figure 1.2. Woman winning salt the communal way (photo credit: Nyani Quarmyne)

Figure 1.3. Atsiakpo individual salt pans in the Songor (photo credit: Nyani Quarmyne)

INTRODUCTION

STRUCTURE OF THE BOOK

The next chapter takes the time to situate the Ada case in an African social movement context. Drawing a connection between independence movements and contemporary movements in three regions of the continent (North Africa, Sub-Saharan/West Africa, and Southern Africa), the chapter establishes a historical and a contemporary context for each of these regions with which the Ada case dialogues – thus establishing six movement contexts. Social movement learning is further developed through reference to these six movement discussions, thus responding to Mamdani's call that opened this introduction to situate African phenomena in African contexts. The chapter further connects movement learning in these six contexts to social movement learning theory. The end of the chapter elaborates a subaltern social movement learning lens that informs the way in which the Ada case is understood in the chapters that follow. Central to this lens is the way in which movements themselves describe and debate their actions and learnings – in other words, the ways in which movements think, learn and produce knowledge.

This knowledge production is the focus of Chapter 3, where the knowledge produced in the past and in the contemporary period of struggle concerning the Songor lagoon forms the basis through which the story of these struggles is told. It is through movement knowledge production that the movement story and history is framed. The Ada struggle's link to the pre-colonial, colonial and independence periods in Ghana is laid out. Of particular importance is the way in which one type of national development project, the Volta Hydroelectric Dam, had a deep negative impact on the Songor Lagoon, and how, through movement articulations, the Songor, and its history of communal access to salt, could represent a different form of national development than the mega project format that damaged the people of Ada's livelihood. And yet, despite this damage, the salt winners of Ada did not sit by when, in the 1980s, their lagoon was enclosed and turned into a corporate concession. They fought back, and managed to reclaim their resource. This chapter ends by describing the new struggle in the lagoon against dispossession by forces internal and external to the Ada area. It also introduces the most recent movement knowledge production that documents the current struggle of women, especially, to maintain the communal access of the past, and argues this communal approach is the way to make the Lagoon a healthy and a vibrant contributor to the nation now and into the future.

Chapter 4 looks at the strategy of the movement in Ada to make arguments, such as the importance of communal access as a contributor to national development, through the use of storytelling. These stories, their production, and their restorying over time provide a longitudinal window into learning in the movement. Two important stories that emerge through this chapter speak to the overall frame of this book. First, literacy is reconstituted in this chapter as being first and foremost something that emerges from struggle, and that being literate in this movement

CHAPTER 1

has nothing to do with being able to read and write, but rather means being versed in Ada's history of struggle, and the contemporary realities of life in the Songor. Second, this chapter reveals the deeply participatory learning process at the heart of the Ada movement, which both allows the movement to produce the knowledge used in Chapter 3, and adapt to new challenges as they come. The role of Radio Ada, the local community radio station, in keeping this dialogue open is noted here. However, the chapter also notes that this learning is sometimes ambiguous. Nonetheless, through the collective process of restorying, the movement has been able to adjust over time to meet emerging challenges with new and creative strategies.

This leads into Chapter 5, which focuses specifically on the current iteration of the Ada movement, the Yihi Katsɛmɛ, or "Brave Women" of the Songor. The chapter focuses on their use of creativity as both a learning technique for teaching and knowledge production within the movement, and as a popular education technique for outreach to the broader Ada, Ghanaian, and international audiences. In particular, it documents the use of song, art and theatre as mechanisms to learn, teach and create knowledge. As a result of the depth of the documentation of movement learning this chapter shares the moments when new creative strategies emerged through collective dialogue. The chapter ends by sharing how this creativity has culminated in the movement becoming visible on the international stage, when the Yihi Katsɛmɛ's songs and stories were shared at a side event at the first United Nations High Level meeting of the new Sustainable Development Goals.

The final chapter concludes by highlighting the emergent contributions the Ada movement case makes to understanding social movement generally and in an African context in particular. It points out how the way in which the Ada movement has restored itself over its many iterations reflects ongoing learning and theorizing through action. African movements of the subaltern thinking and acting of their own volition is clearly dangerous to those in power, as efforts have been made to discredit the Ada movement, as well as similar movements in other parts of the continent for challenging power from the basis of their lived experience and cultural identity. This thinking and acting based on their own analysis is part of what has led the most recent iteration of the movement to defy critics and not only challenge what is happening in their resource, but also the way in which decisions are made in Ada, and the role of women's voice in this process. In this sense, the current iteration of the Ada movement is prefiguring a future that is not a break from the past, but a restored reading of the past that recognizes women's importance in the story of the resource, and therefore in its future. The contribution of Radio Ada to the open way in which the movement has become a source of popular education and mobilization on the resource is also a crucial part of the concluding thoughts. Similarly, the recognition of the way in which the Ada struggle is embedded in a history of non-violent change in Ghana is also important – even while the decision of Adas, and particularly women around the Songor to stand up and take action is not to be overlooked. This movement, ultimately, is one of rural Ghanaians, and rural women most recently, who have stepped into a void of leadership, and who are struggling for a better situation for their communities and families. No one invited them to do this, they have taken on this task because others would not. Therefore, the movement needs to be seen for not just the results it has achieved in changing the situation in the Songor, but also for the potential it has opened for the struggle to continue by those inspired by the decision of movement members to step up, learn in, through and to struggle.

CHAPTER 2

AFRICAN SOCIAL MOVEMENTS AND LEARNING

In 1947, ten years before the Gold Coast colony of the British Empire gained its full independence and renamed itself Ghana – before this success was even a possibility – Kwame Nkrumah was buying a printing press in instalments (Nkrumah, 1973). Once the press was assembled, the man who would later become Ghana's first president began printing a daily one-page (front and back) newspaper. In it he recorded his ideas on ending British rule, and also used it to share rumours about those siding with the colonial edifice and against their fellow colonized. Despite Nkrumah's constrained movements at that time, this newspaper helped to organize the general strike that shut down the colony in 1950, after Ghanaian ex-servicemen were gunned down on February 24th, 1949, for demanding equal benefits to their European counterparts for the role they played in winning World War II. Through this general strike, Nkrumah had learned the power of distributing ideas, and giving people the space to make them their own. This precipitated his "Veranda Boy Revolution," where Nkrumah connected with and mobilized those figuratively and literally on the margins of colonial society. This mobilization enabled him to easily win the colony's first election of a legislative assembly in 1951 – where he went from political prisoner to Prime Minister – and set him on the course to uttering those famous words on March 6th, 1957, "At long last, the battle has ended! And thus, Ghana, your beloved country is free forever!" (Nkrumah, 1957).

These interlinked snippets of Ghana's history reveal that social movement organizing, and learning, are anything but new in the country, and indeed across the continent. Unfortunately, African movements, and movement learning, remain woefully understudied (Branch & Mampilly, 2015; Hall & Turray, 2006). This chapter introduces movement and movement learning on the continent as an important phenomena of study. In order to study them, however, one must be mindful of Mamdani's (1996) warning to avoid studying African phenomenon through analogy. As one of the few scholars to study African social movements in the 1990s (with Wamba Dia Wamba, 1995), Mamdani's warning carries particular weight. It is echoed by many other movement scholars who warn against the all-too-easy transposition of understandings from one context to another (Kapoor, 2008; English & Mayo, 2012). Branch and Mampilly (2015), in particular, echo this when looking specifically at protest movements in Africa. They argue that studying these protest movements:

CHAPTER 2

> Requires nuanced understanding of the social forces involved in protest so as to grasp the diverse transformations that collective action can bring about. It demands that those taking to the streets be contextualized within African political history and not be taken merely as representatives of universal economic or political identities. (Branch & Mampilly, 2015, p. 7)

Of particular focus to all of these scholars, then, is the contextual history of the movements being examined, and each movement's own articulations of its actions, analysis and learnings. This book is largely a product of these two thoughts.

In order to situate the Ada case study in an African political and historical context, this chapter begins by first developing the argument for a movement-centric approach to theorizing movement learning. Building on the work of others in this respect, the chapter lays out the framework for studying social movements and social movement learning, first, from the context within which they emerge, and, second, based on their own articulations and theorizing of this learning. In doing so, it touches upon broader trends in social movement studies and social movement learning literature, but does not make any claims to being an exhaustive delving into this terrain. In fact, this text makes a political choice to draw on subaltern studies, and those informed by it, to turn away from these broader discussions at a certain point and "narrowcast" – as is discussed in community radio – the particularities of the Ada case. This particular focus is scaffolded though, moving from broader discussions to a discussion of African social movements and movement learning. Although not exhaustive, it paints a backdrop that begins with the social movements that arose across the continent that were working to end colonialism and craft new nations to join the post-war world order. It is important to recognize this history as this period of struggles for independence was an incredible time of ideas about how the world could work from African perspectives. Many of the thinkers of these times, let alone the thoughts they brought forth from the struggle, continue to inform movements across the continent today. These independence movements include not only those of Ghana in the post war years, followed by Algeria in 1962, but also, for example, the more recent Zimbabwe liberation movement that led to the end of white rule in 1980 in this Southern African Nation.

Building on Branch and Mampilly's (2015) use of three waves of African protest movements, Table 2.1 illustrates how the chapter goes from the 1st wave of independence movements to draw on examples from the 2nd wave of democracy movements and 3rd wave of contemporary movements – some of which were part of larger shifts in geopolitics, and some of which were much more particular to a specific area. What is aimed for here is a sense of how each movement manifestation is grounded in particulars of that context – even if it is part of a larger shift – and a sense of how diverse African movement manifestations have been. The choice of these particular movements examples is driven by an ability in each to speak to social movement learning dynamics – a rarity across the continent. In doing so, I have tried to achieve some level of regional representation, with an independence-era and more

AFRICAN SOCIAL MOVEMENTS AND LEARNING

Table 2.1. African movements

	North Africa	Sub-Saharan Africa	Southern Africa
1st wave (African independence movements)	Algerian Independence movement	Ghanaian Independence movement	Zimbabwean liberation movement
2nd wave (African democracy movements		Ghana's 1990s Democracy movement	
3rd wave (recent African protest movements	Egypt's Tahrir Square and People's Spring movement		South Africa's Abahlali baseMjondolo movement

recent-era movement from each of the North, Sub-Saharan and Southern Africa regions. Before turning to this, though, I wish to first draw from social movement studies and then social movement learning literature in ways that are responsive to the phenomena in question.

SOCIAL MOVEMENT STUDIES AND SUBALTERN MOVEMENTS

Cabral understood the long tradition of resistance in Africa and its emergence in Guinea-Bissau as a response to Portuguese colonialism carried on from the early appearance of Portuguese traders and settlers through to the Portuguese pacification campaigns. This resistance assumed the form of overt spontaneous uprisings as well as passive resistance such as tax evasion, reduction in cash-crop production, and so on. Thus, national liberation struggles often are preceded by cultural resistance. (Chilcotte, 1991, p. 39)

Social movements, protest movements, resistance movements, and liberation movements are dynamic projects of collective change. Amilcar Cabral, the African revolutionary theorist and leader of Guinea-Bissau's liberation struggle understood this dynamism. His notion of national liberation built on cultural resistance that preceded it, but also saw its success intimately linked to cultural liberation, or the way that liberation "necessarily opens up new prospects for the cultural process of society in question, by returning to it all its capacity to create progress" (Cabral, 1979, p. 143). There is a long view of struggle in this vision, of movement across time, and there is learning implied in this movement – learning from the cultural resistance of the past to inform the national liberation struggle, and recognizing that this struggle opens up cultural creativity after colonialism's defeat. Cabral's thoughts here underscore two important themes in the section that follows. First, he grounds the discussion of social movements, and of social movement learning, in an African context. Second, his thinking highlights the movement in movements – their dynamism, both in action and in learning.

CHAPTER 2

This idea of movement is the cross-fader through which movements and movement learning will be explored in the section that follows. I use the term 'cross-fader' because it implies the dynamic of moving the fade along a slide of focus, allowing the tension between different positions to be unpacked, but also a cross-fader foregrounds the intentionality of which voices we eventually hear. Robin Kelley (2002, p. ix) hints at a dynamic approach to analysing movements with his critique of standard analyses of movements:

> Unfortunately, too often our standards for evaluating social movements pivot around whether or not they "succeeded" in realizing their visions rather than on the merits or power of the visions themselves. By such a measure, virtually every radical movement failed because the basic power relations they sought to change remained pretty much intact. And yet it is precisely these alternative visions and dreams that inspire new generations to continue to struggle for change.

Branch and Mampilly (2015), in their analysis of protest movements across the African continent, echo both elements of this sentiment. Instead of focusing on whether protest "achieves its explicit demands," they are "concerned with the evolving political imaginations forged by the divergent forces involved in African protests and with the efforts made to transcend the structural dilemmas out of which protest is born" (Branch & Mampilly, 2015, p. 10). Much like Kelley, the two elements that surface here are resisting a tendency to evaluate movements based on their direct impact on state policies, and shifting to focus on the imaginaries made possible by movements and their struggle. Kelley, much like Cabral, points out the potential long term and multi-generational impact of challenging the status quo with alternative visions. Branch and Mampilly (2015) also point to divergent forces involved in protest movements. This alludes to the ambiguity in movements, something I will focus on below. This divergence between a short-term and longer view on impact is also suggestive, though, of the various divergent ways movements have been interpreted by academia.

For instance, there is a fundamental disjuncture in the study of mass mobilization, between those who see mobilizations as a part of positive social change and those suspicious of such mobilization and their potential for mob rule. Le Bon (1895) began the later tradition, reacting to the Paris Commune of 1871. Several theorists in sociology have followed in this tradition, or have seen movements in instrumental ways, focusing on how they mobilize resources (e.g. Tilly, 1988). Branch and Mampilly (2015) document how concerns of mob rule, or the emergence of "dangerous classes," preoccupied colonial and post-colonial officials across Africa.

Marxist traditions of social movement studies have been far more focused on how movements become grounded in clear, class-based analysis and strategy and move away from being reactive. Holst (2002), for example, draws on the work of Luxemberg to underscore the importance learning plays in shifting spontaneous protests by the working class into a class-conscious movement towards scientific socialism. Carroll (1997), drawing on Gramsci, describes how deteriorating conditions in capitalist society can provide the basis for the emergence of a counter-hegemonic block that can provide an alternative social vision. At the same time, Marxist analysis has been dominated by a focus on movements emerging from worker mass mobilization – especially in urban contexts. Cabral's use of Marxism stands in contrast to this, with its focus on the potential of the peasantry in a colonized African context. He reconfigures Marx's stages away from the orthodoxy of Luxemburg and others, towards an emphasis on productive forces, and the potential to jump over entire stages based on how the productive forces work together, rather than who owns the means of production.

Melucci (1980) also broke from this focus on the means of production by focusing on movements emerging around identity rights in Western Europe in the 20th Century. Called New Social Movements (NSMs), Melucci and others argued these movements were contesting the state in new ways, demanding their identity be legitimized in State institutions. Melucci and other NSM theorists provided an important theoretical frame to describe the emergence of movements that often crossed class boundaries, and spoke to other forms of exclusion, such as the women's movement, and the LGBT2SIS+ movements. NSM theory provided a language for forms of cultural resistance, and the way in which the state could be pressured into recognizing the rights of different identity-based groups.

Picking up on Gramsci's notion of the subaltern, Guha (1983) and others called for a different approach to studying movements, especially in colonial and neo-colonial contexts. Subaltern Studies argues for paying attention to the voices of those struggling, not just in working class contexts but also in other marginalized and oppressed contexts, in framing theories about movements. In Guha's (1983) work this meant reconstructing the agency of those resisting British colonialism in India through the colonial record of their impact, since knowledge of the resistance in Indian records was minimal. The ideal was to find accounts from within movements themselves, but barring this, Guha inverted the British record, showing how even the most marginalized and oppressed resisted colonial oppression. Cabral echoes this focus, analysing the historical and present mobilization of peasants as opposed to just urban workers in Guinea-Bissau. Much like Guha did in India, Cabral built his knowledge of resistance to Portuguese colonialism through Portuguese records, since very little is captured elsewhere (Chilcote, 1991). Kapoor (2009) has argued that it is subaltern social movements (SSMs) that represent the greatest challenge to globalization as they contest not only material, but also epistemic neoliberal reality. This resonates well with Cabral's focus on cultural resistance as the starting point of national liberation. The notion of subaltern social movements will be returned to at the end of the movement learning section that follows.

SOCIAL MOVEMENT LEARNING AND CRITICAL ADULT EDUCATION

Returning to Kelley and Cabral's conceptualization of movements as dynamic momentums over time, Dixon (2017, p. 33) echoes the importance of this dynamism

CHAPTER 2

and names it learning "lessons for and from the long haul." This long view is not, however the only way that movement learning has been understood. In fact, social movement learning also has a wide variety of "breadth" (English & Mayo, 2012, p. 110) to its composition. In looking at some of this breadth, I will continue to use the cross-fader approach, exploring lines of dynamic range of motion in movement learning analysis.

At the outset of a recent collection of social movement learning studies, the editors of the collection recount their experience at an academic conference focused on issues of "injustice, violence against women, the deeply destructive nature of unbridled capitalism, the willingness of most political regimes to sacrifice both human and natural welfare in the interest of economic growth" (Hall, Clover, Crawford, & Scandrett, 2012, p. ix). They describe how their session on arts and social movement learning provoked a heated debate of views on social movements, co-optation, violence and repression. The spectrum of these reactions both evokes the divergent range of thoughts on movements laid out above, and highlights how even within progressive movement spaces there can be widely differing views on fundamental aspects of movements, what they do and how they learn. This ambiguity is important as it implies the possibility in movements – that they literally represent something not easily pinned down. Griff Foley (1999) also sees the ambiguity of movements, especially concerning how they learn, and what one learns within them as part of their positive potential, but also as what may undermine them.

Echoing Mamdani's framework for examining African phenomena, Foley asserts movements must be understood in their context. 'To understand the complexities of [movement] learning in struggle,' he writes (1999, p. 9), 'we need an analytical framework which connects learning to its context.' The framework he proposes is an analysis of 'learning in struggle.' Foley's notion of learning in struggle is attractive because it combines a sensitivity to incidental and informal processes of learning and knowledge production within movements with an awareness of the ambiguous nature of this learning (i.e. learning can contribute to as well as erode efforts at emancipatory social change). In describing incidental and informal learning, he notes:

> While systematic education does occur in some social movement sites and actions, learning in such situations is largely informal and often incidental – it is tacit, embedded in action and is often not recognized as learning. This learning is therefore often potential, or only half realized. (Foley 1999, p. 3)

Because it is unrecognized, this learning 'is not emancipatory in some linear, developmental sense, it is complex and contradictory, shaped by intrapersonal, interpersonal, and broader social factors' (p. 4). The fact that much of this learning is unrecognized provides the reason for studying it, as well as the potential to better ensure emancipatory outcomes from it:

> To more fully realize the value of such learning we need to expose it. In doing this it helps if we understand that people's everyday experience reproduces

ways of thinking and acting which support the often oppressive status quo, but that this same experience also produces recognitions which enable people to critique and challenge the existing order. (Foley 1999, pp. 3–4)

In this way, Foley is arguing not only for 'social science accounts [of movement learning] ... that convey a sense of "being there"' (p. 13) (in other words, grounded in context), but that also contribute to the deeper possibility, or potential, of these movements to bring about emancipatory change. His concluding remarks on the uncertain nature of social movements capture this normative desire well: 'we need to recognize the complex, ambiguous and contradictory character of particular movements and struggles. Analyses of these complexities provide a necessary basis for future strategies' (1999, p. 143). His framework is also sensitive and open enough to incorporate movement within movements, or their inner and outer dynamism.

Foley's framework very much informed the study of social movement learning in Ghana upon which the Ada case is built. In an effort to provide more nuance to the complexity Foley describes, his framework was expanded by the Participatory Research group in my earlier (Langdon, 2009) study of social movement learning in Ghana since the return to democracy in 1992:

First, there was a sense of the long-term incidental learning that takes place within a struggle over time. Second, there emerged a clear description of the concentrated learning that is produced during the course of a particular engagement, action, or even campaign. Finally, there emerged pronounced opinions on the normative link Foley suggested above – namely, "how" movements should best integrate processes of learning into action in order to ensure the identification of the most effective "future strategies." In order to recognize the link to Foley's over all framework, these three categories were named by the author, 'learning *in* struggle,' 'learning *through* struggle' and 'learning *to* struggle' respectively. (Langdon, 2011b, p. 155, emphasis in original)

Taken together, this expanded framework provides a sensitive set of tools for describing the learning emerging from social movement contexts, but also providing room for this description to not only serve a documentation purpose, but also, as Foley notes, to "provide a basis for future strategy." This framework aside, there are other important cross-fades within social movement learning that need to be acknowledged.

John Holst (2002) establishes the two opposite ends of one such cross-fade, as he lays out two ways in which social movement learning has been understood. "First," he argues, "social movements, through public protest that can take various forms, attempt to educate and persuade the larger public and politicians" (2002, p. 81). "Second," he continues, "there is much educational work internal to social movements, in which organizational skills, ideology, and lifestyle choices are passed from one member to the next informally through mentoring and modeling

CHAPTER 2

or formally through workshops, seminars, lectures, and so forth" (2002, p. 81). This distinction between insider and outsider learning is useful, as it distinguishes the educative strategies of movements from the learning of these movements and their membership. However, as the cross-fade metaphor suggests, there is usually a dynamic balance of these types of learning always being navigated by movements.

Another cross-fade in social movement learning is between the learning of individual activists, and the collective learning of movements. Several studies have looked at the experiences of activists, including their learning, in many contexts around the world. For instance, Larzilliere (2016) looks at the experiences of activists in Jordan; Gellner (2010) has edited a collection of activist experiences in South Asia; and Harley (2012) has looked at the learning from activists in the Abahlali movement in South Africa. Harley's study, focused on more in depth later in this chapter, makes the explicit link between the experiences of these activists and social movement learning – especially anti-hegemonic learning. Chovanec (2009) has also used the experiences of movement activists to speak to larger social movement learning themes in the women's movement in Chile. As mentioned earlier, my previous research (Langdon, 2009) presents the cumulative thinking of activists involved in the democracy movement, as well as other movements, in Ghana about learning *in*, *through* and *to* struggle since the country returned to democracy, and in the lead up to this transition. As with the above note, both of these learnings are always ongoing, but the emphasis on one or the other can move the cross fade in one direction or the other.

At the same time, others have been more focused on what movements have produced as clear indications of their collective learning. Choudry (2015), for instance, focuses on the knowledge production of movements as captured in various different types of texts (written, audio, visual, video). Barndt (2006) has explored the creative expressions that have emerged from movement activism. Kapoor (2009, 2011) has looked at the knowledge produced and mobilized by Adivasi movements in India, contesting various forms of external attacks on their ways of being. And Newman (2006) has documented the ways in which activist knowledge can be turned into teaching material.

Another major cross fade involves the ways in which learning is theorized. Walter (2007) notes that much social movement learning theory "has followed either in Marxist traditions of class analysis (Holst, 2002; Spencer, 1995) or adopted European traditions of New Social Movement theory (Finger, 1989; Holford, 1995; Kilgore, 1999; Welton, 1993, 2001)" (p. 251). Kapoor (2007, p. 33) has warned against the portability of these theories into what he calls "recently independent countries and regions of Latin America and the Caribbean, Asia, and Africa." English and Mayo (2012, p. 109) echo this concern:

> One must be wary of the fact that western models of social movements and their learning are often brought to bear on the analysis of people coming together in action for change or survival in non-western contexts.

From this vantage point, Euro-American traditions of the OSM, or Marxist, position and the NSM, or radical pluralist/postmodern, position need to be inflected with a post-colonial and African-centred lens if they are to be useful to a study of African social movement learning. This point is especially important in the realm of social movement learning theory, where "a healthy body of theoretical debate" has emerged, while at the same time "very few empirical studies [have emerged] to inform this theorizing" (Walter, 2007, p. 251). This critique is important, especially when one considers Mamdani's invective against the application of foreign analogies on African phenomena. Along similar lines, Shirley Walters (2005) – who studies learning within South African social movements – argues that the learning forms that movements take are in large part determined by the cultural and material conditions in which they are grounded. Cabral argues along similar lines in stating a national liberation movement needed to be understood through the context of its struggle.

At the same time, this cross fade includes another element, namely where the analysis of movement learning occurs. Choudry and Kapoor (2010) have argued that movements need to be understood through their own articulations, rather than through academic analysis of them. Mentinis (2006), for instance, has documented how the Zapatista movement in Mexico has been understood to exemplify several different theoretical traditions. Kapoor contrasts this "portability," as he calls it, with a Subaltern Social Movement (SSM) approach that first and foremost foregrounds movements themselves as theorizers of their own learning. Kane (2001) echoes this approach. English and Mayo (2012), building on Kapoor (2009), describe SSMs as situated in marginalised and subaltern resistance, and note that the manner in which this resistance manifests itself is variegated. Movements may pragmatically use essentialist human rights and class-based positions to insist on their right to survive. Spiritual and religious frames may also be used. Choudry (2010), as well as English and Mayo (2012) argue that in some cases these positions may lead to fundamentalist and right-wing nationalist movements that are exclusionary, rather than inclusionary.

Harley, Langdon, Larweh, and Zikode (forthcoming) add to this discussion an African SSM learning viewpoint that understands movements as being driven by a right to live, and to be who they are, but they are not, ultimately exclusionary. In fact, in the South African as well as Ghanaian cases the authors draw from, the experience of exclusion generates a decision to work to better include. The Ghanaian example used in the framework is the Ada movement. Given this, the framework Harley et al. (forthcoming) develop warrants quoting at length. The third point of this African SSM framework in particular focuses on inclusion:

1. Rooted in grassroots organising, and remaining accountable to that, over time. This means that subaltern social movements are always fluid and shifting; they are by their very nature temporal, rooted in the burning issues and the analysis of their members.

CHAPTER 2

2. Integrally connected to people's livelihoods. By livelihoods, we do not mean 'jobs,' but rather the 'doing' (as Holloway (2010) discusses it) that is necessary for both social reproduction and for being fully human. That is, the physical work of production of food, clothing, shelter, and so on, but also of care, nurturing; and the social, creative and emotional work of building and maintaining human relationships, communities and cultures of loving, belonging and creating.
3. Connected to a strong sense of identity, and committed to protecting this. This sense of identity is neither exclusionary nor elitist; there is no central authority determining insiders and outsiders, although there are insiders and outsiders – there is a boundary, but this is relatively porous, and resists colonial boundaries and constructions of identity. Identity in this sense is about the singularity and temporality of experience; but contains within it the possibility of universality. It is a sense of identity that does not deny or negate the humanity of others.
4. Non-partisan, in the sense that subaltern movements occupy a different political territory from the political party. This is not to suggest that such movements are not deeply 'political.' Indeed, subaltern movements are inherently 'political,' occupying the space of real, living politics, rather than that of the 'police,' as Rancière (1995/1999) frames it: "Politics exists when the natural order of domination is interrupted by the institution of a part of those who have no part. Beyond this set up there is no politics. There is only the order of domination [and the police] or the disorder of revolt" (p. 11). In this sense, politics links the singular and the universal: "Politics ... is the art of the local and singular construction of cases of universality" (Rancière, 1995/1999, p. 139).
5. Ontologically spaces of learning. By this we mean, it is the very nature of such movements to think their experience and their politics; and therefore to challenge pre-existing truth-procedures and ideologies, and to create new epistemologies. Because of the temporal nature of subaltern movements, their thinking and learning is fluid.

Each of the above points will emerge in the discussion of the Ada movement, and its learning to follow. In this sense, it resolves the cross-fade tension concerning where the articulation of movement learning analysis needs to start, at least for the Ada case. Nonetheless, the various other cross-fades and tensions laid out above are evident in the chapters that follow, from a focus on the knowledge the movement has produced, to individual learning, to learning along different timelines. All of these frames have been informed by movement articulations of learning. Before looking more closely at the Ada case, however, it is important to situate this complex, multivalent movement learning story in a series of snapshots of movement learning across the African continent.

AFRICAN SOCIAL MOVEMENTS AND LEARNING

1ST WAVE: AFRICAN LIBERATION MOVEMENTS

Branch and Mampilly (2015) identify three important waves of protest movements across the African continent. The first of these waves was the rise of liberation movements in the 1940s, 50s and 60s. The second of these waves focuses on the re-democratization processes that happened in the 1980s and 1990s. The third wave is the one we are currently in, where close to 100 mass protests have taken over the streets of nations across the continent just between 2010 and 2014. These protests have targeted corrupt leaders as well as institutions that fail the ordinary person. To begin exploring African social movement learning, the first wave is the natural place to start. This section will share accounts of three liberation movements: Ghana, Algeria and Zimbabwe.

Ghana's Independence Movement

Returning to the story of Nkrumah assembling his printing press that began this chapter, C. L. R. James (1977) famously described the attack by British colonial police on the ex-servicemen's union March, and the riots that resulted from this attack. Accra was shut down for two days as a result. While the colonial administration tried to describe those rioting as a "lawless mob," James (1977, p. 45) insisted "that was precisely what it was not." Based on the clear ability of a well-orchestrated mass action to shut down the capital of the colony, Nkrumah began to develop what he later called his "Positive Action" campaign. This campaign did not involve "riot, looting and disturbances, in a word, violence," but rather involved:

> The adoption of all legitimate and constitutional means by which we can cripple the forces of imperialism in this country. The weapons of positive action are:
>
> (1) legitimate political agitation;
> (2) newspaper and educational campaigns, and
> (3) as a last resort, the constitutional application of strikes, boycotts, and non-cooperation based on the principle of absolute non-violence. (Nkrumah, 1973, pp. 93–94)

The use of the newspaper and educational campaigns should stand out here. Taking advantage of the clear links between 'Veranda Boys' in Accra – young unemployed youth who would wait around for small bits of work on the verandas of businesses, colonial offices, or the houses of the well-off – and the rural communities from which they came, Nkrumah was able to both build urban and rural communication networks as he deepened his connection with these largely disregarded youth. "Existing formal and informal organization among urban populations was developed by [Nkrumah's] party, as were existing rural-urban linkages, to create new forms of association and consciousness among the population" (Branch & Mampilly, 2015, p. 27). The emphasis on new ways of thinking was central to the Positive

CHAPTER 2

Action campaign, where the call for "Self-Government Now!" broke with the more traditional Ghanaian leadership who called for self-government in the shortest time possible. This break provided disaffected rural youth with a clear line of thinking that enabled them to turn their backs on traditional authority figures – often seen to be in league with the colonial administration. Similarly, this contrast gave urban Veranda Boys a glimmer of hope that change was possible. When Nkrumah called for a general strike in early 1950, the response was overwhelming (Branch & Mampilly, 2015). Describing it at the time, Nkrumah (1973, pp. 118–119) noted:

> All the stores were closed, trains were stationary, all Government services had closed down and the workers were sitting at home. The whole economic life of the country was at a standstill.

While this resulted in an immediate crackdown and arrest of Nkrumah and other leaders of his Convention People's Party, it revealed to ordinary Ghanaians the power of collective action:

> The hitherto omnipotent colonial administration had been confronted for the first time by organized people's power, and its rottenness and inherent weaknesses had been exposed. (Nkrumah, 1973, pp. 90–91)

This clear example of what Foley refers to as learning *in* struggle reveals the educational impact of this movement action. Nkrumah captures this learning eloquently in his concluding reflections on Positive Action:

> There is no surer way to learn the art revolution than to practice it. The experience of shared effort and suffering engenders a political awareness that no amount of armchair theorizing can evolve. The people had seen with their own eyes the economic life of the Gold Coast brought to a halt by unified people's effort in the form of a general strike. Never again would they accept that it was hopeless to attempt to attack a seemingly mighty power structure as that represented by the colonial administration. The 'paper tiger' had been exposed, and this was the essential first step in its destruction. (Nkrumah, 1973, p. 91)

Despite being imprisoned for his leadership of the strike, his party still won a landslide victory in the new assembly brought in by the colonial administration in 1951. This set the colony on course for full independence in 1957. Nkrumah went from prison to the Office of Prime Minister. And yet his mind was constantly focused on how Ghana's independence was bound up in the independence of all of Africa. He concluded his Independence Day speech, on March 6th, 1957, by stating:

> We again re-dedicate ourselves in the struggle to emancipate other countries in Africa, for our independence is meaningless unless it is linked with the total liberation of the African continent. (Nkrumah, 1973, p. 121)

Nkrumah was convinced that his successful use of the non-violent Positive Action was a lesson for all of Africa on the potential to end colonial rule without blood shed. Frantz Fanon, working with the liberation efforts in Algeria had a very different opinion.

Algeria' National Liberation Front

Arriving in Ghana in 1958, the year after its independence, Fanon called for support from leaders of other African liberation struggles for the Algerian National Liberation Front (FLN) in its ongoing armed struggle against France for independence. He argued,

> We have tried this [non-violent] method, but the French came to the Cabash, broke down door after door and slaughtered the head of each household in the center of the street. When they did that about thirty-five consecutive times, the people gave up on non-cooperation. (Branch & Mampilly, 2015, p. 38)

It would be a further four more years, to 1962, until the Algerian War of Independence was concluded and Algeria became independent. Unlike Ghana, Algeria had a large French settler population, which added to the bitterness of the struggle. Nonetheless, Fanon argued that depending on the violence of the colonial state, some processes of liberation may need to match this violence. In response to such colonial violence, violence was necessary both to ensure the revolution would completely break with the former colonial master, but also to engender a new consciousness in those formerly colonized. According to Fanon (1963), "New men" with a "new language and a new humanity" (p. 130) emerge from rebellion, whether violent or not, as it "invests their character with positive and creative qualities" (p. 93) that "are rehabilitated in their own eyes and in the eyes of history" (p. 130). Fanon based some of these conclusions on his psychiatric work during the war. For instance, he noted the impact of radio in subjecting the colonized, when used by the French, and liberating them, when used by the FLN. Prior to the beginning of the armed rebellion, which began in 1954, "voices Algerians suffering from hallucinations [heard] constantly pointed out the presence of ... highly aggressive and hostile radio" (1959, p. 88). Yet, what Fanon found after 1956 (once the FLN began broadcasting) was that "in hallucinatory psychoses ... the radio voices became protective, friendly." In other words, hearing their own language, and a radio defending their own existence created space for those suffering anxiety to begin to breathe, to feel comforted. This non-violent potential of radio to impact the psyche of the oppressed is important to note when we later discuss the role of Radio Ada in the Songor struggle. This aside for now, Fanon's (1963) other main concern in underscoring the importance of violent rebellion was the temptation of the middle class in each liberation context to try and coopt the struggle, and either agree to a settlement with the former colonial master, or simply replace it with a new elite. For him, an armed path was the most

CHAPTER 2

likely to lead to the "whole social structure being changed from the bottom up" (1963, p. 36). Branch and Mampilly (2015, p. 38) note, "As the era of decolonization proceeded, Fanon's diagnosis and warnings appeared increasingly prescient … Over the course of the 1960s, armed struggle came to be seen as the norm for decolonization." And yet, what Fanon revealed through his work was a deep theory of learning through these struggles, and that this learning could enable a break with colonized mindsets and new potentials to emerge both through violent and non-violent means.

Zimbabwe's Liberation Movement

Zimbabwe, the final example of liberation movements, gained independence two decades after Ghana and Algeria. An example of the shift in approaches Branch and Mampilly (2015) noted, Zimbabwe followed the path of armed struggle, rather than that of non-violence. This struggle began after the white supremacist Rhodesian Front gained power in 1962, and lasted through several phases of armed conflict until the 1980 landslide victory of the Patriotic Front in the first universal suffrage election in the settler colony. Griff Foley (1999), whose work on learning in struggle is discussed above, conducted interviews of liberation fighters in the first couple years after independence to pull together an account of the learning in struggle that emerged in this emancipatory conflict. His account, in many ways, gives us the most concrete sense of social movement learning in a liberation movement itself. It resonates with Fanon's analysis, but also underscores that armed conflict alone could not prevent "the development, in post-independence Zimbabwe, of a form of neo-colonial capitalism, presided over by a black ruling class" (Foley, 1999, p. 128). Foley further contends that the "political learning and education in the armed struggle played an important, and ultimately conservative, role" in this development as it "emphasized the racial nature of colonialism, de-emphasized class and legitimized the old-guard leadership" such as Robert Mugabe. In describing exploitation, for instance, guerrilla fighters were only given enough political education to frame this in racial terms:

> It is whereby the other race is felt [to be] inferior […] and the opportunities in jobs and many other things, posts and what have you, were granted to the other, were just too rare to Africans, these were granted to the race. (Foley, 1999, p. 123)

Those fighters who, through the struggle and access to more thorough forms of critical education, became critical of the limited political education, were purged by the movement leadership (Foley, 1999). Nonetheless, Foley (1999, pp. 126–127) notes the ambiguity of the situation, as the mass political work these guerrillas engaged in throughout the rural countryside "created a solid popular base for the armed struggle" and "enabled people to reject colonialism and it prepared them to vote for a particular party" come independence. It did not "enable them to participate in transforming the unequal and oppressive society that was Zimbabwe's inheritance at independence" (Foley, 1999, p. 127).

Branch and Mampilly (2015) propose Nkrumah and Fanon as two trajectories liberation movements took in Africa in the 1950s, 60s, 70s, and even into the 80s. Nkrumah's vision was to gain the political terrain through non-violent Positive Action, and through it transform colonial power relations. This worked initially in Ghana, though Nkrumah was deposed in a coup in 1966. Fanon argued, rather, that in some cases armed struggle was necessary to transform not only the colonial relations of power, but also the colonized mindset in order for true independence to be possible. The Algerian War of Independence was certainly long and bloody, and left the FLN unopposed in power for many years after independence – though through its own repressive measures. Meanwhile, the case of Zimbabwe shows that an armed struggle without a commitment to deep educational work aiming at transforming not just who is in power, but the very nature of social relations is bound to replace a White settler elite with a Black elite. And yet, what must be noted here is that each of these examples reveals clear approaches to learning within each of these liberation movements. It is interesting to reflect on whether, in the end, Nkrumah's non-violent approach, even with several bloodless coups and now with three successive peaceful transitions in government represents the greatest potential for change for what Branch and Mampilly (2015) call the 3rd wave of African social movements. It is also worth noting that even this short account provided here details the cross movement learning occurring across the African continent throughout the liberation struggles. If one was to add the contributions to learning in struggle of Cabral of Guinea-Bissau, or Nyerere of Tanzania, or the learnings from the South African liberation struggle, volumes could be written. And this is without mentioning the countless women who contributed to this learning, but whose contributions have been largely overlooked. For instance, in Ghana the popular educational campaign of the Ghana's first independent government was carried out by Leticia Quake, Hanna Cudjoe, Ama Nkrumah and Madam Sohia Doku (Manuh, 1991).

FROM THE 2ND WAVE OF DEMOCRATIZATION TO THE 3RD WAVE OF CONTEMPORARY STRUGGLES

In moving from liberation movements to contemporary protest movements, Branch and Mampilly (2015) speak of two more waves of movements in Africa. The first of these is a wave of democratization movements that goes from the 1980s into the 1990s. While we will not spend a great deal of time on this wave, it is important to speak to it as it both represents a crucial moment of social movement mobilization across the continent, and also helps situate contemporary movements that in many ways respond to what these democratization movements were able to or failed to achieve. The Ghanaian democratization movement will be used as the example through which this period will be linked to the present, but before turning to it, it is relevant to point out some of the ways this wave has been understood.

CHAPTER 2

2ND WAVE: AFRICAN DEMOCRACY MOVEMENTS

Ghanaian Democracy Movement

Branch and Mampilly (2015) note that critical scholarship of the 1980s and 90s often focuses on how the form of democracy that emerged through movement activism failed to overcome the austerity politics that precipitated it. Drawing on Bratton and Van de Walle (1997), they note over two-thirds of African states had anti-austerity protests during the late 80s and early 90s, and the frequency of these protests grew enormously over this period (Branch & Mampilly, 2015). As these movements shifted from being reactions to World Bank Structural Adjustment Programs (SAPs) to demanding not just economic but political change, state after state across the continent began holding multi-party elections. For instance, "in 1989, thirty-one states were under single-party rule and eleven under military rule, by 1994 only two de jure single-party states were left" (Branch & Mampilly, 2015, p. 40). And yet, by the "mid-1990s, discussion of the protest wave and multi-party elections it had ushered in had already come to be marked by a tone of disappointment" (Branch & Mampilly, 2015, p. 41). Analysts either blamed external, neo-colonial forces that had coopted the democratization process (cf. Abrahamsen, 1997), or blamed the neo-patrimonial character of African politics for leadership that failed its people (c.f Bratton & Van de Walle, 1997). Branch and Mampilly (2015), however, propose another point of view, one that focuses on the protest movements themselves, and the potential they produced, rather than what they failed to achieve. This view very much resonates with Mamdani and Wamba dia Wamba's (1995) collection from the period, where even the view of what movements are was determined from within each context rather than labelling them using such categories as OSM or NSM in use in Europe at the time. This view also resonates with the views of Ghanaian activists who were part of the democratization efforts who saw their movement as a reaction to the military government at the time, as well as a compromise between different political ideologies (Langdon, 2009).

Bound up in the global politics of the end of the cold-war era, the democratization movement in Ghana nonetheless was a product of its own internal dynamics. My earlier study (Langdon, 2009) describes how movements associated with the two socialist-espousing uprisings of the late 1970s and early 1980s learned a clear lesson after the second of these two uprisings, which brought the People's National Defence Council (PNDC) to power in 1981. As the Ada case will illustrate, the early days of this revolution saw the emergence of locally led People's Defence Committees, intended to bring about socialist change on a local scale (Shillington, 1992). And yet, within just a couple years, these committees were being rebranded as Committees for the Defence of the Revolution (CDRs), and fell under central control (Yeebo, 2007). At the same time, the central government took on austerity structural adjustment plans from the World Bank (Hutchful, 2002). These plans opened the economy to foreign investment like never before, increasing neoliberal control over the resource economy in direct contravention of the nationalization of these resources begun by Nkrumah (Hilson, 2004). At the same time, those critical of the regime soon found themselves facing state sanctioned violence. This brought many leftist activists to the conclusion that there was a need for a baseline respect for human rights if they had any chance of truly transforming power relations in the country (Langdon, 2009). This led members of the several left leaning movements to reach out to their political rivals in the run up to a national referendum on the return to democracy – a referendum that was a product of their organizing and the wave of democratic transitions taking place across the continent (Abrahamsen, 2000). The PNDC government was espousing a local form of democracy that would have no partisan contestation, while the Movement for Freedom and Justice – the name of the unified left and right political elements – was pushing for the return of multi-party national elections. The MFJ won the referendum, but then fell apart in the electoral contest that followed, as it split into the New Patriotic Party (NPP) that inherited the anti-Nkrumaist tradition from independence, and a number of smaller parties aligned with the Nkrumaist tradition. Jerry Rawlings, the leader of the PNDC, successfully transformed from a military head of government to an elected head of state, forming his own party called the National Democratic Congress (NDC). Ninsin (2007) notes the form of democracy that emerged from this transition was elitist, and was deeply embedded in the neoliberal austerity project that had actually helped spark the move to democratic transition in the first place. Importantly for this account, though, many of the left-leaning factions who had taken part in the democracy movement decided to eschew party politics, and instead engage in social movement activism. A longtime activist, formerly involved in the socialist movements of the 1980s reveals this new attitude:

> I am an opportunist in the sense that if these are the things we are critiquing, and people want to come and join us and build momentum with us, fine let them do it, but don't call me an NPP man or an NDC man; you call me this today and that tomorrow, but you will always see me fighting for the same things. (Langdon, 2009, p. 86)

When the newly elected NDC – Rawlings' party – tried to bring in a new tax targeting the poor, a broad section of the labour movement rose up in resistance to it. As many in the general public joined the anti-austerity movement, the initial resistance sparked weeks of protest known as the *Kume Preko* demonstrations. One activist describes the importance of *Kume Preko* as "the defining moment of the 4th Republic" and another said:

> *Kume Preko* was the most successful demonstration in Ghanaian history [with] larger crowds than political parties attract. (Langdon, 2009, p. 226)

It also avoided co-optation by the leading political opposition, the NPP, which taught the organizers a lot about the potential of mass demonstrations in this new democratic context. This tradition of large-scale street protests in several urban contexts in

CHAPTER 2

Ghana has continued throughout the current democratic period, regardless of who is in power. An activist who has been part of these protests, as well as the democracy movement, captures this feeling well: "democracy has come to mean contestation, not just contested elections" (Langdon, 2009). At the same time, activists involved in the democracy movement also helped spark protest movements against the impacts of mining activities, while others have played pivotal roles in launching an autonomous women's movement – wrenching the movement away from partisan party control (Prah, 2007; Langdon, 2009). Anyidoho and Gariba (2015) note how the tradition of contestation in Ghana's democracy has contributed to the potential for collective change in the country. In the story of Ada that follows, this history is illustrated in depth; but another recent example of this is how Occupy Ghana's interventions led to recent policy shifts (Langdon & Anyidoho, 2017). In this sense, the impact of the democracy movement on the long term learning in social action of Ghanaians since the wave of democratization in the 1980s and 90s is clear and ongoing.

My previous study of learning in this movement (Langdon, 2009), as well as the movements it helped generate, documents the take-aways from this time period, from the perspective of activists involved in these movements. Along with the learning noted above – that consistent contestation, rather than state capture, is the most effective way to make change in the Ghanaian context – long-term activists also noted the importance of staying rooted in the struggles of those impacted by neoliberalism, but doing so from a Ghanaian framework, including recognizing the power of movements embedded in defending people's identity and defending their livelihoods. Furthermore, these activists also underscored the importance of operating in a context that respected people's right to organize and contest that is part of this democratic terrain – even as they contested the way in which this terrain is contained by neoliberal global capital. Anyidoho and Gariba (2015) draw on this study in underscoring a crucial learning that emerged through collective action in this period in Ghana – the realization that by coming together they could change their world.

3RD WAVE: PROTEST MOVEMENTS IN CONTEMPORARY TIMES

In more contemporary times, other movements of significance have emerged. Branch and Mampilly (2015) describe this as the third wave of African uprisings. While this surge includes the North African elements of what has been termed "The Arab Spring," they warn against minimizing the protest movements occurring across the continent, and suggest instead their interconnection. They describe similar trends across the more than 105 mass protests that occurred in 40 countries across the continent between 2005 and 2014. "[T]oday's protest wave represents a vehement rejection of the neoliberal economy by the urban poor" (Branch & Mampilly, 2015, p. 70). Whether a reaction to a single party or military state, or a multi-party democracy, such as Ghana, "unaccountable and violent state power" is still often "faced by Africa's urban poor" (Branch & Mampilly, 2015, p. 72). Economic indicators may be improving, but are largely benefiting the elite and middle class, and working and precarious classes have been left to pay the bill of structural adjustment. The resource economy is key to this bifurcation, as industrial production has diminished across the continent, and foreign ownership of resources and land has increased. Finally, the rise of a form of civil society invested in co-opting protest through NGOization, has attempted to "steer NGOs' urban beneficiaries away from collective political action and towards individualized profit seeking as the path to social and economic improvement" (Branch & Mampilly, 2015, p. 77). In reaction to these failures and efforts at state and NGO control, protests have erupted that turn their backs on traditional parties, or civil society. These subaltern uprisings take many forms, from localized to general protest (Branch & Mampilly, 2015). What is important though, is their sense of continuity. Far from being individual manifestations, these are cumulative protests of conditions that have not been improving, despite whatever changes may have been promised in the 2nd wave of movements, and they continuously look for an alternative avenue for change. As the Ghana example shows, the elite democracy that emerged from such waves has created elite consensus, not collective change, and movements continue to rise up to point this out. The Egypt example shared below also reveals that the Arab Spring was not a surprising, unique moment, but was the galvanization of momentum that had been building, and it is a momentum that continues to this day, despite subsequent repression. Similarly, the South African case, with its massive hope for change, has given birth to highly effective movements in urban contexts that contest daily the erosion of the hope the end of Apartheid was supposed to usher in. A crucial dimension in all of this is the learning across, within and between these protests over time. The two examples shared here speak to the wider way in which social movement learning is happening across the continent right now.

Egypt's Tahrir Square Uprising and People's Spring

Samir Amin (2012), writing in the midst of the potential of the "Arab Spring" – or what he calls the "People's Spring" – is clear that it is only from mainstream Western perspective that the uprising in Egypt was unexpected. In line with Branch and Mampilly's (2015) analysis above, he points to major strikes in 2007–2008 that clearly critiqued the ongoing impact of neoliberal policies on the urban working class as one example of this building momentum. Philip Marfleet (2016) echoes and builds on this analysis. His work uses 9 years of interviews from before Tahrir square to afterwards, with a wide range of activists to develop an account rooted in the analysis and articulations of those at the heart of the 18 days in January 2012 that toppled Mubarak, as well as the protest movements that came before and those that have continued despite the ongoing repressions that began after the military seized power in 2013. Most pointedly, Marfleet documents how the taking of space, over and over again throughout the uprising, has transformed what is possible in people's mind – alternative ways of co-existing came to life, if even briefly, and that reality

CHAPTER 2

cannot be undone. Though not without acknowledging its importance, Marfleet (2016) also disrupts the common held notion that this was a social media revolution. "Recognizing the value of Twitter in disseminating news about dissent to large audiences," Marfleet (2016, pp. 24–25) quotes Hossam El-Hamalawy, a leading digital activist, in refuting "the notion that social media was the key mobilizing force":

> I saw Twitter helping to exaggerate the power and strength of some activists and/or groups giving a false impression about their abilities [...] Some [people] are under the illusion that it's enough to have a Twitter account with a big number of followers to 'instigate the masses into action,' which is of course a farce. (El-Hamalawy, 2012, as quoted in Marfleet, 2016, p. 25)

Some of the biggest rallies happened, Marfleet reminds us, after the internet had been shut down by Egyptian authorities. From a movement learning perspective, a crucial component of the uprising was the way in which it produced its demands and knowledge. Of equal importance to taking to the streets to create space to come together, was the way in which this space allowed people to collectively dialogue on what their key demands were, and to do this again and again as the situation changed:

> The demands of the streets had been formulated on 25 January. In Tahrir they were agreed at an open meeting in the square [...] activists then rushed to copy centres to make tens of thousands of leaflets for distributions among people flooding the city centre. [...] As the movement swept Egypt debates entered every workplace, generalising the demands of the streets and adding to them or reformulating them in the context of collective discussion and experience. (Marfleet, 2016, pp. 7–8)

These open spaces enabled the movement to move quickly from squares into committees at the village and neighbourhood level, "becom[ing] the heartbeat of Egyptian society – locally rooted and flexibly organized, informal and voluntary" (El-Meehy, 2012, quoted in Marfleet, 2016, p. 9). The movement also transitioned into workplaces that led to widespread strikes that deepened the impact of the street activism (Amin, 2012; Marfleet, 2016). These spaces also opened the door to creativity:

> Creative activity filled the streets they now claimed as their own. Participants in the '18 Days' of protest in Tahrir (between 25th January and 11 February) describe a festive atmosphere, even during bitter fighting with police and armed gangs. [...] the square had become a stage for song, poetry, dance and theatre; on buildings nearby popular artists commented on events with graffiti and paintings. (Marfleet, 2016, p. 9)

Unlike most accounts of the Egypt uprising, Marfleet's (2016) account does not dwell on the failure of the uprising, but rather focuses on what has been learned from it. A key lesson was that after the success of gaining the streets, there was no central organizing structure that could prevent the mobilization being hijacked away from the collectively determined demands. Nonetheless, it was also clear that massive learning from earlier strikes against the regime had identified building local collective structures as being crucial to what emerged in 2011/2012. In this sense, Marfleet's (2016) account ends by sharing that strikes and organizing have continued on the local level, despite the repression by the current military government. This type of learning cannot be driven away, and with an opening, these structures can reconnect and emerge quickly. The conditions that brought people onto the streets in 2011 still exist, and much was learned then and has been learned since.

South Africa's Abahlali baseMjondolo Movement

The last example of contemporary movement learning is from South Africa. Linking the independence movements to contemporary struggles, Mamdani (1996) argues that South Africa should be understood not as an exception to the rest of the continent, but in fact, as the ultimate example of colonial impact. This is important, as it helps frame the idea that the post-Apartheid period is in fact very much in dialogue with the post-independence containment of transformation that occurred across the continent at the end of the cold war. Neocosmos (2006) describes how South Africa has become a neoliberal flag bearer under ANC rule, and, like many, points to the failure of the post-Apartheid government to address the issues of urban shackdwellers – central sites of resistance and destabilization of apartheid, and key to ANC's rise to power.

Richard Pithouse (2006) explains the significance of the shackdwellers' movement, called Abahlali baseMjondolo (AbM). S'bu Zikode, one of the prominent figures in the movement, makes it clear that they are not just fighting for services, but a right to articulate their own vision of their future. This is said in the face of countless academics and government officials that claim the movement members are sock puppets for a disgruntled left intelligentsia. Further to Zikode's statement, Raj Patel (2008) describes the emergence of AbM's own university – insisting on their own rights to knowledge production. Anne Harley (2014) has gone further into learning in the movement, describing the pedagogic elements of movement techniques, such as blockades. Elsewhere, Harley (2012) lays out some of the most important things the movement describes as its learning: speaking for themselves, Abahlali has realized, is a criminal act; at the same time, they have insisted on their ability to think for themselves; their experience has led them to question if the end of apartheid has really brought freedom; their issues are the issues of all poor – they will not be drawn into divide and rule tactics; elections bring no change, and therefore change must be organized outside elections; they have also learned to critique the economic system from within its impacts; their own theory informs their actions. S'bu Zikode (2014, quoted in Harley et al., forthcoming) sums up the long term learning of the movement:

CHAPTER 2

> The only democracy that we have experienced in the last twenty years is the democracy that we have built for ourselves in our own communities and in our own struggle ... Democracy from below assists the whole society in acknowledging the thinking and practices that takes place in our dark confined corners of our society. These corners are shack settlements, flats, hostels, rural communities and farm communities. Democracy from below builds the power of the oppressed. It gives us a platform to take our place in the debates and the strength to take our place in the city.

With its 50,000 members in 13 shack settlements in several South African cities, the Abahlali clearly represent a crucial ongoing challenge to the state. They have experienced assassinations and brutal attacks from police and ANC activists – both proven in court (abahlali@lists.riseup.net, personal communication, June 14th, 2018). They continue to organize in a context where every effort is made to delegitimize their voice. A recent invective from the mayor of Durban told members of AbM to sign up with Shackdwellers International (SDI), an international NGO, if they wanted services and new housing. In the same statement, she claimed AbM was a clear front for a hidden third force of external interests. The irony of insisting members of a South African social movement join an international NGO instead because the SDI is somehow less representative of an external interest is very rich. Linking back to the earlier social movement learning section of this chapter, AbM is the second example from which Harley et al. (forthcoming) developed the characteristics of an African subaltern social movement, along with the Ada movement.

MOVING FROM AFRICA TO ADA

Ferguson (2006) warns against an over emphasis on Africa as a unique unit of analysis. At the same time, he notes that the continent's colonial history has created a similarity of experiences whereby African states have been consistently undermined by external forces. Mamdani's (1996) warning can be read in similar ways, both insisting that the particulars of African history not be ignored or minimized, even while refusing the over generalization of this experience. In the preceding pages, we have looked at three waves of activism in Africa – the decolonization period, the democratization wave and the contemporary time frame. Learning in the social movements in these time periods has been explored, including the theorization around change that they propose. These examples have been placed in dialogue with social movement theory, and social movement learning theory, with an effort to frame these discussions through important voices from within African movements such as Amilcar Cabral, Kwame Nkrumah, and Frantz Fanon. Although it is impossible to truly unpack all the important contributions activist/ theorists from within these movements, I have looked at such voices as Nkrumah and Fanon and how they framed change across the continent. The point, however, in all of this is to underscore three important ideas. First, movements need to be contextualized; second, movements and movement learning need to be understood through their own knowledge production rather than through theoretical frameworks imposed from outside; and, third, movement learning is complex and multifaceted, and documenting it is an important way to deepen learning reflection within the movement. Keeping these ideas in mind, it is towards a presentation of the Ada movement defending communal access to the Songor lagoon that we now turn.

CHAPTER 3

ADA MOVEMENT KNOWLEDGE PRODUCTION, QUESTIONING NATIONAL DEVELOPMENT

My wife's statue has been erected at Bonikope. So that each year the communities can be reminded of the struggle and remember that day. I just hate seeing it. When I see it, I recollect so many things. I feel cold and sad. When she was shot dead and I was called to look at her, I felt sad.

It was the death of my wife that led the former President (Rawlings) to make a law to take over the Songor and hold it in trust for the people of Ada. It pains me beyond description when issues concerning the Songor are being discussed and I am not even remembered. I am unemployed and shuttered.

This is a sad thing; it is even worse to observe that there is still no peace at the Songor. The present Government and for that matter the current President Kufuor is also doing all he can to take over the resource completely to deprive the Adas of ownership.

The Adas want the government to hand over the resource to them. They are still struggling over the issue, it has not ended.
  – Thomas Ocloo Lanuer, husband of Maggie Kuwornu, fatal casualty of Songor Lagoon crisis (Radio Ada, 2002, p. 6)

The movement of Adas contesting and resisting the various efforts at taking over the Songor lagoon has produced knowledge not only to counter these efforts, but also to counter the logic upon which they are based. In this sense the movement has produced local histories embedded in subaltern and subjugated knowledges that contest the logic of such truth regimes as National Development, and Neoliberal Globalization. These truth regimes, or global designs as Mignolo (2000) calls them, frame development as large scale projects that marginalize local people and their opinions in order to "make way for development" (Blaser Feit & McCrea, 2004). Ferguson (2006) calls this framing a topography of power, and connects it to the waves of democratization across Africa discussed in the previous chapter.

In the excerpt above, the husband of Maggie Kuwornu, a pregnant bystander killed by a police bullet during a raid on the lagoon, questions not only the fact that the Songor has been taken over by Ghana's government, but also the very logic of this takeover as it has not produced its intended results. Voices such as his have informed the movement of Adas in its critique of national development narratives,

CHAPTER 3

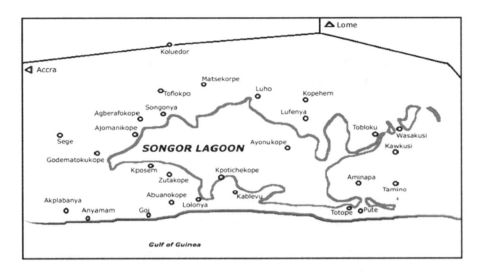

Figure 3.1. Map of Songor (from ASAF, 2016)

and its proposal of a different vision of a national use for this resource. This chapter provides the background context of the Ada struggle, situating it in the broader historical trajectory of Ghana's emergence as a nation state. The chapter then goes on to share how the movement of Adas has attempted to undermine the authority of the nation state to make decisions about the resource by producing alternative knowledge about what it means to use a resource to further national interests. But first, the chapter situates the Ada story in a discussion of the topography of power, and the power of subaltern and subjugated knowledges to destabilize such topographies.

NATIONAL DEVELOPMENT AND NEOLIBERALISM AS TOPOGRAPHIES OF POWER

In an extension of the reflections on democracy of the previous chapter, James Ferguson (2006) argues that the 2nd wave of democratization that swept African nation-states over the last two decades should be understood as a renewed attempt to gain legitimacy for a level of governance that has been seriously undermined by a history of foreign intervention, manipulation and coercion. According to Ferguson, the failure of structural adjustment policies – the most sweeping of these foreign interventions – necessitated a re-legitimation of national governments that had visibly abandoned their populations. Ferguson (2006, p. 100) advances a framework to analyze this wave of democratization of African nation-states, called "topographies of power." It involves a reconceived spatialization of power relations whereby African nation-states are conceived as vertically encompassing civil society, communities, families and citizens, as if the state exists somewhere "up-there" above these other elements in society. Through this conceptualization of power, African nation-states claim legitimacy and supremacy in deciding how people should live at the local level because of their greater claims to generalizability – they understand what is and is not good for the nation. In contrast to this rarely questioned spatial arrangement, Ferguson suggests Africa's history, and its contemporary relationship with neoliberal globalization, tells of a different topography of power, where the local is embedded in transnational forms of governmentality (Ferguson & Gupta 2002).

Following Foucault's lead, Ferguson extends the notion of governmentality – a term Foucault (1991) linked to the mechanisms through which a population is governed by institutions such as the nation-state – to connect with transnational forms of institutions and discourses that govern people, such as neoliberalism. With his colleague Akhil Gupta, Ferguson argues that:

> Rather than seeing processes of governmentality as all-determining, this work sees the historical process of attempts to manage and shape people and their relations to things as always deeply compromised prospects, composed of contradictory movements. (Ferguson & Gupta, 2008, p. 5)

In this sense, their use of governmentality is more closely in dialogue with Mignolo's (2000) connection with Foucault's sense of power, where discursive regimes of truth – or what Mignolo calls global designs – are constantly being challenged by subjugated knowledges, what Foucault (1980) describes as "knowledges that have been disqualified" by dominant discourses and that Mignolo (2000, p. 19) renames "local histories." It is based on Mignolo's reminder of this more complex understanding of power, especially in the post-colonial context, that the description of the global design of transnational neoliberal governmentality is counter-balanced with a description of local subjugated knowledges that contest this governmentality's truth regime.

Returning to the African context that informs this use of transnational governmentality, Ferguson (2006) reminds us that the contemporary African postcolonial state cannot be understood without reference to its colonial antecedent. He further notes that African states continue to "be ruled in significant part by transnational organizations" (2006, p. 100). At the heart of these topographies of power is the question of resources, and who can make decisions, and therefore profit, from them. Harvey (2004) has described how attempts to accumulate wealth and power through dispossession of common property are a crucial dimension of contemporary neoliberalism. The Ada story, laid out here, reveals assertions of topographic power, largely shown through legal assertions, and attempts at local and national accumulation by dispossession. It also shows the ways in which subaltern and subjugated knowledges have contested these forces.

CHAPTER 3

THE ADAS, A SALT PEOPLE FROM THE START

The foundation stories of the Ada state describe an encounter between a prominent Ada hunter and an old woman in the forests surrounding the Songor lagoon. This old woman is purported to have shown the hunter the lagoon and offered it to him and his people so long as he followed her teachings concerning its care and maintenance. To this day, she is known as the Yomo – a literal translation of "old woman" – of the lagoon, and is considered its spirit. Here is the account of this foundation the Ada movement produced in its 2016 book, *The Struggle of the Songor Salt People* (ASAF, p. 15):

> An eagle, or perhaps an antelope is spotted by the hunter, and is subsequently injured, but escapes into a nearby forest. When the hunter pursues it, he comes to meet an elegantly attired Old Woman, attended by two younger women, and perhaps many more. Her regalia is pure white, and according to some she sits upon a white stool – possibly made of salt. She welcomes the hunter, who is frightened and starts to retreat, but is then convinced to stay. She tells the hunter she is the animal he chased, and that he has been brought here to learn of the spirit of the forest, and the lagoon beyond. This lagoon, she shows him, carries fish, but also yields salt. She tells him that he and his descendants can fish and win salt in the lagoon, but only if they promise to uphold certain rules. The most important of these is to not dig to the gold underneath the salt. The hunter agrees to these rules, and subsequently becomes a priest of her spirit. He returns to his people gathered in the plains beyond and guides them to their new home, where they agree upon a division of the resource that sees each of them benefiting from its mutual protection.

This telling makes it clear that the Adas have been connected to salt and to the lagoon since the foundation of the state. Further evidence of the depth of this cultural connection is woven right into the language, where speaking Dangme – the Ada language – is literally the same as eating salt: "E yon ngo?," the question one asks to know if someone speaks Dangme, translates literally as "do they eat salt?" (Langdon & Larweh, 2017).

There are two important elements to pull from this origin story, as they are foundational pillars of the pre-colonial Ada state. First, the teachings of the Yomo have provided important principles of what Manuh (1992, p. 111) calls "community management of a natural resource." One of these teachings is described above – not to dig beneath the salt in the lagoon. The rest are elaborated further in the movement-produced text:

> First, she said, you must not bring anything red into the lagoon, including blood. This therefore excludes menstruating women from entering the lagoon. Furthermore no one should wear gold, bronze or bring a metal implement into the lagoon. Also, it is only when the Libi Wornor, the Tekperbiawe priest of

the Libi spirit, has deemed the salt is ready, and has performed the necessary rites, that people may enter the lagoon to fetch salt. This is done first by the Libi Wornor tasting the salt, and then placing sticks on the paths to the lagoon for two weeks after the tasting. When the sticks are removed, the salt-winners may enter the lagoon, and collect salt using a calabash and, later, a flat bottom canoe. Finally, it has been mentioned that there were only 3 days in a week that could be used for salt winning.

Many of these teachings continue to play a role in the struggle over the lagoon. For instance, in the chapter that follows on creative dissent (Chapter 5), there will be a discussion on the issue of blood in the lagoon also meaning there should be no conflict in the lagoon, and the traditional mechanisms in place to deal with such conflict. However, important at this point is the teaching about gold, as well as the power invested in the priest, the Libi Wornor, in opening the salt winning season. To this day, traditional leadership in the lagoon wear no gold as a sign of respect for what the Yomo taught. Likewise, the Libi Wornor's regulation of the access to the salt, as well as limitations placed on winning by the number of days one can do, have meant historically Adas have used the resource as a source of livelihood, but have not abused it, or monopolized it. This last point is important and will be returned to further below.

There is a second point raised above that needs further discussion – the settlement around the lagoon after the initial introduction by the Yomo. At the time of settlement, it is said there were four clans that made up Ada, namely, the Tekperbiawe, Lomobiawe, Dangbebiawe and Adibiawe (ASAF, 2016). They are known as the Okor clans. A book produced by an earlier iteration of the Ada movement describes how the Okor term is connected to this foundational moment:

> It is believed that the word 'Okor,' the traditional name of the Ada, was coined from what Korley [the hunter] said in Dangme: 'I ma ye o kor no,' meaning 'I shall observe your taboos.' (Ada Salt Cooperative, 1989, p. 18)

Hence, the traditional state foundation acknowledges the importance of the Yomo's instructions. What is important to emphasize is the way these four clans developed a mutual defence pact that enabled each clan to both have access to the resource, and also benefit from its mutual protection. Unlike many areas in contemporary Ghana that hold traditional cultural festivals to celebrate the harvest, Ada to this day celebrates the mutual defence pact that started with the Okor clans, and their settlement, and the way it allowed them to maintain control of the lagoon through several pre-colonial wars. Amate (1999, p. 111) notes, "For well over 2 centuries, from the second quarter of the seventeenth century until the third quarter of the nineteenth, the history of the Adas was troubled and dominated by one war after another." These wars were fought over the Songor and control of the salt it produced:

> As a result of this external interest in the Songor Lagoon, the people of Ada, for a long time, had to heroically defend the lagoon in numerous tribal wars.

CHAPTER 3

> Two of such wars fought over the Songor Lagoon in the last century were the Kantamanso war of 1826 and the Battle of Dodowa of 1866. These were battles fought between our people – the Adangme supported by the Ga and Ewe (coastal tribes) on one side against Ashanti invaders on the other. The Ashanti were ignominiously routed and driven away. Up to this day we, the Ada, celebrate these victories in our traditional annual festival, the Asafotufiami festival. (Ada Salt Cooperative, 1989, p. 24)

The success of the Adas in these wars is connected to the fact that all Adas would come when called to defend the Ada nation (Amate, 1999). This collective response is still performed today through the swearing of the oath of war at the Asafotufiami festival and other moments, such as the enstoolment of a new chief (Amate, 1999). And yet the spirit of the Yomo also informed the openness of Adas to those who chose to settle amongst them, rather than trying to seize the resource from them. Ada now consists of ten clans – the four Okor clans, and six other clans that emerged from those who came to join the original four. In fact, Nene Ada, the Ada Matse, or paramount chief, comes from one of these late-comer clans, the Kabiawe clan. Kofi Larweh (Langdon, 2015, p. 131) describes the key feature of overlapping ownership as crucial to the success of this pact:

> The [Songor] movement is deeply rooted in the culture of the people, why? Because of the way ownership is conceived. Ada is made up of different clans, about 10 or so 12 clans, and one clan [the Tekperbiawe] is seen as the owner of the water body. And there are four others who are owners of the surrounding lands. You look at the wisdom in this … So when you say the owner of the water body is there, and the surrounding lands have also got owners it is a convenient agreement for joint ownership and defence of the resource.

When one adds the natural expansion and evaporation of the water through the rainy and dry seasons, this overlapping custodial relationship becomes literal – the borders of authority change depending on the time of year. This mutuality does not end with the Okor clans, as they also opened the winning of salt to all interested Ada settlers, so long as they respected the Okor custodial rights and the teachings of the Yomo. Kofi Larweh (Langdon, 2015, p. 131) explains,

> You have this big salt resource … and you have millions of tons forming there for the people to collect, and anybody at all, the people are so liberal, whatever you are able to collect is yours, you only give some small part as tax to the chief and … the owners.

Albert Apetorgbor, a key member of the 1980s activism, shares just how far this generosity stretches,

> People from all walks of life come to the Songor Lagoon for salt. Some come from as far as Tamale, Ewe land, Kumasi and other places. (Radio Ada, 2002, p. 3)

ADA MOVEMENT KNOWLEDGE PRODUCTION

Nene Akwada, a Songor community chief, expands on this openness,

> Harvesting of the main of the lagoon is open for all people in Ghana even the Nigerian. Open to harvesting and then you pay tax. The priest in Ada and the Ada Paramount Chief are who operate the tax operation. Because we are open the harvesting to all Ghana, all Ghana knows that Ada has something precious. (ASAF, 2016, p. 23)

Added to this, Manuh (1992) describes how historically Adas used salt winning as one form of livelihood amongst others, such as fishing and trading. She quotes historical accounts of the trade that noted this balanced approach, and that the majority of salt winners were women or children (cf. Dickson, 1969; Sutton, 1981). Furthermore, she describes how when the salt formed, it would be stored by households for years. The French traveller, Isert, described how in the 1780s "To each house at Ada where attached huts each of which could store at least fifty tons of pure salt" (cf. Isert, 1793, quoted in Manuh, 1992, p. 111). Victoria Kpodo, one of the members of the Ada movement and a salt winner, describes salt's importance for women such as her,

> My name is Victoria Kpodo. I'm fifty years old. I'm from Sege. The Songor is there for everybody, so I also go and win the salt. When I win the salt, I use to preserve, and sell some to look after my children, pay school fees, buying their clothes, and look after the house. (Garbary, 2016)

In this sense, the lagoon was not just broadly beneficial in the past, but also gave women control over their labour and financial independence in the household. These are important points that will be returned to more deeply in the chapters to come.

To summarize, in its precolonial formations, the Ada state effectively defended this resource, but not in order to keep its benefits for its elites, its men, or even its members alone, but rather to ensure the resources was managed according to Yomo's teachings. As described below, the emergence of the Ada Matse position [known today as Nene Ada] was a result of the need to defend the lagoon, but as with the mutual defence-pact, his power was kept in check by the traditional priests, like the Libi Wornor, as the Ada Matse had no control over the Songor, or the land. This foundational attitude is a crucial touchstone that the Ada movement has returned to in its current contestation of National Development narratives. In order to properly situate this contestation, it is necessary to expand on the colonial and post-independence experience in Ada and the Songor. Rather than being valued, this careful balance of power in the "community management of a natural resource" was exploited for colonial gain.

ADA SONGOR FOCUS OF BRITISH COLONIAL DIVIDE AND RULE TACTICS IN AREA

Gerschiere (1993) documents how Britain's colonial administration created division between various factions within a particular traditional state in what is now known as

CHAPTER 3

Cameroon in order to more effectively rule over the territory. Through this example, Gerschiere (1993) illustrates the divide and rule tactics of British colonialism. In the case of Ada, the emergence of this divide and rule tactic was gradual. The two centuries of war Amate (1999) describes above saw the Adas consistently looking for allies beyond their borders to maintain their existence. In the early to latter half of the 19th century a growing British presence in forts along what is contemporary Ghana's coast made it a potential ally in the battles especially against the inland Ashanti Kingdom. Thus, Ada joined "other coastal communities in accepting British protection in the mid 1800s":

> In this sense, the British did not conquer the Adas, but rather entered into a protection, and later judiciary agreement with them [...] Colonial magistrates would supersede local authority if disputes arose that could not be handled locally. This was an important introduction, as it saw the rise of internal conflict concerning the Songor, where different British magistrates, over the later part of the 19th and early part of the 20th century, ruled back and forth on behalf of different parties within the ruling structure of the Adas on which of them would control proceeds from the Songor (Amate, 1999). This process of creating internal tensions in states through the manipulation of how customary law is interpreted is one of the ways in which the British enacted divide and rule processes. (Langdon, 2017, p. 233)

A series of magistrate and later the colonial supreme court rulings (1904, 1942, 1943 & 1946) pitted different clans against each other for control of the proceeds from the taxation of salt winning. Amate (1999) describes this tension,

> Years after Ada fell under British colonial rule, the ownership claim of the Tekperbiawe [clan] to the Songor lagoon, which had been traditionally accepted from time immemorial by all of the Ada clans, began to be seriously challenged, firstly by the Ada Matse [Nene Ada] and subsequently by the other Okor priests. Much later on, it also became a bone of fratricidal contention within the Tekperbiawe [clan] itself. As the head of the traditionally acknowledged owners of the Songor, the Libi Wornor had been performing the ceremonial rituals that pertained to the lagoon and its acknowledged goddess, the Libi. He had been ceremonially closing and opening it for salt collection and for fishing. Furthermore, he had been levying, as of right, tolls on the salt collected or fish caught from it. By convention, he had been taking one-third of the salt tolls, while the Ada Matse and the other clans were content with having the remaining two-thirds. (p. 166)

The inability to resolve these disputes within Ada, and the growing reliance on a colonial judicial system to reinforce rulings undermined the unity and autonomy of the traditional Ada state, and increased the legal rights of the colonial administration (Langdon & Larweh, 2017). If nothing else, this loss of autonomy and unity facilitated the topographic power of, first, the colonial state, and later the post-independence

Ghanaian state in the Ada area (Langdon, 2015). The tensions would also later be exploited by those interested in taking over the salt resource from outside, and thereby dispossessing the Adas of the Yomo's legacy.

GHANA EMERGES FROM THE GOLD COAST COLONY, BUT THE POST INDEPENDENCE STATE PROMOTES THE NATIONAL OVER THE LOCAL

While Ghana's independence movement is discussed in the previous chapter (Chapter 2), the Nation-state that emerged at the end of formal British colonization took over the contours of this colony. At the time, with Kwame Nkrumah's call for pan-African unity, and his spearheading a push for a decolonized Africa that would contest the borders established during Europe's scramble for Africa, it was possible to believe these borders were not fixed. And yet, as McMichael (2009) has pointed out, the emergence of self-emancipation over self-definition during such decolonization processes – even in contexts like Ghana – meant the nation-state, based on European norms, became the de facto frame of post-independence Nation-state formation. Coupled with the cold war, along with US post World War II ascendency meant national development was embedded in a web of international power relations that reinforced former colonies transforming themselves into countries. Despite Nkrumah's adept tightrope walk in the cold war period between the US and the USSR, Ghana's government still emerged as focused on large-scale infrastructure projects partially supported by the World Bank, and international donors. In other words, very quickly after independence, a form of National development focussed on large scale, industrial projects began to take shape in Ghana.

One of the largest of the post-independence period projects undertaken by Nkrumah was the Akosombo dam. Like so many internationally funded dam projects the world over, the mega project displaced 80,000 people, and wreaked havoc on ecosystems that drew from the dammed Volta river (Gyau-Boake, 2001). According to Nene Pediator, head of the Kudzragbes, the Ada clan closest to the Volta river:

> The Akosombo Dam was erected in 1965, roughly 85 kilometers upstream from Ada. The hydroelectric power facility was created to contribute to the further industrialization and modern development of Ghana. Despite Government efforts to lessen negative effects of the dam on communities surrounding the Akosombo itself, including the relocation of roughly 80,000 citizens, the dam was built without consultation or mitigation efforts to any of the downstream communities of Ada. Soon after the establishment of the dam, the people and environment of Ada suffered numerous side effects with large consequence on traditional livelihood practices […] Prior to the dam, the Ada area had an annual flood that aided in salt production, farming, as well as fishing. Once the dam was complete, all three sectors suffered greatly due to a decrease in water flow through the Volta. (ASAF, 2016, p. 27)

CHAPTER 3

Thus, this national development project did not properly take into account its impact on all Ghanaians that were connected to this river. The Amissah Commission, a commission of inquiry established by the Ghana Government to investigate the conflict that led to Maggie Kuwornu's death, alluded to at the outset of this chapter, acknowledges this oversight:

> Before the construction of the Volta River hydro-electric projects at Akosombo and Kpong, sea water flowed into the lagoon through tributaries of the Volta from Big Ada which fed the lagoon and made possible the formation of salt in due season. With the commissioning of the dam and control of the flow of the Volta into the sea at Ada, (this put an end to the seasonal flooding of the Lower Volta Basin) sand bars have formed and are still forming along the coast and the river estuary making it difficult for sea water to reach the tributaries and streams which fed the Lagoon in the past; they have become silted thus affecting salt production in the Lagoon. One witness before the Committee alleged that for seven years before the granting of the 1971 lease to Vacuum Salt Products Limited [discussed below] salt had not formed in the Songor Lagoon. If so, one could appreciate the ready willingness to co-operate with a Company which sought to revive the salt industry. Two specialists, an agriculturalist and a hydrologist, who gave evidence before the Committee stressed the seriousness of the formation of the sand bars and the effect on salt formation and emphasized that sea water would need to be brought into the Lagoon by artificial means for salt production. Seepage of seawater into the Lagoon through the seashore will not be adequate for producing a reliable quantity of salt. The visit of the Committee to Akosombo and Akuse to check on the effect of the dam on the Lower Volta Basin revealed that the emphasis had been on monitoring the flow of the river rather than the effect on the environment and ecology. (Government of Ghana, 1986, pp. 37–38)

Not only did the design of the dam not take into account its impact on those down river, but, as suggested above, monitoring of the effects of the dam in the mid-1980s was limited to flow, and not the ecological impact. Gyau-Boake (2001) has provided more recent independent evidence of the long-term impact on many communities down river from the dam – underscoring this major oversight in the ongoing management of this mega-project, over and above its initial impact. The seven year break in the formation of salt, along with the Volta dam's impact on other livelihoods meant the traditional Ada state was under pressure to figure something out, especially since the national government seemed to have its attention elsewhere. This crisis, and the existing tensions between Nene Ada and the Tekperbiawes resulting from British divide and rule, provided the opening for outside interests to come in and dispossess the people of Ada.

The account of this dispossession is well documented in both *The Making of Ada* (Amate, 1999) and *Who Killed Maggie* (Ada Salt Cooperative, 1989). *The Struggle of the Songor Salt People* (ASAF, 2016) also documents this episode in the life of the

Songor. I will draw mostly from the two movement-produced texts to illustrate the knowledge production of both iterations of the Ada movement, but also add Amate's account as and when it adds to the nuance and texture of the telling.

ADAS DISPOSSESSED, FIGHT BACK THROUGH LEGAL, POLITICAL AND PHYSICAL MEANS

With the overthrow of Kwame Nkrumah's government in 1966, Ghana began a long period of coups, counter-coups and brief periods of democratic rule. It was in the midst of this unstable period in the country's history that one company in particular, Vacuum Salt Limited (VSL) and its main owner Mr. Apenteng, began working to acquire a major concession in the Songor lagoon. Up to then, smaller salt companies had existed, but had never acquired significant concessions (Ada Salt Cooperative, 1989). Another company, Star Chemicals Ltd. also got a much smaller concession, but they remain peripheral to what happened, and therefore are not focused on in this account.

The initial approach of VSL to the Ada Traditional Council, and to the Tekperbiawe clan chief, Nene Korley II, was rebuffed. Manoeuvres behind the scenes then led to the deposing of Nene Korley II in favour of C.O.C. Amattey, a more amenable candidate (Ada Salt Cooperative, 1989). Amate (1999) describes in detail how this was made possible through a rift in the traditional leadership of the Tekperbiawe brought on by the years of fights over the Songor. C.O.C. Amattey, ironically, quickly fell out with the company, when he learned the concession size VSL registered was 11 square kilometres bigger than what he had agreed on (Ada Salt Cooperative, 1989). It was he, then, who brought the first court case against VSL, though it couldn't be heard before he was arrested on charges of misrepresenting the Tekperbiawe as having the right to lease a concession of the Songor to VSL in the first place (Amate, 1999). This then led, in 1974, to the first National political intervention specific to the Songor – Executive Instrument 30 – in which the military government expropriated the entire lagoon (Ada Salt Cooperative, 1989). After this expropriation, the government "granted a lease of a portion of the lagoon and its adjacent lands covering an area of about 12,000 acres to Vacuum Salt Products Limited" (Ada Salt Cooperative, 1989, p. 30). In reaction to this reestablishment of the company concession, traditional leaders from the Tekperbiawe clan brought:

> a petition through counsel for the revocation of the government acquisition. The apparent response to the petition under reference was an amendment to the acquisition by Executive Instrument 57 passed in 1975. This amendment [...] excluded portion of the lagoon is called the Yomo at the eastern part of the main lagoon. (Ada Salt Cooperative, 1989, p. 30)

Thus EI 30 (1974) had been amended to now become EI 57 (1975). This situation remained unchanged through a change in military leadership in 1976, a revolt by the junior ranks of the armed forces in 1979, and a return to democratic rule, also in 1979. Through this period VSL was able to establish and legitimate itself with the assistance of the National government, and to lay claim to a vast majority of the Songor Lagoon – yet at least the Yomo section remained to allow artisanal salt winners to collect salt in a limited fashion. In 1981, the situation changed in the people's favor. Mrs. Eunice Ametor-Williams, the MP that won the Ada constituency in the 1979 elections and member of the governing party, had promised during the election campaign that "if she was voted into office, she would do everything within her power to restore the Songor Lagoon to the people of Ada" (Ada Salt Cooperative, 1989, p. 32). Two years into the government's mandate they passed Executive Instrument 10, which cancelled "the leases granted to the companies in 1975 through Executive Instrument 57. The government acquisition through Executive Instrument 30 of 1974 was, however, not revoked" (Ada Salt Cooperative, 1989, p. 32). However, before the decision to maintain EI 30's government acquisition, or expropriation, of the Lagoon could be contested, the government was overthrown by the December 31st revolution. Jerry John Rawlings, the Flight Lieutenant who led the brief revolt of the armed forces lower ranks in 1979, led this people's revolution at the national level. At the local level, People's Defense Committees (PDCs) emerged that were to carry out what Rawlings said would be "nothing less than the total transformation of society" (Shillington, 1992, p. 80). They were guided by two principles:

1. Eradication of all forms of exploitation and abuse of power;
2. Organisation of the various communities to set their own developmental goals to be financed principally from local resources (Ada Salt Cooperative, 1989, p. 34).

Yeebo (2007) describes how these PDCs would be changed to Committees for the Defense of the Revolution (CDRs) when the central government, the People's National Defense Council (PNDC), shifted from local control to central control, and as the regime drifted away from its socialist rhetoric to take on neoliberal structural adjustment plans from the World Bank from 1984 onwards (Hutchful, 2002). However, in those early days of the revolution, uncertainty over what was happening enabled VSL, through their long-standing relationship with police, to reassert by force their control over the lagoon, and the salt trade in Ada in general. There are several accounts of the abuse the company, and agents of National state security under their orders, inflicted on Adas, including the force feeding of brine to those found winning salt in the lagoon, as well as the seizure of salt wherever it was found. One incident from this time was described by Albert Apertorgbor on Radio Ada:

> The late Apenteng [the owner of VSL], especially his son Stephen, would not allow anybody to win salt, let alone keep it in stock around the Lagoon for a better price.

> One day, in 1982, he brought some soldiers to the Kasseh market some 20 kilometers away from the Lagoon. The soldiers were led by Lt. Awuah. They

were well-armed. The soldiers started beating all the women selling salt at the market and all the vehicles loaded with salt were attacked. Almost everybody took to their heels. Everybody was scared. I gathered courage and went closer. I mean, I approached the soldiers to find out what they were looking for. I stood by a man who introduced himself as Apenteng, the son of the late Apenteng. He opened his palm and hit his chest boastfully, saying that he was Stephen Apenteng and the whole Ada state was under him and that he could do anything to the people at anytime he wished. He went further to say that even when Adas managed to go to university, they, the Ada scholars, would automatically come to him for employment to be able to live. His final provocative statement was that no Ada man or woman could challenge him.

I was on the verge of slapping him, but the presence of the guns surrounding us made me change my mind. That was the era of Rawlings's revolution era. The time the soldiers were ruling Ghana. I was scared to the marrow. (Radio Ada, 2002, p. 3)

In response to this and other incidents similar in nature, the PDCs in Ada moved to take over the VSL salt factory. The "14th October 1982 was set for the take-over":

On D-Day the inhabitants of the villages around the Songor Lagoon converged at Koluedor at dawn drumming and singing patriotic songs. And those from far-off places came in vehicles placed at their disposal free of charge by transport owners in the community. There was also a donation of one keg of 'akpeteshie' (local gin) from the Paramount Chief of the Ada State, Nene [Ada] Kabu Abram Akuaku III, to raise the spirits of the crowd.

At about 9 o'clock in the morning, the crowd moved from Koluedor towards the Vacuum Salt Products Limited site singing war songs. They stopped on the way at a village called Toflokpo-Kpalamkorpey where the Asafoatsengwa Otu Anim IV, the war leader of the Tekperbiaweh clan, poured a libation calling on the ancestors and the gods to lead the crowd to victory. After the libation the march continued through Bonikorpey to the Agbedrafor Presby Primary School compound for the final rallying up of the crowd in preparation for the onslaught on the company's premises where several policemen were positioned to maintain peace and order.

The leaders of the crowd seized the Site Manager of Vacuum Salt Products Limited, Mr Allotey, and demanded the keys to the offices of the company. He initially resisted and would have been mercilessly beaten into submission but for the timely intervention of the police. He then handed over the keys of the premises to the leaders of the crowd. Having gained control of the premises, the leaders went ahead to take inventory of moveable and immoveable property of the premises under the close supervision of the police. [...] Immediately PDC volunteers mounted security guard at the premises until the [appointment of]

CHAPTER 3

an Interim Management Committee (IMC) to run the affairs of the company. (Ada Salt Cooperative, 1989, p. 37)

This seizure of the VSL compound was quickly followed by an announcement by the IMC allowing free winning of salt for all in the lagoon, much to the "relief and joy to the communities of the area [... this] dealt a devastating blow to the monopoly profit enjoyed by Vacuum Salt Products Limited" (Ada Salt Cooperative, 1989, p. 38). Unfortunately, this relief did not last long. *Who Killed Maggie* (Ada Salt Cooperative, 1989) describes a number of local and national political maneuvers at this time that castigated the PDC running of the factory, and aimed to reassert the VSL and Apenteng claim on the operation. However, with the benefit of hindsight, *The Struggle of the Songor Salt People* adds some reflective self-critique, as well as placing this situation in the context of the larger shifts happening in the PNDC at the time:

> as some of those involved [in the PDC seizure of the factory] have noted, the trips to Ada's new rural bank to deposit the large earnings from the salt sites were long and some of the monies were lost along the way. It is partly as a result of this failure to manage the factories well, through internal siphoning off of the proceeds, that the same police units that oversaw the seizure of the factory by the PDCs came to kick them out on December 22nd, 1983. The Government took control of the factories at this point [..., but] it became clear the Government had the intention of restoring the factories to the companies. While this may have had its root in the misuse of funds by the IMCs, the decision was also clearly a result of broader shifts within the PNDC. In contending with the economic hardships being experienced in Ghana at the time, the PNDC decided to source help from the World Bank, taking a dramatic right turn away from a people's revolution towards neoliberal unfettered capitalism. Many of the leftist elements within the PNDC were either purged at this point, or left of their own accord – some fleeing the country, pursued by accusations of counter-coup plots. Those progressive elements that remained did so in a changed context where the PDCs were no longer given the room to offer a localized parallel source of power to the agenda of the National PNDC directives. Thus, in late 1983, the PNDC leadership implemented the first World-Bank-negotiated structural adjustment program, called the Economic Recovery Program (ERP-I). (ASAF, 2016, p. 33)

Shortly after, the Ada Songor Salt Cooperative was formed. Its emergence is taken up by both texts produced by the Ada movement. It is a central piece of knowledge sharing in *Who Killed Maggie*. Almost 30 years later, it also remains a key part of the knowledge that *The Struggles of the Songor Salt People* shares. One of the chief architects of the cooperative, Lawer Hushie, shared his version of its emergence in *Who Killed Maggie*. He described how, despite being a native of Ada, he had little knowledge of the Songor until going there as part of his duties with the PNDC central government. Upon seeing the poverty of the local communities contrasted with the wealth he knew came from this resource he decided to get involved in helping the artisanal salt winners improve their livelihoods. When he became aware VSL was likely to resume its management of the factory he was "alarmed [...] wondering whether the state of repression would not return" (Ada Salt Cooperative, 1989, p. 43). It was in this context that he had a flash of insight:

> The idea of a co-operative for the salt miners came into my mind in a flash one morning in March 1984, whilst I was sitting on the edge of my bed, my head resting in my palms and reflecting on what the fate of the salt miners would be. It was as if someone was talking to me: 'Go and form a co-operative for your people.'
>
> I immediately moved out of my room to tell my colleagues [...] about my sudden awareness of the solution to the problem of the salt miners that we had been thinking about for some time now. [...] I obtained a copy of the Co-operative Societies Decree (NLCD 252) from the Department of Co-operatives in Accra and started working on a draft for our co-operative byelaws. We moved to the lagoon area and contacted Narteh Nardugbey, Nene Klokpah II and Francis Azinah, [Songor salt winners] all from Koluedor, and discussed the idea with them. Their response was favourable and we decided to begin our organisational work toward the formation of co-operatives at Bonikorpey. (Ada Salt Cooperative, 1989, p. 44)

Very soon after, on June 1st, 1984, a Ghana Radio announcement restored the factory to VSL control, but also added, "the Ada Traditional Salt Miners should be encouraged to form co-operatives" (Ada Salt Cooperative, 1989, p. 40). With this announcement, a new stage of the struggle for control of the lagoon began, with the people having a new formal structure to contest the company's dispossession and monopoly of control. This development was indicative of the presence within the PNDC government of a real tension between two competing narratives of development, one focused on companies, and capital-intensive resource extraction, and the other focused on community-led development. While this period was seen as a time of massive deregulation and foreign investment in gold and other mineral mining (cf. Hilson, 2004), it was also the time of a large focus on developing community run cooperatives – especially to help contend with the massive influx of Ghanaians expelled from Nigeria in 1983 (Berry, 1995). The original NLCD 252 cooperative decree was brought in during the 1960s, and built on earlier colonial cooperative policies from the 1930s. However, with the economy in shambles and the return of the expelled Ghanaians, it was only in this PNDC period that cooperatives were actively encouraged (La Verle, 1994). It is important to keep these two narratives in mind, because they also speak to the presence of two factions within the PNDC itself, with one pushing for a deeper commitment to structural adjustment and foreign investment to help boost the economy, and another still linked to the

CHAPTER 3

PDC era of the early revolution and a people-first policy approach that contested exploitation. The Ada story is a clear illustration of these tensions.

By the time the announcement was made, the Cooperative had been registered, was engaged in mobilizing community members in Bonikope, and had even managed to acquire customs and tax waybills that allowed artisanal salt winners to bring their salt to market. In previous times it was VSL that collected these taxes and issued waybills, something they refused to do as "a deliberate act rendering the disposal of salt by our people impossible" (Ada Salt Cooperative, 1989, p. 46). Hence, getting these waybills was an important way to ensure the company's return could not prevent artisanal salt winning. After the June 1st announcement and confirmation by press release, it was this capacity to issue waybills that came under attack by the company through what Mbembe calls the "privatization of state violence" – a key component of the structural adjustment Ghana was now undergoing (Höller & Mbembe, 2007, p. 8). One such incident is described in *Who Killed Maggie*:

> For seven weeks after the 25th of June 1984, Vacuum Salt Products Limited had been making conscious preparations to launch a heavy raid on the salt miners. And on 16th August 1984 a detachment of the Ghana Police Force led by Assistant Commissioner of Police in charge of Tema Region, Michael Asiedu, raided the offices of the co-operative and chased hundreds of the traditional salt winners out of the lagoon. The raiders came in about eight police jeeps, two motorbikes and a police car driven by Asiedu himself. About 300 winners were forced into six cargo trucks intended to be loaded with salt and driven to the premises of Vacuum Salt Products Limited where the very young ones and the weak, aged ones were set free. The others, about 66 in number, were forced into a cargo benz truck with registration number TRA 3259 purchased by the People's Defence Committee during their take-over of Vacuum Salt Products Limited and later seized by the same company. As the captives were being conveyed to Dawa Police Station, three people, [...] jumped out of the truck and escaped. At Dawa Police Station the rest were packed into a tiny cell and detained for three to five days. One can imagine the horrible conditions in the cell at this time. Some of the captives, like Mekporgbey Lawerteh, fainted as a result of the excessive heat and stench in the cell. After the third day the captives were charged with stealing salt and were asked to pay 600 cedis each, totalling several thousands of cedis. (Ada Salt Cooperative, 1989, p. 50)

It was on May 17th, 1985, during a similar raid that targeted the cooperative and artisanal salt winners, that Maggie Kuwornu was shot and killed by a stray police bullet. Pregnant at the time, Maggie had stopped at a friend's house in Bonikorpey to have a drink of water, and became the innocent victim of VSL's ongoing campaign of dispossession. Her tragic death, and the fact that Doris Ocansey – the cooperative's lawyer – was able to get word of it to the head of state, J. J. Rawlings, changed the fate of the salt winners of Ada. *Who Killed Maggie* documents what took place:

ADA MOVEMENT KNOWLEDGE PRODUCTION

Figure 3.2. Memorial Statue of Margaret Kuwornu (photo credit: Nyani Quarmyne)

Live ammunition. Rifles and truncheons. Policemen. All this was needed to carry out an unprovoked raid on a defenceless community. The result? An incredible number of brutally assaulted people and the cold-blooded murder of a young pregnant woman. […] That morning the sun was unusually hot, probably confirming the saying that 'coming events cast their shadows before them.' Our people trooped with their working implements – hoes, baskets, sacks, shovels, carts, pieces of wood and pans – into the lagoon. Some arrived there after having walked several kilometres barefooted in the hot sun. The actual work began. But the salt miners in the lagoon and also those staying behind in the villages were unaware of the danger that loomed ahead. […]

At Sege, a town five kilometres away from the lagoon, the police were preparing for an attack on them. A scouting party was sent in order to locate the actual places within the lagoon where our people were working. Having sighted them the party returned to base. After having received their final instructions, the policemen collected their ammunition, jumped into their vehicles and zoomed off in the direction of Bonikorpey sending clouds of red laterite dust into the air. Everyone was startled. Goats, sheep, pigs and dogs took to their heels for dear life.

Ezekiel Amanor, a member of our newly formed co-operative, on duty at the office, was quickly seized by the police, slapped several times in the face and hit on the head with a truncheon that left a deep gash from which blood flowed freely. When he attempted to defend himself, he was hit in the stomach with a rifle butt. He fell flat, looking helpless, groaning and with blood oozing

CHAPTER 3

from his mouth. He was then dragged on the ground and finally heaved into a waiting police van.

While this was going on, a section of the raiders went into action in the lagoon. A rather cunning approach was adopted in their attack. Behaving as if they came on a friendly mission, having hidden their guns and other ammunition in their vans, the policemen beckoned the large crowd working in the lagoon to come out. A small group of courageous persons, however, came out of the village and started to sing war songs, our usual practice to inform one another of impending danger. […]

Just then, a reinforcement of policemen arrived in police vans and tipper trucks belonging to Vacuum Salt Products Limited. The people back in the village, realising the precarious situation of the miners in the lagoon, mobilised to their rescue. This made the police focus all their attention on the village providing those in the lagoon with an opportunity to escape. The sun at this time was at its zenith leaving the temperature of the brine extremely high. Running on the crystallised salt in the lagoon was hell. Some miners who drifted towards Okorngmleku, an island on the eastern part of the lagoon, discovered to their consternation that some of the raiders had also laid an ambush for them there.

Therefore they returned the way they had come, back into the hot brine. Some stumbled and fell and were trampled upon. Some with their feet seriously bruised by the sharp edges of the crystallised salt, hopped painfully. Hunger and thirst weakened those trapped in the hot lagoon. Our people were thus forced to give up for loss of energy. They were like the innocent lamb ready for the slaughterhouse. The police beat them up, shoved them into the waiting vans and carted them off to the offices of Vacuum Salt Products Limited. More people were arrested in the Bonikorpey village. There was heavy traffic: from Bonikorpey to Vacuum Salt site. The journey to the slaughterhouse was not comfortable either, as victims on board were mercilessly beaten. Other policemen busily engaged themselves in seizing our stockpiles of salt and the tools we use for work. People were shot in the legs. Others were vomiting blood as a result of the severe beatings they had received from the police.

Back in Bonikorpey, there was a fierce clash between the [police] raiders and members of the community. Our people defended themselves by hurling stones and sticks at the policemen. In the process, some of the policemen took shelter behind a baobab tree while others fired warning shots. […] Then, suddenly, there was a loud explosion. A trigger had been pulled and a live bullet had been shot. The original target was missed but the bullet found other victims. It tore through the arm of a lady, Amakwor Anim, then grazed the stomach of Christiana Abbio, a pregnant woman. There was a loud scream. Ao!, A fiami tu!' (Ouch! I have been shot). The bullet finally penetrated the chest of another young pregnant woman. She fell dead with blood gashing [sic] from her body. Her name was Margaret Kuwornu, known to her people as Maggie. The entire village was thrown into confusion and panic. There was wailing as our people swore to their ancestors. There was running in all directions for safety, but nowhere was safe. [...]

Having fully satisfied themselves with the day's raid, the raiders finally retired to the Vacuum Salt site leaving behind Maggie's dead body. When the dust finally settled, the village of Bonikorpey was virtually deserted. [...]

On that very day Doris Ocansey, [Ada PDC chairperson] hearing the news, rushed to the village to ascertain the truth. After having met the elders of the community and members of the bereaved family, she left with the promise that Chairman Rawlings would come down.

At about 10 p.m. on that fateful day, the Chairman and his entourage arrived at Dawa Police Station, where he ordered the immediate release of those arrested and locked up in the cells. He then continued to Ada-Foah where he met the District Secretary, Mr James Ayiku Nartey. From there the Chairman moved towards Bonikorpey. Frightened by the sound of the approaching engines and the sight of lights some of the villagers sneaked into the nearby bushes and watched the trucks of the Head of State approach the village. Those watching over the corpse pretended that they were asleep. When the Chairman arrived, it was midnight. After formal customary greetings, Chairman Rawlings requested to see the body. A libation was poured [...] after which the corpse was uncovered.

After having observed some minutes of silence, the Chairman promised that he would do all in his power to resolve the Songor issue once and for all. The Chairman finally left for Accra with the corpse. Some members of the bereaved family accompanied them. (Ada Salt Cooperative, 1989, pp. 10–13)

This extended quote illustrates the violence, chaos, confusion, tragedy, and sorrow of the day. Its events, and the loss of Maggie continue to be remembered to this day – an aspect of the story chapter to follow (Chapter 4). The quote clearly shows the privatization of state violence through the collusion of the police with VSL. In *The Struggle of the Songor Salt People*, Maggie's death is remembered, but the changes it brought about are also prominently featured:

Subsequently in the days that followed, a [government] probe into the situation in the Songor was established, called the Amissah Commission. Over the course of 1985 and well into 1986, the Commission heard testimony from the various parties involved in the Songor dispute. During this time, an announcement came [from central government] that the cooperatives and the salt-winners should be allowed to do their work unmolested. (ASAF, 2016, p. 34)

CHAPTER 3

The Amissah Commission looked at all dimensions of the situation in the Songor. The commission sat for 70 public meetings, focused on investigating "the grievances and complaints of the people of the Ada Traditional Area" with regards to VSL's behavior, whether this behavior "resulted in undue hardship to the people in the area and to make recommendations to redress such hardship, if any" (Ada Salt Cooperative, 1989, p. 70). Meeting in Accra, the commission members also undertook a visit to the Songor to see for themselves the quality of life in the area. The final results of the commission recommended the annulment of the company concessions in the lagoon, and the development of the lagoon to the benefit of both cooperatives and potential private interest. It was from the recommendations of the commission that a Cuban engineering firm, ECIMAT, was appointed by government to undertake the creation of a Master Plan for the Songor that would see the lagoon:

> used as a common resource for brine management. The local co-operative societies registered and duly recognized will also be located at the "shores" of the lagoon and will crystallize salt in their own crystallizing pans from brine partly concentrated in the evaporating ponds. (Ghana Government, 1991, p. 4)

This would, according to the plan, ensure a capacity of:

> over 1,200,000 tons per year. This capacity is enough to afford operation of the different concerned parties. This means that if the technological solutions being proposed are accepted, then the source/basis for the conflict in the area will be removed. (Ghana Government, 1991, p. 4)

Considering the theme of this chapter, it is relevant to note that this plan was developed in consultation with Songor communities and cooperative members and remains the only planning process to do so. Albert Apetorgbor, one of those involved in the Ada PDC, and who later worked for the National Commission on Civic Education (NCCE), describes this process:

> [The Cubans] were meeting the communities explaining the concept of salt production, the modern way, and the modern production of salt, they came around with pictures and moved from community to community around the Songor Lagoon. Now [the communities] were also afraid that salt is corrosive, if the salt industry is set up then gradually it will seep into the soil and destroy their various communities. These fears were also alleged. Then the Cuban team with my assistance went round and explained to them and they were doing their survey, it was my own level background in geography and my local knowledge I was able to assist them a lot. And then somewhere along the line there were a lot of consultations with the people on the ground. In the course of all these things I even suggested to them that there is a need to put the cooperative idea into the program of salt production in the area and then secondly, that now, if salt is produced in Cuba, there should be that sort of exchange program between the Cubans and the Ghanaians who are producing

salt so we can have that exchange of salt and technology and some of these things benefitted from in [sic], they trained some people and one of our people even went to Cuba and was trained, I think for one year of so. So that yearly, there can be that exchange program so that we all learn from each other, which they put in. So finally, when they completed everything, we met at the lagoon side. A lot of people came round and then the final document, it's not the final document, but the work done so far was read out to the people and, at each stage, their minds or suggestions were solicited and there were a lot of inputs. So that is why at the moment most people prefer the Cuban Master Plan to the Land Use Plan [discussed below] because it is people-centered. (ASAF, 2016, p. 76)

After this plan was produced a crucial law was passed, PNDC law 287, which codified the Master Plan in the preamble of the law, and states emphatically that the Songor should be developed for the benefit of the contiguous communities:

Whereas the Provisional National Defence Council is desirous of acquiring the land [...] and has developed a masterplan for salt production in the Ada-Songor Lagoon to ensure the efficient development of the salt potential of the Ada-Songor Lagoon by undertaking infrastructural work to benefit the contiguous communities and the public interest. (Government of Ghana, 1992, p. 1)

The law also says the lands taken over from the companies "are vested in the Council in trust for the owners and for the development of a salt industry" (Government of Ghana, 1992, p. 2). By owners it means the original Okor clans (especially the Tekperbiawe) of Ada. In this sense, and according to a, PNDC law 287 provides the communities surrounding the lagoon and its the traditional custodians a clear right to be included in whatever development happens in it. This interpretation was recently echoed by a legal opinion presented to the Ada community on July 27th, 2018, by Law and Development Associates. This law is an exception in the Ghanaian context, and provides something close to what the UN Declaration on the Rights of Indigenous People calls Free Prior and Informed Consent – more on this below. However, the law also revealed that the lagoon had been returned into the company hands in 1988, despite the killing of Maggie and the Amissah Commission deliberations. This revelation made clear the ongoing tension between development narratives in the PNDC that is described above.

Prior to the finality of PNDC law 287, VSL was still manoeuvring to regain its concession. Some of this only surfaced after the fact, so it is *The Struggle of the Songor Salt People* that describes it best:

Meanwhile, again unbeknownst to most in Ada, a new threat was emerging from those supportive of the neoliberal agenda. The new mining act, PNDC law 153, was established in the mid 1980s. It allowed much more foreign access to gold mining sectors – part of the ERP-I program of structural adjustment – and it contained a new clause that considered salt a mineral to be governed in

> the same way as gold. This meant that any mining of salt had to be done with the permission of the central Government. Concessions, such as those held previously by Vacuum Salt [...], needed to come from central Government, and not from the traditional landowners. This arrangement very much favoured the large companies, and made it difficult for artisanal salt producers to operate legitimately in front of the law. What led to the addition of salt in this law can only be guessed at, but it appears to have been another attempt to assert company rights over that of the Cooperatives and communities around the Songor. Sure enough, in 1988, just after the establishment of the new District Assembly [DA] system, the PNDC Government re-granted the leases to Vacuum. [...] However, their tenure did not last long, partly as a result of the new DA system that brought its own dynamics to the Songor situation, but also partly because the White Paper issued by the Amissah Commission clearly stated that they should be removed from the Songor. (ASAF, 2016, p. 35)

The new mining law, PNDC 153, was an important building block of the solidifying neo-liberal agenda of the PNDC National government. Established in 1986, right at the time the Amissah Commission was deliberating, it was later adopted almost wholesale into the 1992 Constitution, upon Ghana's return to democratic dispensation (Ayine, 2001). Ayine (2001, p. 100) notes how "the wording of the 21st Chapter [of the Constitution] is the same as section 1 of Law 153 except the addition of the word "trust."" The insertion of "trust" is indicative of the shift to Constitutional rule (Langdon, 2015) but it also interestingly surfaces in PNDC law 287 where, much like E.I. 10 of 1981, the lagoon is not returned to the Adas after annulling the company lease, but is rather, "vested in the Council in trust for the owners" (Government of Ghana, 1992, p. 2). PNDC law 287 also incorporates the central government legal rights established in Law 153 over salt being a "property vested in the Provisional National Defense Council" (Government of Ghana, 1992, p. 1). In this sense, while PNDC law 287 is in tension with PNDC law 153 in the sense of giving local contiguous communities as well as owners clear claims on the lagoon, it still expands the legal rights of the central government, both in solidifying salt as a state-controlled mineral, and also by layering in the notion of "trust" to comply with the Constitution introduced later that same year. Ayine (2001, p. 98) has argued that the inclusion of "trust" has opened up Ghana's current democratic executive, including the President, to being "in breach of trust imposed on them by the Constitution" because of the way communities impacted by mining have been treated. Ada, with PNDC Law 287, has the potential to contest the benefit of National Development, and perhaps open the door to other communities challenging the choice of large-scale development over people-focused development. Despite this potential, it remains unimplemented in concrete terms:

> To this day, PNDC law 287 remains the primary document governing the Songor Lagoon. Yet, the tensions within the PNDC previously mentioned

continued to play a part in the swirling wind even up until PNDC Chairman and Head of State, J.J. Rawlings signed the law. There are rumors that the law kept disappearing from his desk between April 24th, when it was drafted, and when he finally appending [sic] his signature in August. There were many in Ada and elsewhere that may have believed that with the signing of this law some of the intrigues would be in the past. The tensions in the PNDC transferred into the National Democratic Congress – Rawlings' new political party, through which he won both the 1992 and 1996 Presidential elections. The GNPC [Ghana National Petroleum Corporation] was part of this; Tsatsu Tsikata, brother to the lawyer Fui Tsikata who had defended the cooperatives during the Amissah Commission, was in charge at the GNPC and visited Ada regularly throughout the early 1990s. He saw the GNPC as a place where Government revenues could be generated in a way that was pro-people – a point of view that ran counter to the prevailing neoliberal atmosphere at the time. It is perhaps this discord with a pro-capitalist agenda that led to the failure of the implementation of the Master Plan. In any case, after 1992, the people of Ada were expecting something good to surface, and found themselves waiting and waiting and waiting instead. (ASAF, 2016, p. 71)

At the same time that this internal tension was evident in the PNDC, there was also growing tension and conflict within the cooperative. The final chapter of *Who Killed Maggie* (Ada Salt Cooperative, 1989) reveals this tension, accusing several of the senior members of the cooperative of corruption and embezzlement. The *Struggle of the Songor Salt People* (ASAF, 2016, p. 53) describes the conflict:

At this time, the Cooperative – having emerged as a major revenue collector in the Songor – also faced challenges due to internal conflicts with regards to accounting for monies. This is one of the points in this text where there is an attempt to share multiple points of view regarding what happened. In essence, the conflict had to do with the leadership of the Cooperative. By this time, some breakaway cooperatives had also formed to collect tolls on salt. In addition, in late 1986, a major rift had developed within the top leadership of the Cooperative. Accusations of misuse of funds that were taken to the National Cooperative Secretariat resulted in 3 court convictions of the Vice Chairman of the Cooperative, Lawer Hushie, his brother, Dornu, and the Chairman, Lawer Agblo. Other members within this same executive, namely the Treasurer, Ofoe Blaise Mankwa, as well as Tsatsu, his brother who was Financial Secretary, initially raised these charges. Though the 3 spent several years in prison, they were able to eventually appeal and overturn the convictions in the early 1990s. In many ways, the damage had been done: Cooperative members, as well as Songor community members had serious doubts about their leadership. These doubts were related not just to the fact that these convictions had occurred, but that the leadership was so divided against itself.

CHAPTER 3

As this quote mentions, several different cooperatives had emerged in this period of internal conflict. Manuh (1992), writing based on research done in the area in this period, describes this emergence as being directly related to the leadership issues that had emerged in the main cooperative. She also describes how absent women's voice was within leadership of all cooperatives in this period – a point she critiques especially given women's heavy involvement in the practice of salt winning. In this sense, the tensions and conflicts within the cooperatives were coming to a head at the very moment that the government was about to remove all concessions in the Lagoon.

Kofi Larweh and I (Langdon & Larweh, 2017, p. 239) have named this the *trorkpe period*, "being in the middle between two major events, where people are waiting for the proverbial second shoe to drop." Adas had successfully contested the dispossession of their resource by private interests, and had returned to artisanal salt winning, but they were fighting with each other. At the same time, the impact of the Volta Dam remained, and the solution VSL had put into place was not enough to replenish the sea water in the entire lagoon, and it began to deteriorate – something the Master Plan pointed out (Government of Ghana, 1991). Furthermore with the national government's increase in legal rights over the lagoon, the provisional return of artisanal salt winning could be undermined with a new government – which is exactly what started to happen after the democratic change in government in 2000. This led to new contemporary efforts to dispossess the Adas of this resource, and new ways to resist these efforts.

A NEW DISPOSSESSION ON THE HORIZON MEANS NEW TACTICS ARE NEEDED

Look behind us, there comes Government after us Okor People. I repeat, turn and look behind Dangme People, Government is catching up with us.

But what is the issue? Atsiakpo is consuming the whole Songor. And all attempts to stop it have proved futile, the fire rages on.

Government could not help but to step in. They told our Elders, they are going to take over Songor, to quell conflicts so that we live in peace.

Radio Ada heard of this development, took on their broadcast armour, mobilized us; we entered the communities and started informing the people; we are spreading it. (Akpetiyo Lawer, "*NƆ NƐ NƆ KO LI Ɔ, NƆ KO LE,*" ASAF, 2016, p. iii)

There are two interlinked elements to the dispossession Adas face today in the Songor. The first is the intentional failure to implement the Master Plan since it was first put forward in 1991, and the seemingly intentional continued diminishing conditions of the lagoon. The second element is the local and national elite's allowance, encouragement, and even involvement in '*astiakpo*,' the ongoing atomization of the lagoon edges through the creation of large- and small-scale private salt pans. The communal practice of old, where everyone would win salt together, and what you won was yours after paying the owners a tax, is gone, and has been replaced by a thick belt of private pans, sponsored by chiefs as well as other wealthy Adas and political elite from outside Ada, and predominantly run or owned by men – leaving Ada women dispossessed of a crucial livelihood for their independence. This issue is taken up more fully in the story and song chapters that follow, but nonetheless, the analysis of Akpetiyo Lawer, troubadour of the current iteration of the Ada movement, is another example of movement knowledge production. She astutely identifies the growing conflict in the lagoon as providing the opening central government has been waiting for to come in and exercise the legal rights it has expanded. This foray has already been tried twice, once in both of the governments that have come to power since Rawlings finished his two terms as President. It is these two attempts that will be focused on here, but in order to do so, it is important to acknowledge the entrance of a new people's organization into the Songor struggle:

> In the mid 1990s, another prospect of a people's organization emerged. Radio Ada, Ghana's first community radio station was founded in 1997, after a two-year period of participatory dialogue. As part of its mandate to be both the Voice of the Dangme People, and the Voice of the Voiceless, the station regularly broadcasts on Songor issues – keeping the Ada community connected with these issues even when they do not earn livelihoods from it. (Langdon & Larweh, 2017, p. 240)

The presence of Radio Ada has contributed directly to push back on both of the two state-led attempts to physically take over the lagoon. The station has also led the only successful campaign to date to stop atsiakpo – if only briefly.

After the 2000 change in government, President John Kufuor and his New Patriotic Party took power. Atsiakpo was still in its beginning phase. As the quote that started this chapter points out, Kufuor's government made moves early to sidestep the Master Plan, and create a new plan for the Songor, called the Land Use Plan:

> as it began its consultative process, it also began excluding voices that challenged its approaches. This led to a series of press conferences by a group representing the Songor landowning [Okor] clans [Tekperbiawe, Lomobiawe, Adibiawe, and Dangbebiawe]. At one such press conference, in 2005, the police were actually sent in to disorganize the meeting. Fortunately, some of the invited press members were able to bring the police actions to the attention of one of the main radio stations in Accra, and it carried the evolving situation live. As a result, the group was able to get its message of concern about the Land Use Plan across. 2 primary issues were raised through the process. First, there was concern that the landowning clans' desire to continue to be involved in the decision making process was being disregarded. Second, there was deep worry at the prospect of saltwinners being given alternative livelihoods, and

even some communities even being relocated out of the Songor area. Cecilia Bannerman, the new Minister of Mines was not able to overcome these concerns. When the Land Use Plan finally saw the light of day in 2006, it could not be implemented before the end of the NPP's tenure in office [in 2008]. (ASAF, 2016, p. 98)

The Land Use Plan ignored the broad consultative approach of the Master Plan, and instead looked to turn the lagoon into a concession granting area, with clear intensions to treat it similarly to other minerals under the mining act, thereby stripping local authorities from any say, and also raising the likely specter of relocation for communities in the way. This threat helped to unite the traditional leadership of the Okor clans with those living around the lagoon – an intimidating combination going back to pre-colonial times. Together, through the series of press conferences they held, and their on-the-ground support, the land owning clans rebuffed the Land Use Plan. Learning from this mistake, central government's next attempt at asserting legal rights over the lagoon would aim to drive a wedge between these elements. But before we turn to this, it is important to share how the origins of atsiakpo are directly attributable to the intentional neglect of the lagoon through the failure by government to act on the Master Plan.

Having waited most of the 1990s for the implementation of the Master Plan, people around the Songor began to get restless:

When the [Master Plan] was failing to commence work, and where the Cooperative leadership continued to operate with a question mark associated with it, related to the court cases, and internal wrangling that had occurred in the late 1980s, a Chief in Adzomanikorpey decided to take matters into his own hands. After discussing things with the [Ada Songor Salt] Project[1] Interim Management Team, he received permission to draw water from the same section of the lagoon the factory used to fill a communally built pan in his community. The salt that was collected from this pan was divided into thirds, where one third was given over to him, and the saltwinner kept two thirds. Through this he was able to set up electric lights in the village. Nonetheless, this process was attacked by a number of other traditional authorities, and eventually he was de-stooled on the charge that he was selfishly using the resource. The local court case on this matter is ongoing. Ironically, those who accused him are now purported to be leading figures in the atsiakpo process. (ASAF, 2016, p. 72)

Hence, this idea by the Adzomanikopey Chief that was begun with a desire to push the Master Plan forward in the face of government inaction, and to create communal pans outside the lagoon became the blueprint for its critics, as well as other elite, for similar individually-owned pans around the lagoon:

After [the Chief's] de-stoolment – related to how he was using 1/3 of the landowners' share collected to develop new saltpans for himself – the practice of setting up pans outside the lagoon for salt production seems to have caught on. Certainly, there are now a number of large saltpan projects that can be seen on the roadside opposite where the Songor Salt Project factory sits. Rumours abound as to whom these pans belong to, with the late Vice President Aliu Mahama being one. The rumours allege these personalities have front men as decoys. Rumours aside, it is clear that many Adas have set up small pans on land around the lagoon and draw water into them to make salt. (ASAF, 2016, p. 99)

The spread of the outside pans was initially resisted by local Chiefs and youth well aware that individually oriented pans contravened Yomo's teachings on proper respect for and maintenance of the Songor. At a very recent community forum in Lolonya, the Libi Wornor described his fight against this abomination:

In 2005, during my normal tour of the Lagoon, I came across an atsiakpo. I quickly destroyed it, and the pumping equipment it was using. As a result I was arrested and forced to pay compensation for these damages. I have stood against atsiakpo ever since, and have never gotten involved in it. (statement made at Lolonya and carried on Radio Ada, July 27th, 2018. Translated by Jemima Larweh)

Similarly, Nene Doku Anim III describes how:

We had a meeting for the atsiakpo to be abolished, [... and] we decided that the atsiakpo would be abolished or that we would stop the atsiakpo in the community but unfortunately people were not compromising with us, they don't want to do that. So we went to destroy their things, we destroyed their atsiakpo. So we were taken to court at Ada Foah and we were asked to buy their machines for them and we were still in the cells when the machines were bought before we were granted bail. And this was about 10 years ago. (ASAF, 2016, p. 120)

A youth involved in a similar action described how getting punished for stopping atsiakpo actually led him and his peers to start the practice:

Atsiakpo was being constructed, some of us stood up against it. We destroyed some of the Atsiakpos and were arrested. But we've been released and as the [sic] released us they [the authorities] also went and did the Atsiakpo, we all jumped into the Atsiakpo end and do the Atsiakpo. As a way to cater for our families. But when we were coming to destroy it we were arrested. (ASAF, 2016, p. 120)

This defence by national and local authorities of private salt pan developers, despite the fact they were operating without state dispensation, and contravening long held teachings and local regulations was a deep moment of learning for these youth. The local chiefs and youth stood up, but none of the authorities nor the older generation of Songor activists came to their defence (Langdon, 2009b). This set the stage for many of the schisms in community level activism later on, and opened the door for women to step forward as the only ones who could legitimately organize Songor community resistance (Langdon, 2011a). This is discussed in greater detail in the chapters that follow.

With government and upper level Ada traditional authority backing atsiakpo, if only indirectly at this point, it was allowed to spread – with some of those who couldn't beat it joining it. The next major effort to stop it came in 2008, when there was a realization even by the Ada Traditional Council that it was getting out of hand. Radio Ada had also begun carrying it as an issue from 2002. Kofi Larweh described how it was becoming a major source of conflict in the lagoon at that point:

> People have called in [to Radio Ada] on some other programs that we have organized in the community. People have hinted … if you are talking of water, there is a more serious case. If action is not taken, if people do not, if the people who are cheating us are not prevented there will be war in the Songor. (Langdon, 2009a, p. 262)

He goes on to say how it wasn't just those in Ada complaining of the growing conflict in the Songor:

> This is not only an issue of Ada. We had calls from the Volta region, saying that, look we don't like what is happening, the Adas are not selfish, we know them to be very embracing. (Langdon, 2009a, p. 263)

This point harks back to the consistent argument the Ada movements have made that this resource has never just been for Adas. This reminder by callers outside Ada underscores how the communal approach to artisanal salt winning represents a counter argument to large-scale national development, as the Songor has been for generations an artisanal source of livelihood for a wide spectrum of people who now call themselves Ghanaian. Atsiakpo not only threatens the livelihood of Adas, especially women, who generally don't own pans, but also threatens the way the resource benefited people far beyond the borders of Ada (Langdon, 2015). At the same time, it should be acknowledged that the atsiakpo practice has its origins in the perhaps misguided, but nonetheless community-minded intentions of a local leader tired of waiting for the Master Plan to be implemented. Furthermore, it became an out-of-control destructive phenomenon because of this same period of state neglect and the prosecution of those who rose against atsiakpo, who were charged for the destruction of private property. Where were the state forces defending the public interest and common property?

In a prescient fashion, Akpetiyo Lawer's song, quoted above, describes how these events have let to the present where "Government could not help but to step in. They told our Elders, they are going to take over Songor, to quell conflicts." After neglecting the Lagoon for years, the rise of Atsiakpo has enabled the central government to reengage with the Songor space with renewed vigour – ostensibly

Figure 3.3. Ada Songor Advocacy Forum members, including Akpetiyo Lawer, third from right, Mary Akuteye, first on right, and Jane Ocansey, second from left (photo credit: Nii Obodai)

to "quell conflicts," but really to secure its legal rights. And, again, it was Radio Ada, along with a newly emerged iteration of the Ada Songor movement, called the Ada Songor Advocacy Forum (ASAF) that took on the new threat to artisanal and communal salt winning. *The Struggle of the Songor Salt People* describes how in May 2011, a government delegation held a series of meetings in Ada to launch a new strategy for the Songor:

> The strategy aimed to make the lagoon into a brine reservoir, to relocate Songor communities and offer them "alternative livelihoods." This delegation included representatives from the Minerals Commission, the Ministry of Lands and Natural Resources and the Office of the Vice-President, and was led by PEF [Private Enterprise Foundation – a parastatal government agency]. It raised deep suspicions by meeting with the 4 original Okor clans separately – a tactic that was perceived to be an attempt to divide and rule. Subsequently, the 4 clans met to compare notes and realized they had been told the same story about moving the Salt Strategy forward, and moving communities out of the Songor area. Radio Ada broadcast news of this delegation to much concern throughout the communities, giving air to the accounts of the various clans at these meetings. (ASAF, 2016, p. 102)

CHAPTER 3

Despite the change in government in 2008, back to the NDC (the same party that was connected to the establishment of the Master Plan), this new plan sounded a lot like the Land Use Plan of the NPP. The newly formed ASAF, along with its ally, Radio Ada, took news of this plan to the people:

> In the months that followed – especially during the rainy season when salt could not be won – ASAF members, along with Radio Ada went to 7 main communities around the Songor (Toflokpo, Agbedrafor, Lolonya, Luhuor, Lufenya, Anyamam and Goi) for 2 main reasons: (a) to continue to solicit their views on atsiakpo, and ways people could try and deal with it on their own, and (b) to discuss the Government hints about relocation and alternative livelihoods. In Anyamam and Goi, they also discussed the deforestation of the Okor forest – the legendary forest where the 4 clans originally stayed together, and where original Korley is said to have met the Yomo spirit. Atsiakpo continued to elicit much debate. There was general agreement that it wasn't a positive development, but that the diminishing returns from the lagoon had made some sort of local action necessary; at the same time, the response regarding relocation and alternative livelihood was a unanimous "No!" The Priestesses of Lufenya summed up the general sentiment by breaking into war songs. They stated they would only agree to relocation if their ancestors and the ones who had yet to come agreed, and if all the buildings, houses, trees, the river Lufenya from which the community draws its name, and the whole of the Songor were to be relocated. (ASAF, 2016, p. 102)

Radio Ada also managed to capture the tension within the ruling party, as it aired interviews with the two local MPs who were part of the government but opposed this plan; "both stated the Government delegation had done a 'bad job' and 'not the right thing'" (ASAF, 2016, p. 103). This quick mobilization on the airwaves and at the community level forced the government to back off, but it hadn't given up as it chose "to operate in secret instead" (ASAF, 2016, p. 103). It was later learned that several prominent chiefs were invited to Accra, where secret attestations were signed by them that gave the government room to stop community salt winning, with the prospect of "alternative livelihoods" offered instead. These attestations, and the Cabinet Memo they were attached to, were leaked to the movement, and they detailed the government plans for the Songor. Though the memo suggested the best plan for developing the Lagoon was a government/private investor/community approach, it then went on to make it clear that the community would not be involved in production, but would rather be given alternative livelihoods in line with the Land Use Plan (ASAF, 2016). This Memo and the attestations became the focus of community and airwave activism the following year. Added to this, ASAF and Radio Ada focused on intervening at the Asafotufiami Festival – mentioned above – where women salt winners marched, and a popular education display was mounted to share the Songor story with the 10,000 visitors that flock to the area:

ADA MOVEMENT KNOWLEDGE PRODUCTION

Women in each of the communities visited were incensed. Not only was atsiakpo continuing to make them labourers in their own resource, partially as a result of the failure of Traditional and District Assembly leadership, but now these same leaders were conniving with central Government interests to deny them once and for all of their ancestral salt winning practice. The women from across the contiguous Songor communities decided to march at 2012 Asafotufiami Festival and insist on the centrality of salt to Ada's identity. […] They demonstrated to much effect, also setting up a popular education display that included a tapestry they designed. (ASAF, 2016, p. 104)

The details of this popular education effort are shared in the next chapters. While the police were left flat-footed by this demonstration, especially as it was by women and was clearly non-violent, there was still a reaction by the traditional authorities:

[A] member of the organizing committee of the festival, Adams, knocked down the placards the women carried that read, "*Salt for Sale, Lagoon Not for Sale*" "*President Mahama, we look to you for help*" and "*Implement the Master Plan.*" (ASAF, 2016, p. 104)

Figure 3.4. Women marching in 2012 Asafotufiami demonstration

Since this unsanctioned foray at the festival, the movement – especially the women leaders – has identified legitimately participating in the festival as an important mechanism for elevating their analysis of the Songor situation to the ears of National and local leaders, as the festival is an important meeting ground for local and national political interests. For instance, "the very political leadership from Accra connected to the idea of alternative livelihoods and relocation" were present on the day of their march and popular education display (Langdon & Larweh, 2017, p. 245). This leadership even visited the display, where a member of the ASAF women's leadership narrated their struggle, ending with this statement:

> Presently the state of Ada is we are mourning, we are so sad, we are in poverty. The question is should this continue, because in those days people were arrested, people were arrested, this is the police. They arrested people, they chased people, some were asked to eat salt. Some were driven away, and this has continued and continued up to date. We are saying the wealth that we have is encased and locked up in this box, what do we do? […] We are saying the Government should implement the Master Plan, so that we can get a lot. (ASAF, 2016, p. 142)

The constant reference back to the Master Plan is an important marker of the link between the knowledge production of past and present iterations of the Ada salt movement, as the plan's participatory design process after the long period of resistance to company rule has made it a touch-stone for a way forward that includes the livelihood concerns of Songor communities, and artisanal salt winners in general.

Since 2012, external central government relocation threats to the lagoon residents have been in abeyance, but the ongoing destruction from atsiakpo – both of the resource itself and of community unity – has continued, despite the continued resistance of the women of ASAF. The activism of these women has become so visible that they have been renamed the Yihi Katsɛmɛ, or Brave Women. Their story is the focus of the two chapters that follow.

RESISTING THE NATIONAL DEVELOPMENT AND NEOLIBERAL NARRATIVE

Kapoor's (2008) work makes it clear that social movement learning literature must be grounded in movement articulations, and that subaltern social movements use a variety of ideological positions to support their projects. In the case of Ada, the two, and possibly three, articulations of the Ada salt movement have defended local livelihoods and the link between Songor and Ada through a variety of arguments and positions. As the above has shown, these articulations have been active through very different times. Lawer Hushie remarked on this at one point, noting how they had to use different tactics to fool authorities during the resistance in the 1980s given the political realities of a military government at the time. However, in today's context, with freedom of association and freedom of expression guaranteed in Ghana's Constitution, community radio makes great sense, as the movement, and its meetings can now be wide open, allowing for broader participation in the movement. This openness has also enabled the movement to critique the secrecy of local traditional authorities, as well as central government. Furthermore, it has helped broaden a knowledge democracy surrounding the lagoon, and it is through this openness that the movement has shared its current and previous knowledge production. In this sense, the iteration of the 1980s, embedded in a far more repressive state, relied on the Amissah Commission and the Master Plan process to share the knowledge it had produced – knowledge it later turned into *Who Killed Maggie*. In contrast to this contained ability to disseminate its knowledge production, the current iteration of the Ada movement uses radio, the internet, mobile phones, as well as open meetings at the radio station and community after community to produce and disseminate its knowledge. *The Struggle of the Songor Salt People* is available online, as is *Who Killed Maggie*. Even more recently, the movement uses songs, dance, and theatre to share knowledge. This will be the focus of Chapter 5.

Recognizing these different times, and their realities, the multiple iterations of the movement have nonetheless returned to similar positions in their knowledge production in defending communal artisanal salt production in the Songor. As emerged in the Amissah Commission, and was re-emphasized in both books created by the movement, large-scale national development has been the source of many of their problems. The Volta dam destroyed their natural salination cycle. The back-and-forth policy decisions (Executive Instruments, etc.) of various versions of the nation-state display of topographic power echoed the back and forth decisions of colonial times, where local unity was undermined through state intervention. The one national development plan the people had a say in, the Master Plan, and the PNDC law 287 that enshrines it, has never been implemented.

At the same time, Ferguson and Gupta (2008) provide an important reminder that even in the shift to a democratized context, the African Nation-state needs to be understood to be embedded in a web of transnational neoliberal governmentality that discursively defines how the state can enact development. The Ada movement has challenged this definition repeatedly by mobilizing the discredited knowledge of those large-scale development would seek to dispossess. In fact, in contrast to the track record of chaos, dispossession and disappointment, the Ada movements past and present have been consistent in offering the traditional communal and artisanal approach to salt winning as an alternative form of national development. So often, the argument for the topography of power of the state is premised on ensuring the wealth of a particular region benefits the rest of the nation (Ferguson, 2006). As was described above a number of times, the Adas have consistently shared with their neighbours, and even those from far away – always ensuring the Songor was beneficial far beyond its borders. The shape of this locally determined, but nationally inclusive approach can be seen in other sectors, such as the small-scale gold mining sector, in which people from across the country engage (Langdon, 2015). Hilson (2004) notes that despite this sector operating largely illegally, it still employs roughly 1 million Ghanaians, compared to the large-scale mining sector that contributes

CHAPTER 3

> ## Songɔ wɔ kulaa wa nɔ yimi tomi
>
> ### Songor For All Manifesto
>
> **Adopted by Songor Women Saltwinner Representatives at Abokobi (8th April, 2016)**
>
> 1. Whereas we the women of the Songor know this to be our reality:
>   - (i) The Songor Lagoon is integral to the identity and history of we, the Adas, drawing from the legacy of Yomo (the "old lady") who handed it over as a resource for all;
>   - (ii) Our forefathers and foremothers maintained and defended the Songor as a resource for all, including through observing traditions for its preservation;
>   - (iii) As women, we use the Songor as a sustaining life force for our families and our communities;
>   - (iv) While simply living a life like ours, a woman of the Songor just like us, and one even pregnant with child, was shot dead by state security;
>   - (v) In the recent past, Songor has become a resource for a few, rather than for all;
>   - (vi) Atsiakpo has divided the Songor, and brought disunity, hunger and suffering among us, the Adas;
>   - (vii) Songor for a few has dispossessed women in particular from our beloved Songor;
>   - (viii) Authorities at the local and national level have not fulfilled their responsibilities as stewards to ensure Songor is maintained as a resource for all;
>   - (ix) For decades, women's voices have been silenced from the Songor struggle, but we now take our rightful place at the forefront of efforts to ensure Songor is for all;
>   - (x) The Constitution of the 4th Republic of Ghana gives us the right to express and organize ourselves to ensure equality as well as equitable development;
>   - (xi) PNDC Law 287 entrusts Songor for the benefit of contiguous communities of Ada;
>   - (xii) Our right to be included fully in the development of the Songor development is supported by the UN Sustainable Development Goals and the UN Declaration on the Rights of Indigenous Peoples, to which Ghana is a signatory;
>   - (xiii) The past has shown that when united as Adas – when the hand is one - we are able to maintain and defend our Songor;
>   - (xiv) We, as Songor women, assume our place as the thumb in the hand.
>
>   *Yihi katseme! Wamasi!*
>   *(Brave women! We are there!)*
>
> 2. As Songor women, our work is guided by the following values and principles:
>   - (i) Songor as a resource for all;
>   - (ii) A united woman's voice for Songor as a resource for all;
>   - (iii) Unity and peace among the people of Ada;
>   - (iv) Humility, courage and integrity;
>   - (v) Sharing what we know, learning what others know;
>   - (vi) A vibrant and healthy Songor, therefore vibrant and healthy families and communities of Ada, for generations to come;
>   - (vii) Commitment to Songor as a resource for all: yesterday, today, tomorrow.
>
> 3. To ensure Songor is a resource for all, we the women of the Songor will:
>   - (i) Engage our communities to include all voices of Ada, especially those who are least heard;
>   - (ii) Work in particular with women to amplify the voices of Songor Women;
>   - (iii) Work to instill unity among all people of Ada;
>   - (iv) Spread the story of Songor and its struggle far and wide;
>   - (v) Maintain and defend Songor as a resource for all!!!
>
> 4. We call on our leaders at all levels to join us proactively in maintaining and defending Songor as a resource for all:
>   - (i) Our Queenmothers to align themselves vigorously with Songor Women;
>   - (ii) Our Chiefs to be faithful to their role as stewards of a communal resource;
>   - (iii) Our local and national authorities to ensure equitable policy and legislation;
>   - (iv) The President of the Republic of Ghana to provide supreme leadership to ensure Songor as a resource for all in line with the Constitution of the Republic of Ghana, PNDC Law 287 and the Sustainable Development Goals.

Figure 3.5. Yihi Katsɛmɛ Manifesto, 2016

very little to the economy. Therefore, what happens in Ada, and the knowledge this movement produces is of direct relevance to another area of national development. Manuh (1992) has noted how the Master Plan and the end of company rule in Ada suggests that with pressure another relationship with the National state is possible.

In its most recent iteration, Yihi Katsɛmɛ, the Ada movement has returned to this position, calling for the implementation of the Master Plan and to respect PNDC law 287. They have also drawn on international accords such as the United Nations Declaration of the Rights of Indigenous People (UNDRIP) to boost their case.

The Yihi Katsɛmɛ, or Brave Women, have sought the advice of legal experts to put together a challenge to the state's topography of power to make decisions without local input on the Songor. Their most recent manifesto, contained in *The Struggle of the Songor Salt People* (ASAF, 2016, p. 148), calls for PNDC law 287 to be respected as it, "entrusts the Songor for the benefit of contiguous communities of Ada." It also links this respect to ensuring, much like in the development of the Master Plan, that they be "fully included in the development of the Songor" and that this right is supported by both the UN Declaration of the Rights of Indigenous People (UN, 2007), and the UN Sustainable Development Goals (UN, 2015). In consultations with public interest lawyers, Law And Development Associates (LADA), PNDC 287 has been identified as a much stronger basis for ensuring local benefit and involvement in development of the resource than Ghana's current Mining Act (LADA, 2018). This is based both on the legal principle that a specific law takes precedence over a general law, and also on the thinking that this specific law is more closely aligned than the general Mining Act with international compacts to which Ghana has agreed. This stance has yet to be tested in court, but nonetheless represents the latest of the important contributions to knowledge the Ada movement in its various iterations has been producing. At the same time, LADA made it clear that a Legislative Instrument (LI) is needed to implement 287, and this is a current focus of the Yihi Katsɛmɛ activism.

NOTE

[1] The Ada Songor Salt Project is what the former VSL salt factory has been called since the government take-over of the Lagoon through PNDC law 287.

CHAPTER 4

STORIES AND RESTORYING AS SOCIAL MOVEMENT LEARNING

> Our work, in the field, is to help people tell their stories, is to help people come out with these images so that it will stick – the images stick better, because that is what people will remember.
>
> – Kofi Larweh (Interview, August 2012)

Stories are central to this research, not only for how they emerge, embedded in the context, the history, and the epistemology of the Ada people, but also for the way they are restoried over time – revealing a pattern of evolving analysis, a series of conclusions that come from learning from experience. Chamberlin (2003) argues that stories are the way in which we write ourselves into the world, and justify the direction we have chosen or would chose to follow. At the same time, Abdi (2008) emphasizes that oral cultures have a deeply refined literacy level that often manifests through stories. Choudry and Kapoor (2010) further underscore the importance of grounding social movement learning studies in movement articulations. Building on the last chapter that illustrated the arguments justifying movement actions emerging from movement knowledge production, this chapter describes how the Ada movement produces knowledge through a process of restorying – revisiting stories and editing them based on learning (cf. Randall, 1996; Kenyon & Randall, 1997).

Here is a quick story to illustrate this process, picking up where the previous chapter ended, with the Yihi Katsɛmɛ having articulated a new vision to return communal access to the Songor, called the "Songor for All" Manifesto. Since the articulation of this manifesto in 2016, the Yihi Katsɛmɛ have consulted with communities around the Songor, as well as with traditional leadership about the plan. The Tekperbiawe clan leader, Nene Korley – who has publically endorsed ending atsiakpo in the lagoon – asked that the Yihi Katsɛmɛ change the title of the manifesto as it seemed to imply the Songor would be owned by all. As an example of restorying in action, the Yihi Katsɛmɛ took the decision to accommodate this request, and renamed the manifesto, "Songor, livelihood for all." This quick example of restorying illustrates how the narratives the Ada movement have articulated over the past decades reveal both the learning of the movement, and the knowledge it has produced.

In this chapter, several examples of the production and restorying of collective stories will be shared. These range from following the shifting narrative of

CHAPTER 4

the movement in response to pressure from authorities, and thereby avoiding containment; to tracing the emergence of overarching imagery that has framed movement members' thinking about their struggle; to the ways in which these narratives are restoried over time, and evolve into the basis of concrete knowledge production; to an in-depth look at the processes that led to the most prominent examples of knowledge production in the movement: the tapestry, the books, and most recently the "Songor, Our Life, Atsiakpo, Our Death" dance drama. But before turning to these examples, we need to discuss a crucial concept that emerged through this research: literacy of struggle.

LITERACY OF STRUGGLE

The literacies here, the best way of looking at it, is to see the communication models that have emerged. One key is Akpetiyo's form of literacy, where she is using her natural voice and the talent of using Dangme idioms and expression to [connect with] people and direct their attention to her music and lyrics. That is one, and it has a strong feeling because she is using the culture, the sound forms that make her presentation attractive. (Kofi Larweh, Interview, August 2012)

Literacy of struggle is a term developed during the course of this research (Larweh & Langdon, 2014). It is a way the research has come to describe the emergence of being literate in the struggle not so much by the facts, signs and symbols that one knows, but through an "attitude of constant learning and growth of understanding of the Songor struggle" (Larweh & Langdon, 2014, p. 230). In such a conception of literacy, a member of the movement such as Akpetiyo Lawer is reconceived as being deeply literate in Dangme idioms and culture as opposed to lacking written literacy or language capacity in English. As her song made clear in the opening of the ASAF book, she is deeply immersed in the challenges the Songor faces, and sings to both share this knowledge and call on all to act. Let me invoke one of her songs, part of which was quoted in the last chapter, to underscore this point:

Hark Almighty, put on the sun light; I say Almighty Radio Ada, put on the sun light forever. Whatever is under water through you comes to light. Whatever is underground through you comes to light. [...]

Chorus (implying; 'what do you think my people?' And they: respond 'we agree.' Applause)

Look behind us, there comes Government after us Okor People. I repeat, turn and look behind Dangme People, Government is catching up with us. But what is the issue? Atsiakpo is consuming the whole Songor. And all attempts to stop it have proved futile, the fire rages on. Government could not help but to step in. They told our Elders, they are going to take over Songor, to quell conflicts so that we live in peace. Radio Ada heard of this development, took on their broadcast armour, mobilized us; we entered the communities and started informing the people; we are spreading it. [...]

What someone does not know; I say, what one doesn't know, someone knows! (Repeat emphatically). (Audience response): What someone does not know; what one doesn't know, someone knows! What someone does not know; I say, whatever one doesn't know, someone knows! (Repeat emphatically). (Audience response): What someone does not know; what one doesn't know, someone knows! (ASAF, 2016, p. ii)

Here, Akpetiyo's call for people to come to know the situation is at once a call for listeners to become critically literate of the situation in the Songor, and it is also an indictment of those who know but do not share the knowledge. In this sense, literacy is both about gaining fluency in a new knowledge context, and displaying the appropriate community-building attitude towards this knowledge. This is not a passive form of literacy, it is a "literacy form that invites ownership, as it implicitly commits people to the struggle" (p. 230). The democratization of knowledge implied by this form of literacy also resists commodification, and "is rather premised on deepening collective ownership of issues and understandings" (Larweh & Langdon, 2014, p. 230). Kofi describes how this form of literacy has emerged in the context of the Ada movement:

We are also using another form [of literacy], you may want to call it gossip, but it is our traditional way of spreading what is new, people have started talking of 'hey, have you heard, I went, I had an experience which is different from what we have been doing' and you can tell that the sort of meetings we [Radio Ada and ASAF] hold are different from other meetings because they leave indelible marks on their minds so the way the meetings are conducted is like, using all the people who are there to go and carry out the message again. There are some ways of handling information, whatever you hear you keep it to yourself and you just shut your mouth. There are others, they are a trigger, you hear and you feel that hey, it empowers you to show others how much you know, how much you care, how much you are part of a certain system and so the driving force is there [to spread the knowledge]. (Larweh & Langdon, 2014, p. 233)

The open space at the heart of the Radio Ada, the Ada Songor Advocacy Forum (ASAF) and now Ada Songor Salt Women Association (ASSWA – Yihi Katsεmε) dialogue encourages this second form of learning. Literacy in the Songor struggle is deepened when "broad based [oral] discussions and mutually constituted understandings of the struggle bump up against one another and enrich people's literate connection with and ownership of the issues at stake" (Larweh & Langdon, 2014, p. 234). When coupled with communication technology such as radio and mobile phones, this form of literacy takes flight, and is no longer bound by the forms of dogmatic written scripts. Oral literacies can be carried far and wide, can be archived for future use, and can be incorporated into edited collections of voices

CHAPTER 4

through digital editing. In fact, Kofi and I (Larweh & Langdon, 2014) have together argued that the digital turn in communication technology has democratized literacy tools to those who are so often excluded from having a voice – allowing those such as Akpetiyo to emerge as living, deeply literate leaders and knowledge producers of their cause.

This concept of literacy of struggle is important as it frames the stories that follow. These stories emerged in the context of building a literacy of struggle, and the literacy of struggle that was born in turn helped produce some of the concrete knowledge products that movement members have used to further democratize this knowledge. In many ways, there is no better place in this book to find evidence of the deeply productive theory and knowledge building of this movement than in the stories below. Their foundation in a "pluralistic literacy allows for understanding to be defined and enriched by marginalized voices, as opposed to elite ones" (p. 234). Inherent in this process of building a literacy of struggle is the production, the articulation of knowledges that undermine dominant discourses and ways of understanding. In rooting these knowledges in local literacies, subjugated ways of knowing, ways of understanding the world rooted in these local literacies begin to disrupt dominant forms of knowledge (Mignolo, 2000).

CHALLENGING HOW THE ROOT CAUSES OF STRUGGLE ARE FRAMED

As noted above, collaborative restorying narratives allow for an epistemic challenge of dominant discourses (even within critical theory) as it foregrounds the ways in which subjugated ways of knowing and being are actually defining struggle – rather than locating this struggle within Euro-American theoretical containers (Marxism; post-structuralism; liberalism; etc.). For instance, the Ada case challenges the false dichotomy between material livelihood and identity concepts as a root source of struggle. In ASAF's work the two are absolutely intertwined, as the history of struggle about the Songor, along with its linkage with foundational narratives of the Okor people is as much a part of the strength of the movement as are the 60,000 people fighting to protect their livelihood. This point can be illustrated through the following narrative.

This narrative concerns the link between livelihoods and resource use. From the outset of the most recent iterations of the movement, ASAF and Radio Ada have not solely focused on the defense of communal access, and inclusive planning processes in connection with government decision-making about the resource. The movement has also consistently emphasized the link between the Songor and Ada identity. Not only is speaking Dangme literally described as eating salt, mentioned earlier, the founding of the Ada nation is intrinsically tied to the lagoon. This connection is spelled out in the previous chapter. Here, I will discuss the use of this link as an example of restorying in action, and how the ability of the movement to think on its feet allowed it to side step efforts at containment by the government and local elite. To do this, I will turn to an incident that followed the women's march in 2012. This incident happened in Goi in the middle of August 2012. Crucial here is not only the way in which Ada identity narratives were used to bolster the movement's position, but also how these were restoried over time to deepen the impact of movement actions.

The importance of the Okor forest in terms of Ada foundational identity cannot be understated. In many ways, this forest – located on the southern edge of the lagoon – symbolically echoes the current situation in the Songor, and also the larger Ada nation. Called "Okorhuem," or home of the Okor, it is heralded as the forest through which the founders of the Ada nation were guided to the lagoon by the Yomo spirit (ASAF, 2016). This forest serves practical spiritual purposes, as it is a major shrine of the Ada people, and is the first place a newly enstooled Ada Matse, or Paramount Chief of Ada in the current lexicon, is to go to be spiritually fortified and educated in the roles and responsibilities of his new position. Although it is still unclear as to when the deforestation of Okorhuem started, it has nevertheless dwindled in contemporary times to a fraction of its original size. It has also been shunned by the current Paramount Chief of Ada, Nene Ada. The only parts of the forest that remain are the four shrine areas of the founding Ada Okor clans. On a number of occasions Radio Ada, along with other members of the movement, linked the degenerated nature of the forest to the atsiakpo encroachment on communal access to the Songor, as well as to the dwindling of the lagoon's salt production levels. In particular, this link was made at a community meeting in Goi on August 16th, 2012, elaborated below. In making this link the movement has both connected with the foundational narratives of the Ada nation and Ada identity, as well as established a strategic support to the movement's consistent message that it is working to improve not just the lives of Songor residents but also revitalizing the culture of the Ada nation – a difficult thing to openly criticize. From a social movement learning perspective, this strategy emerges from long-term learning *in* struggle (Langdon, 2009a, 2011b), connected to previous iterations of the movement.

During the company conflict described in the previous chapter, defenders of communal access at the time were able to have the Yomo shrine site (not the *Okorhuem*) declared outside the purview of the company concessions (Ada Salt Cooperative, 1989). The "strict cultural adherence among the people of the area" was convincingly used to get the military government at the time to "exclud[e] the Yomo section from the acquisition" (Ada Salt Cooperative, 1989, p. 31). In several ASAF discussions, this victory was described as an important beachhead for the later annulment of the concessions. From this perspective, linking spiritual and cultural identity-markers to the Songor struggle was an important lesson to apply to the current struggle. Along slightly different lines, Radio Ada also saw this link with the forest as an important demonstration of the station's commitment to address multiple community issues – a point often used to undermine attempts to paint the station as becoming too deeply involved in Songor issues alone. This sense of the need to show balance emerges from the learning of the station staff in how to deal with contentious issues, enacting the station's mission to be the 'voice of the

CHAPTER 4

marginalized' and ruffling the feathers of the local and national elite, while at the same time performing neutrality, or a form of balance in the station's relationship with traditional authority. As is discussed elsewhere, this is not an easy balance to achieve, and is a constant source of learning and adjustment (Langdon, Cameron, Quarmyne, & Larweh, 2013). But the pragmatic approach this account of learning suggests should not overshadow the very palpable importance this forest has for many Adas, and the very real need to do something to protect and regenerate it – something a wide number of people, including many traditional authority figures, support.

The importance of this many-levelled interconnection was demonstrated at the movement forum in the Songor community of Goi on August 16th, 2012. This meeting was to be a continuation of the series of meetings about the previously mentioned secret Songor attestation that ASAF and Radio Ada had held in 4 other communities (Nakomkope, Lolonya, Toflokpo and Anyamam). At the meeting, ASAF and Radio Ada effectively undermined attempts to paint the movement as anti-Ada and anti-Development by broadcasting live from the community and focusing not only on Songor issues, but also the regeneration of Okorhuem. It was clear from the outset that there would be attempts to disrupt the meeting and to try and undermine the open agenda of ASAF/Radio Ada. For instance, as a number of invited traditional rulers arrived, they received phone calls, and quickly started to leave. Upon inquiry, it turned out someone claiming to speak for Nene Ada had threatened them with removal from their positions, a process called destoolment in Ada as Traditional Authority figures sit on stools. Adapting to the evolving situation, the assembled members of ASAF and Radio Ada quickly restrategized and restoried their approach. They sensed an effort to discredit the open approach they had been using, and so decided to air the entire meeting live on Radio Ada to show they had nothing to hide. They also made sure to draw links between the issues they were raising about the Songor, the secret attestation and the plans around it, and the way in which the nearby sacred Okor forest had been allowed to become run-down. This connection was immediately picked up on by the assembled community members and the outpouring of concern about this important Ada symbol was captured on air. For instance, one community member said in the live on-air broadcast:

> [W]here our elders settled in the Okorhuem, we've neglected it; people are building in the Okorhuem; it is vanishing. And the Okorhuem is there for the four main clans, so when they enter there they have these certain roles and the rites they perform over there, and the duties to mention at the Songor. And when Songor is full of water, they journey with canoe from the Songor, land and then walk to the Okor forest. Now none of these things are happening. (Unnamed speaker in Goi broadcast, August 16th, 2012)

This strategy allowed the movement to effectively position itself as defender of both livelihoods and Ada identity. The use of genuine concern for both the Songor and Okorhuem took the foundation narratives of Ada's history of defending these two symbols of the Ada nation from threats, and wedded them to the movement's work. This conscious use of narratives, reworked and restoried as the movement moves and learns, is illustrative of the effectiveness of narrative restorying as a method for documenting this movement's deepening and democratizing literacy of struggle.

This approach had the desired effect of positioning the movement as a defender of Ada values, and backfired against the Traditional Authorities. As a result, the Ada Traditional Council were forced to meet with ASAF and Radio Ada members, where some openly discussed their mistake in signing the government's secret attestation. Kofi Larweh describes how the Ada Traditional Council requested:

> a formal meeting with ASAF today as part of the day's agenda. [...] We had to strategize so that they do not turn the meeting into a trial. We got the Women advocates to lead the group – ASAF/Coops/Radio Ada/DESPA. Rev Sophia Kitcher did the delivery supported by Rebecca and Jah. The women did the talking so Jah ended up with permission to take leave and the vote of thanks. The meeting slated for 10:00am took off 11:45. The presentation was received with claps, smiles and a frown. There were questions, clarification and commendations. The frown came from Nene Okumo of Dangmebiawe. He admitted openly that he was one of those who signed the attestation and has not been happy with attacks on the reputation of Chiefs who signed. He referred to ASAF as the enemy of Ada Chiefs. He was cautioned diplomatically by Nene Pediator who was in the Chair for Nene Ada. One other Chief who signed said he was grateful for the awareness being created thru Radio Ada. Different Chiefs spoke about their appreciation on the [*Okor Ng kor*] drama series and the weekly Tuesday evening Coop Salt Programme. (Kofi Larweh, personal communication, January 5th, 2013)

During the course of the conversation, the central point was that any plans for the Songor need community input and involvement, and that this is crucial for the overall development of Ada. The openness of the Goi meeting, where Songor development was linked with ensuring conservation of other Ada sites, like *Okorhuem*, buttressed this argument – in contrast to the secret agenda of the government discussed earlier. This kind of transparency, and also grounding its narratives within what Mignolo (2000) calls 'local histories,' have been the two legs upon which the movement has had success, and has built its literacy of struggle. Mignolo describes how such histories, grounded in subjugated knowledges, destabilize what he calls global designs, or sweeping logics such as that of neoliberal globalization. In this he draws from both Foucault's (1980) notion of local subjugated knowledges that destabilize truth regimes, such as large discursive logics like neoliberal globalization, and Gramsci's (1971) belief around subaltern knowledges being the place to begin challenging hegemony. Gramsci's work also inspired Subaltern Studies scholars such as Guha (1983) whose work proposed challenging colonial dominant knowledge claims through the stories of those who resisted colonial power. In this sense, restorying of local histories of struggle not only reveals collective learning through

CHAPTER 4

their ongoing production, but also shows the ways in which dominant knowledges, such as National Development as shown in the last chapter, are challenged in an ongoing, shifting way. It is the shifting, the restorying, that both reveals learning, and the emerging efforts to contend with the global designs of neoliberalism.

Delving deeper into how these subjugated and subaltern local histories/ local imageries emerge, then helps us follow the path of learning in struggle in this movement. The three symbols and surrounding narratives described below document these paths of learning. Kofi Larweh helps to open up this site of local history by describing the importance of this narrative approach in connection with the epistemically rooted symbols at the heart of this chapter:

> When we were growing up, knowledge and wisdom was presented in the form of Ananse Stories and you have animals and trees talking and it helps to build the imagination so that one is led in the spirit to experience what is good. Now, our people are storytellers. All the history of the community is, is written in songs, in stories that are handed over from one generation to the other and so, people would even say what is going on in the community in the form of animals or trees, birds or whatever, in a certain way. Our people are great storytellers. That is the reason why I started by saying that what has been expressed has two forms, the spirit and the letter. And so, if you take the thumbless hand, the dog and the chameleon, this is the letter, that is what is physical. The spirit behind it is the feelings that the people are able to express, looking at the whole thing, at these things as they said or as they live with the humans. The understanding is that, normally you will hardly, for example, if you have a bad leader, our people would not say that, "you have a bad leader," you would say that "our leader has bad advisors." The same way you don't want to talk to the people in the face. And so, the simple thing is to use the logic of the thumbless hand, the dog and the chameleon in the form of objects that can give meaning to what they feel, deep down their hearts. And our work, in the field, is to help people tell their stories. Is to help people come out with these images so that it will stick, the images stick better, because that is what people will remember. Even up to this day, those who said these things and those who heard will know that, when you're talking of the thumbless hand, the dog and the chameleon, they know what they are talking about. (Langdon & Garbary, 2017, p. 9)

With this analysis in mind, we can now turn to look at the "hand, the dog and the chameleon" symbolic, restoried narratives that inform much of the ongoing strategic analysis of the two most recent iterations of the Ada movement – ASAF, and the ASSWA-Yihi Katsɛmɛ.

THE THUMBLESS HAND, THE CHAMELEON, AND THE DOG

With so much history of struggle in this movement, one of the major issues identified by movement members early on in collective conversations was a need to share inter-generational knowledge, while also learning from the past in today's struggles. As was mentioned in the previous chapter, and as is discussed in the Chameleon section below, there has been a disconnect between the generation of older male activists and youth protestors (Langdon, 2011). It is in part because of some of these tensions, and a desire to regenerate organizing around the Songor, that the initial conversations around this research began in 2008. At the same time, cross-cutting this issue, and very much linked to continued mobilization and concern by women in the Songor communities regarding atsiakpo, is the point that Manuh (1992) had made previously that it is especially women who are affected when communal access to the Songor is restricted. It was based on these three key elements (older male activists, younger activists, and older female activists) of the current iteration of the Ada movement, called the Ada Songor Advocacy Forum (ASAF) at this point, that the organic perspective of these groups emerged during a workshop, held on June 6th and 7th, 2011. Divided into age and gender-based groups, each group had taken on the task of detailing their understanding of the issues confronting the lagoon, concluding with sharing a symbol that captured the core issue for them. It is from this process that three images – now deeply entrenched in the movement's popular education processes and public analyses – emerged.

The Thumbless Hand – Older Male Activists

> For me, this whole thing is like somebody without thumbs, who is cutting morsels of food, he is hungry, but he wants to cut, you know, banku, you have to cut a morsel, and you need to roll it into a certain shape, before you can [eat it] ... You need, you need a thumb ... so for me it is a thumbless hand trying to mold a morsel of banku ... So, we had, we had everything, but we lacked something, we lacked something to make our intentions and our aspirations complete. And for me, the thumb is important. (Nomo Abayatey, Traditional Priest, member of the older generation of male activists)

In their group discussions, the older generation of male activists, including Nomo Abayatey, shared their version of the history of struggle, detailing the layers upon layers of intrigue and undercover moves associated with the 20 years plus of company presence in the lagoon (1970 to 1992). While being a combination of older men from both within the Songor community, including some elders, chiefs and traditional priests, and from the educated Ada civil servant community, the group members were all involved in the last wave of struggle over the resource. The group reflected on the difficulties they had in meeting under successive military regimes, the challenges they had in finding out what was planned at the national level, and the intrigue of discerning who within the broader Ada community, and within the Songor communities themselves, were aiding the companies in their operations. With the revolution in 1982, this all became more fraught, with a belief that the resource would be returned to the community. According to Manuh (1992, p. 115),

CHAPTER 4

the revolution opened the door for one of the local People's Defense Committees (PDCs) "formed in communities and workplaces following the events of 31 December 1981" to take "over the operations of Vacuum Salt Limited." As was detailed in the previous chapter, this seizure was not handled well, and short-term looting overtook putting in place a long-term, people-centered management plan.

But even as this was going on, the companies, especially VSL, had gone behind the scenes and were quietly pushing for the concessions to be re-granted. This came to light in an ambiguous moment where, on June 1st, 1984, the revolutionary government both re-granted the concessions of the companies and issued a proclamation on national radio that "the traditional salt winners in the Ada Traditional Area must be encouraged to form co-operatives to win salt in the area allotted to them" (Ada Salt Cooperative, 1989, p 46). As part of the transformation away from monopoly capitalism, and also to contend with a major return of Ghanaians expelled from Nigeria in 1983, the PNDC called for the formation of various forms of production cooperatives (Berry, 1995). Anticipating a need to secure traditional artisanal salt winner access to the lagoon, as well as taxation and customs forms to trade the salt won from the lagoon, a group associated with the PDC management committee had already begun forming cooperatives in the lagoon. The foresight in pursuing the formation of the cooperatives meant the people of Ada now had a tool through which they could reassert their right to win salt. And yet, this tool was necessarily blunt, as it had to face repeated police raids, intimidation, etc. It was one of these raids that led to Maggie's death. Through her death, as the previous chapter explains, the Amissah Commission was formed and PNDC law 287 was eventually passed, cancelling the company concessions.

It was in the midst of reflections over what was regained, but also the terrible price paid in the process, that the notion of the thumbless hand emerged. As Abayatey said, "we had, we had everything, but we lacked something, we lacked something to make our intentions and our aspirations complete" (ASAF Focus Group Discussion, June 6th, 2011). This idea of the hand with the missing thumb became important, as it captured the way in which the mobilization in Ada was successful at regaining access to the lagoon, but there was a lack of something to concretize the aspirations of the people to guarantee this access. Upon presentation to the plenary, broad agreement emerged that this was the perfect image to describe both the success and the shortcomings of the last struggle over the lagoon.

However, of perhaps greater pedagogic interest, the issue of the missing thumb provoked a debate that instigated critical analysis. First, discussion centered around whether the missing thumb was mismanagement of the resource by those who managed to seize control at particular moments during the 1980s. Then a discussion emerged, provoked by Kofi Larweh who said:

When we had the opportunity to manage the resource, was management composed of women? And, for, for that special ability of women to be added, or, management of the time was so made up of men, that the missing thumb could be alluded to the missing role of women in managing at the time that we took over? (ASAF Focus Group Discussion, June 6th, 2011)

Thus, the inability to use the resource well was connected to Manuh's (1992) critique that the previous organization around the movement provided very little room for women's leadership. This is discussed further below, but it should be noted here that the Yihi Katsɛmɛ *Songor for All* Manifesto states, "We, as Songor women, assume our place as the thumb in the hand" (ASAF, 2016, p. 148).

Debates also surfaced regarding who removed the thumb: was it removed by internal strife, or by external threats? The companies were still operating behind the scene to regain their stranglehold on the resource – even as the Amissah Commission sat to review the situation that led to Maggie's death. At the same time, Manuh (1992) documents growing internal tensions within the cooperative over the mishandling of money, which led to the criminal proceedings against cooperative leaders, on the one side, and the proliferation of cooperatives on the other. *The Struggle of the Songor Salt People* shares voices from both sides of this internal conflict (ASAF, 2016). Upon reflection, these and many other answers were found for both what the thumb was, and how it came to be removed. Importantly, though, many of these answers provoked lines of action that were grounded directly in learning from the past. This is what restorying can do in an action-reflection cycle. For instance, the discussion of missing women's leadership within the previous movement led to a conscious effort within ASAF to ensure women are not only playing a lead role in the movement, but also in articulating the struggle. Ultimately, it was the emergence of women's leadership in ASAF that led to the formalization of the Yihi Katsɛmɛ (Brave Women) movement.

The Chameleon – Youth Activists

> The symbol that we selected was a chameleon, and, it was in reference specifically to the chiefs, who were participating in Atsiakpo, and to how the chiefs would be doing, some – would be involved in Atsiakpo, but at the same time, like I mentioned, they would be saying "oh yes, Atsiakpo is very bad, I'm gonna stop it." And so, like a chameleon, they would be in one environment looking one way, but then they would change when they went to another environment, they would change their appearance. (Tom, representing youth activist group, ASAF Focus Group Discussion, June 6th, 2011)

The next symbol came from a group that was self-described as a mixed gender youth group, but was mostly composed of young men. Being much less versed in the history of struggle than both the older men and women, the focus of the youth was on the current situation – atsiakpo. It was the internal betrayal by those in leadership positions, saying one thing and doing another, that rose most firmly to the surface of their analysis. As can be gleaned from the above quote, there is a common understanding that many traditional authorities – those who have the power

CHAPTER 4

to grant land usage – are directly involved in the atsiakpo process. The traditional priest, Nomo Abayatey, confirmed this, saying "what the youth said is so effective, it affects [and touches] the chiefs." He went further to link the importance of publicly declaring on radio this chameleon behavior as being crucial to ending atsiakpo, as well as to building a strong, united front to undermine any attempts by central government to expropriate the resource:

> The [radio] drama, as it's going on, showing that a chief is giving money to somebody to do Atsiakpo for him. And, the same chief, in the drama, was asked to arbitrate over a case where the person he was sponsoring is caught constructing Atsiakpo, and the chief fined the, the culprit, and the chief gave money to the culprit to come and pay at his own court, that was in the drama. That it is true, that is exactly what is happening. (ASAF Focus Group Discussion, June 6th, 2011)

This avowal by a key traditional priest is crucial to legitimating the critical analysis of the movement, especially by its younger generation. As important as it is to be rooted in women's articulations of this struggle, the voice and energy of youth is also critical to the success of this movement. What was so important, if also disheartening, was that the community discussion forums that followed this workshop around the atsiakpo issue and the threat of government relocation confirmed both the applicability of the chameleon image, and the stories of elite involvement in the astiakpo phenomenon. For instance in Toflokpo, the heart of atsiakpo activity, one of the youth spoke of a contemporary company being "formed by some of the elders and chiefs in the community [who] came together to form this company to win salt, to construct atsiakpo along the lagoon" (Unnamed young man, Toflokpo community meeting, July 10th, 2011). As was mentioned in the previous chapter, young men in the area did not take kindly to this development and initially "stood up against it" (ASAF, 2016, p. 120). After being arrested for defending what was right, they became atsiakpo practitioners themselves "as a way to cater for [their] families" (ASAF, 2016, p. 120). Another youth made clear the hypocrisy of Chiefs calling for an end to atsiakpo out of one side of their mouth, while being involved in it:

> the Atsiakpo, there are bigger ones along the lagoon. And if they should stop the Atsiakpo they should start destroying those ones. Because when the decision, the chiefs having been making the call because they want to stop the Atsiakpo, but they are not really doing it because those ones are there and they are winning salt from them. Because if those ones are not destroyed, they cannot destroy the smaller ones. (Unnamed young man 5, Toflokpo, July 10th, 2011)

This analysis of the duplicity of leadership has led to the return to this image again and again over the last seven years. It was this analysis that led ASAF and Radio Ada to steer clear of working with Chiefs for some time. The secret attestation that was discovered showed even more clearly that those in positions of authority were only too happy to hand over the Songor to the government, and give the Songor inhabitants "alternative livelihoods." The Goi example was equally revealing, even amongst those chiefs who had been getting closer to the movement. They were easily scattered by a phone call and text message. Despite the meeting with the chiefs after the Goi incident, and the subsequent visit of Nene Ada to an ASAF meeting in the latter part of 2012, the restoried narrative of the chameleon has taught the movement members to keep both eyes on the Chiefs lest they change color again. In March 2016, Jane Ocansey, Treasurer of the Yihi Katsɛmɛ, noted:

> The Chiefs have a place where they call "the Chiefs are eating," we call that place Small Harbor because the Chiefs will come and talk and talk and go in and get money from that place and then will keep quiet on what is happening. The Chiefs have paid people to do the atsiakpo; people even said they will go and show them, this is for the Chief and they will show them with proof so still, the Chiefs are part of the thing.

This continued duplicity teaches movement members to stay vigilant, and through the use of the Chameleon imagery, their literacy of struggle deepens.

The Dog – Older Female Activists

> "What symbolizes the group's view?" We said dog. Our reason for choosing dog is that the dog works for us, when we [are] going for hunting, take the dog along. When we need an animal to take care of our house, we take the dog. But what do we do to the dog? What, when we, even when we go to hunt with it, do we even give it the meat? After cooking, do you remove some meat for the dog? No! It's what we've chewed, the bones that you feed it with, that's what we do to the dog. So, that's it, that is what the Songor is. (Jemima, representing older generation of female activists (ASAF Focus Group Discussion, June 6th, 2011)

> Look behind us, there comes Government after us Okor People. I repeat, turn and look behind Dangme People, Government is catching up with us […] They told our Elders, they are going to take over Songor, to quell conflicts so that we live in peace. Radio Ada heard of this development, took on their broadcast armour, mobilized us; we entered the communities and started informing the people; we are spreading it. (Translated excerpt from *"NƆ NƐ NƆ KO LI Ɔ, NƆ KO LE"* song by Akpetiyo Lawer, ASAF Focus Group Discussion, June 7th, 2011)

Akpetiyo is a leading voice within ASAF and the Yihi Katsɛmɛ. Her social commentary songs, like the one drawn from here, capture the essence of the current struggle in Ada. She was not present the first day of the 2011 imagery discussion. Yet, when she joined the following day, she immediately connected with the symbol

CHAPTER 4

of the dog that Jemima describes above. She sees the lagoon in a similar fashion, calling the salt from the lagoon, "abomination salt":

> My family and I no longer win salt because we consider the current salt from our lagoon to be abomination. We were not using this atsiakpo method of salt winning in the past. I grew up to meet the Songor lagoon free to all. It was the main source of livelihood for our mothers and also served as their source of income. Today, people are balkanizing Songor lagoon and selling them. (ASAF Focus Group Discussion, June 7th, 2011)

This analysis by Akpetiyo is crucial at grounding the current struggle in the livelihood contexts being felt by communities around the Songor, and by women in particular. During the plenary presentation from the women's group they applied the notion of the taken-for-granted and mistreated dog to themselves, and not just the lagoon. This was an important link, as it foregrounded in the midst of discussions about the history of struggle around the resource, how women's labour has always been at the heart of salt winning, and yet how their opinion has never been sought when decisions are being made about the lagoon. This analysis further connected with the conversation of the missing thumb, described above, where women were also excluded from leadership of the previous iteration of the movement.

In a follow-up women's leadership session in July, 2012, women organizers from across the Songor communities, as well as those in the district capital, came together at Radio Ada to deepen their analysis, as well as articulate together the role they could play in changing both the situation of the Songor, and how women are perceived within the Songor. It was during this session that their plan to march in the Asafotufiami Festival was developed, and also where the idea of the tapestry took shape. First, it was decided that Songor community women would organize themselves to come to the park where the festival durbar (culminating celebration) is held, and bring salt to carry on a march around the park. The aim was to ensure that all know who it is who wins salt in the Songor:

> The reason for carrying salt for the public will know that that is our source of livelihood and so we should add, people will know that we are serious about ours and your property and someone is coming to take it from you, we will make banners and placards. On the banners we will write "leave our salt for us, leave our land for us," one will be direct for the Atsiakpo people. (Unnamed woman 1, Women's Leadership Meeting, July 13th, 2012)

Following this, the women also decided to display the salt for sale:

> one advice I'd like to give is that we could win some salts to come and sell, so if you can bring them in the little sacks that you sew and you know we could bring those ones, and then come and sell, you should bring the different levels of salts that you have, you could also, and you should have some little,

maybe packaging stuffs to come and that you could package some of the salt. (Unnamed older woman 1, Women's Leadership Meeting, July 13th, 2012)

At the same time that these roles were taken on by women from the salt winning communities, the Queen Mothers – the recently established women's voice in traditional authority – and Rev. Sophia Kitcher took on the role of producing "an artistic work." Reverend Kitcher is an important voice of professional women in Ada, as she is both a reverend and a veterinary doctor. They decided to engage an artist who "will listen to what the Queen Mothers and I say and put it into a drawing or a cartoon" (Rev. Sophia Kitcher, July 13th, 2012). This effort ended up surfacing as a beautiful six meter long tapestry that depicts the story of the Adas, and also highlights crucial roles played by women in this history.

Figure 4.1. The story of the Songor Lagoon Tapestry, by women's leadership in ASAF (photo credit: Nii Obodai)

This restorying has used the subjugated stories, experiences and knowledges of women to destabilize male-dominated versions of Ada identity to make room for women's leadership. Betty, a speaker at the women's forum noted:

Most of the [C]hiefs are forgetting that they are run by females, not just them, most of the males are forgetting that they are run by females, their mothers, they forget the role that females [play] ... let's not always, try to look to the men, now let's get over those fears that we have, so that we will do what we need to do as women ... even if you are a kid, a little girl or boy, and you are given a leadership position you should be able to go and be just as [one of our women leaders] is here. (Women's Leadership Meeting, July 13th, 2012)

With this clear vision that women have always played leadership roles, and that young ones, girls and boys, should be taught to emulate women leaders – not just male leaders – a popular education mission was born. Not only would this tapestry present visual evidence of women's prominence in the Ada story, but its attractiveness would also offer an opportunity to go deeper into this restorying. This would be done by creating an oral walk through that would accompany the history represented in the art work. This restorying is perhaps the finest example of sharing the literacy of struggle this research has documented. The Queen Mothers and Rev. Kitcher worked with a small number of women from the Songor communities to develop this oral

CHAPTER 4

presentation, and worked out how to tell it in four languages: Ga, Twi, Dangme and English. This work was done with the intention of setting the tapestry up at the Asafotufiami Festival agricultural exhibition being organized by Rev. Kitcher – also a veterinary officer with the local Ministry of Agriculture department. This was also where the women set up their salt mining exhibition – with salt for sale. On the day of the Asafotufiami Festival Durbar in Big Ada, with thousands there to take part, the beauty of the tapestry, as well as the scrutiny the women's unsanctioned march drew, resulted in enormous attention from locals and visitors alike.

Figure 4.2. Jane Ocansey shares the women's Songor Tapestry story with a group of Ada children (photo credit: Leah Jackson)

Having women trained to take groups through the story of the tapestry in several languages meant they could share their restoried vision of the history and future of the Songor with over 2000 people on the day of the Festival. Radio Ada, broadcasting live from the festival grounds, carried one of the women's descriptions across the airwaves that day, reaching thousands more. Here is a translation of this live broadcast, in its entirety as it captures restorying in action, as the movement builds its narrative for change:

> The whole legend is that you know Adas originally came from Nigeria, Ile Ife, and we walked all the way to Osudoku area in those days, history that is

92

what we got to know, and midway there was some friction, some conflicts, that is why we have the name Ada, Ada means separated or dispersed, and our ancestors' intention was to relocate, come down and look for a suitable place to resettle, so they walked along the coast, right down from Ningo area and as they were coming, one of our ancestors was coming, was thirsty, that is Tekperbiawe, the name of the man was Korley, he was thirsty, he was looking for water to drink. Fortunately there was an eagle, over the Okor forest, so he saw the eagle, the eagle flew and directed him to water, and then fortunately he saw the sea, and the Yomo, you know where the source of our salt is a small catchment area. And it's been named Yomo. So it was this Yomo, the old woman, who led, she was a spirit, who led Korley to this. That was how he discovered the Lagoon. And so what happened after that, after that there have been developments. And in those days what normally happens is when the salt is the salt forms, our chief, that's Nene Ada, goes there. To open the lagoon for everyone to come and mine. This is him, he comes all the way from Luhesi and then he comes with a boat, and he walks to the Lagoon so that people will start mining.

So this is the mining process. All these years we've been expecting him to come, to interlink our leaders, so we could have created something. The booklongs [academics], the bourgeoisie, the chiefs, our leaders the assembly who would say something [against the companies], they couldn't do anything until this lady was killed and they came out with the Master Plan, that is Maggie, they came up with the Master Plan, unfortunately nothing has happened up to date. We have gold, the white gold, but unfortunately people are dying because of the white gold. Maggie was of value, womanhood is of value, of value. She died as a pregnant woman. Presently the state of Ada is we are mourning, we are so sad, we are in poverty. The question is should this continue, because in those days people were arrested, people were arrested, this is the police. They arrested people, they chased people, some were asked to eat salt. Some were driven away, and this has continued and continued up to date. We are saying the wealth that we have is encased and locked up in this box, what do we do?

Now it's selfishness, because the place is not developed, selfishness has set in, individuals have been able to allocate small portions of the plots to themselves and they are doing their own salt production, and they in turn will hire women to come and mine, before they give them just peanuts. Should this continue? We are saying the government should implement the Master Plan, so that we can get a lot. Salt, the uses of Salt: first it can be used in the textile industry, we use it for food seasoning, we use it for fish and meat preservation. We use it for the petrol chemical industry. We use it for the soap industry. Through electrolysis it can be used for chlorine and the chlorine products, and then when salt matures it turns into gypsum, you can use gypsum for vessels, ship building. You can use gypsum for chalk making, you can use gypsum for

CHAPTER 4

> even cutleries, you know the handles, the white handles you can use it for that. We can use it for numerous things, we have over one hundred forty uses, thousand uses of salt and Ada is one of them. Why do we continue importing from Brazil? So many potentials, the youth will be employed and we will go a long way. Coming and contributing our quota to the nation and the district, and whatever, so that's what we are expecting. (Rev. Sophia Kitcher, August 4th, 2012)

This account of the Ada story places women in key positions. It is the spirit of the lagoon, the Yomo, the old woman, who guides the Adas to the lagoon. It is Maggie's death and the question mark it raised that finally forces the chiefs, the assemblymen and the book-long bourgeoisie – impotent until then – to say something. Finally, it is women's current status of being subjugated through the selfishness of some that has raised the current round of demands to implement the Master Plan. Women are portrayed in this account as crucial to Ada's progress, to answering the question "what do we do?"

In order to unpack this unfurling of women's leadership and activism within ASAF, we can return to the planning session in July, 2012. It begins with an analysis of how women are perceived in the Ada community:

> [In] the church and then the home, we are given a little respect, but when it comes to the community whether you are a youth or an adult, you are not given any respect at all. (Unnamed older woman 3, Women's Leadership Meeting, July 13th, 2012)

This analysis echoes the "dog" connection made in the 2011 focus group discussion. At the same time, women boldly asserted they have real knowledge about the Songor situation to share, and have begun sharing it despite this lack of respect. Martha, a women's representative from Goi, shared a story of courage in standing up to the atsiakpo process:

> I told one old man there, why are you allowing this person to do this, create a pan at this place, that's the passway for the water, water could collect for tilapia to come so they could fish from that place too. (Women's Leadership Meeting, July 13th, 2012)

This confidence in knowing the situation in the Songor better than others – even older men – laid the foundation for women within ASAF to take the lead with the analysis and activism in the movement as well. Not only did women such as Akpetiyo insist that the issue of atsiakpo be kept at the center of movement work, but it was also women who led the planning for how to demonstrate against the secret attestation and planned relocation of Songor communities in 2012:

> We said we will wear trousers, we will go with Gong-gongs and some people will carry, and some said they need to wear red tops so that they know they are

very serious. (Unnamed older woman 2, Women's Leadership Meeting, July 13th, 2012)

Wearing trousers is something generally reserved for men, while wearing red is a traditional sign of going to war. Putting these two together would symbolically register that the women were marching to take the leadership men had failed to provide, and that they were prepared for figurative war on this issue. This collective planning and organizing process had its challenges, but coming together also emerged as a story of overcoming adversity:

> it's about time we, all the communities also come together, and we are able to work or speak whatever they say to us here and [...] bring out our voices as one, [...] today I pray to God that, I'm an illiterate and any time I come here so many issues come up and I need to go and report all those things to my community, but unfortunately I can't put it down on a note so that I can remember everything. But today God's been so good, I've been able to keep everything and I hope that when I go I will tell them, I will inform them about everything that we have discussed here today, so that we will be able to also, come up. (Unnamed older woman 1, Women's Leadership Meeting, July 13th, 2012)

This sense of coming to know, to understand, and to be able to share this knowledge is crucial to the women in moving from their self-avowed status as dogs to their yet-to-be-named status as wolves, from passive to active stakeholders in the Songor's future. This is the process of becoming literate in the struggle:

> I would have lost a very important and vital information about the lagoon which I have been winning salt from. If I had not come here I wouldn't have known what is going on. Things that I have not hear, or I've never heard, which are secret issues I've come to hear those things here. (Unnamed woman 2, Women's Leadership Meeting, July 13th, 2012)

It was out of this sense of purpose and knowing that the 2012 Asafotufiami Festival intervention occurred. And by a year later, after the demonstration at Asafotufiami, after the launch of the tapestry, after Reverend Sophia Kitcher led the ASAF delegation to get an apology for the Goi incident, after Radio Ada had carried Akpetiyo's songs countless times as well as aired the Songor drama production, after all this, the sense that they had transformed from dogs to wolves was articulated by the women leaders. When asked for an image to describe themselves in 2013, one woman said:

> So with the women now the discussion, our proverb is the woman is the one who knows what the child eats. Our symbol is that we are like a wolf standing in front of the Songor and is scaring away all destroyers of the Songor. So that is our symbol and that is our proverb. So we are standing by Songor like

CHAPTER 4

wolf scaring away all other animals with the aim of destroying the Songor. (Margaret, Yihi Katsɛmɛ Focus Group, July 3rd, 2013)

The women, by their own admission, have gone from being dogs to wolves. A key learning that has emerged in this iteration of struggle is that women must play a leadership role in the Songor movement. The combination of this shift in imagery, along with the idea of the missing thumb articulated by the older male activists, and the women's grounded analysis has made this conclusion clear. Over the course of 2013/14, the women's leadership within ASAF began to take on their own voice and structure, and it was through this that the Yihi Katsɛmɛ were born.

Akpetiyo is a key example of this leadership, as her voice, and her songs have emerged as the crucial popular education tools of this movement. For her it is the atsiakpo-ization of the resource that is the key example of the disregard for the lagoon and the livelihoods that depend on it. Her thoughts back in July 2011 reminded all present that being a chameleon is not just for the Chiefs:

Some atsiakpo practitioners are seated among us. We are the same people making noise against such atsiakpo. If we really want to change, it must start with us ... because we need to unite and fight for Songor. (ASAF Focus Group Discussion, June 7th, 2011)

This statement reflects the dialogue and learning space at the centre of ASAF and then Yihi Katsɛmɛ, where group discussion often involves both calling people out on their contradictions, and at the same time offering a path to collective action. Unafraid to call it like she sees it, Akpetiyo illustrates how having a "thumb" like her might have changed the last iteration of struggle, even as she composes songs in the current one that point out people's duplicitous colour changing. As part of the Songor for All community level focus group sessions, the Yihi Katsɛmɛ developed a mechanism for visually navigating people's positions on atsiakpo collectively:

[T]he 345 women who participated in these focus group discussions voted overwhelmingly for Songor to return to being a resource for all. These votes were a visual method in themselves, in that the vote began with eyes closed, with arm positions showing how people felt (i.e. arm up if you wanted a return to Songor for all, down if you didn't, and in between if you weren't sure), and then participants would open their eyes to see how they all voted. The visual vote was also then turned into an open discussion where those who voted in different ways explained why they voted the way they did. This open, transparent process meant women in communities surrounding the lagoon could delve into the complex feelings in their midst, while also building a consensus for action. (Harley & Langdon, 2018, p. 199)

This process will be elaborated on more in the next chapter, where the creative use of songs to frame this voting will be discussed. Nonetheless, what has emerged over time is a women's group first being part of the analysis, then leading the analysis, then leading the action on the Songor, and now, in the contemporary period where women salt winners, very few of whom can speak English, or read or write in either Dangme or English, are deeply literate in their struggle. This was brilliantly illustrated when Mary Akuteye, the President of the Yihi Katsɛmɛ, restoried the image of the dog, shared above, at a popular education conference in Cape Town, South Africa, on June 26th, 2018. She reconfigured the image of the dog to now embody how they bark at threats until the threat feeds them, at which point they bow their heads to eat. She likened this to Chiefs and other leaders in Ada who make noise about what is happening in the Songor, until they are given something to quiet their bark. In this sense, Mary linked the dog analysis to the chameleon image the youth had used previously.

CHALLENGING MALE DOMINANCE THROUGH ROOTED RESTORYING

The story of the missing thumb is indicative of one way in which the movement itself is undermining male dominance in the movement from within. The conscious decision by ASAF to center movement strategy on the analysis of women, and the subsequent emergence of Yihi Katsɛmɛ as an autonomous element within ASAF, now leading the activism on the Songor, has opened an opportunity to spread this thinking beyond to the broader Ada context, restorying Ada gender power dynamics more generally. A great example of this is the radio programming Radio Ada undertook in support of the activism in the lagoon.

Much like ASAF was being more and more guided by women's analysis and action, Radio Ada began to delve deeper into women's leadership potential in the *Okor Ng Kor* drama series it was developing alongside the movement's activities throughout 2011, 12 and 13. This series focused on the Songor, and fictionalized the ongoing conflicts in order to comment on them. For instance, the whole of episode 10, called 'Trusteeship: Males or Females?,' was dedicated to the potential of women's leadership, given the failure of male leadership to solve long-standing issues in the Songor. Here is an excerpt from the opening of this episode, in which an old wise woman, Wana, speaks to one of the traditional priests and elders of the community, Nomo Gbleetse:

Wana: ... So if I may ask, who are the elders choosing to take the position [of the head of our clan]? We are still searching but no one has been decided on yet. It shall be well ... it definitely will be well but don't you think Songorteytse's first daughter may be a good choice? The girl he had with that lady who stayed in that mud house close to the forest.
Nomo Gbleetse: Yeah ... yeah ... yes I think I remember her.
Wana: Yes, that is the girl I am talking about. Her name is Yohupeeor ... Yohupeeor is the daughter's name ...
Nomo Gbleetse: Is she not the one schooling in Accra or so? –

CHAPTER 4

Wana: Exactly, she is very humble and very-very respectful. I will be very happy if you will consider allowing a female to take the chief trustee position because I believe the gods had prepared her specially to bless us through her.

Nomo Gbleetse: Oh ... o Wana, it is a good idea that you are bringing though but do not forget that it is the over-all chief of the Songorbiawe clan. If you have forgotten, let me remind you that this position has since time immemorial been occupied by males so why are you suggesting a female. Will this be possible?

Wana: Oh yes I know but the issue here is this; those who we will say qualify for this position are the same people who are misbehaving and making up stories to cover themselves up. Are we going to stoop that low to getting people with ill manners to rule this clan? No way, that cannot work. You [elders] really need to digest this issue better before things get out of hand. And do not forget that this is the one unto who all assets and properties of our noble clan is going to be trusted to. Think ... think and think well my elder.

Nomo Gbleetse: Ok I have heard what you said but ...

Wana: Let me leave you with this, whenever the hen lays its eggs, it protects and incubates it for good twenty-one days before it hatches. Her care does not end there, it continues to care for the chicks till they come of age. Within this period, mother hen provides food for its chicks, protects them from the hawk as well as serpents. Whenever it feels any danger, it quickly gathers its chicks under its wings. Whatever food she finds, she opens it up and scatters it for its chicks. Aw females (mothers) are better care providers.

Nomo Gbleetse: Wana, you have really broadened my catching net and I promise that in a few days time, the chiefs and elders will be meeting so I will sell this suggestion to them and whatever the response will be, I will inform you. Thanks so much for all you have shared with me. These are the advices we need day in day out from you [elderly women]. Thanks so much once again and I pray the gods bless and keep you longer on this earth for our sake. (Radio Ada, 2011)

This documented effort to restory gender relations and power was clearly tied to broader efforts by women to organize to affect the framework of their lives. Lisa Gunn (2014), a research assistant on the Songor work, did her undergraduate thesis work on women's organizing in Ada, beyond the women in ASAF, but also informed by their organizing. She begins her work with the following statement:

STORIES AND RESTORYING AS SOCIAL MOVEMENT LEARNING

> Everyone seems to acknowledge in Ada how the women are of fundamental importance to fighting to regain control of the Songor. They are the missing thumb to mould the resource. They are the wolves protecting the lagoon from outside threats. They win salt year round on their own accord and use that money to better their families and communities. The women in Ada have formed their own groups on a number of levels. They are their own group in ASAF. Some of the communities have women's groups where they support each other financially and offer a space to discuss issues that affect them. They attend their church fellowships more than men. … In Ada, women are the driving force behind every child and every family. While dismissed by their husbands in a variety of ways, including financially, women work tirelessly to ensure that there is food on the table, a roof over their heads, and education for their children. They are the holders and keepers of indigenous languages and customs. (Gunn, 2014, p. 5)

Gunn goes on to show how women in a number of other contexts in Ada parallel to the Yihi Katsɛmɛ, such as the market women's association, were coming together to articulate their needs. While noting the organizing women were doing in other livelihood sectors, such as seamstresses and market sellers, Gunn (2014) highlights the emergence of Ada Queen Mothers as representing the recognition by male traditional authorities that women should be involved in leadership. Furthermore, she goes on to share the controversy that emerged in trying to install a Paramount Queen Mother for all Adas:

> [T]he power and importance Queens have in traditional council is not denied. This was no more apparent than [when] I was in Ada in 2013 when the whole community was talking about the installing of a Paramount Queen for the whole of Ada, and that the founding clans of Ada were going to withdraw their participation from the Asafotufiami Festival if the Paramount Queen was not installed properly with the consent of the other original Ada clans. (Gunn, 2014, p. 74)

This issue has remained a point of contention between the four Okor, or foundational, clans and Nene Ada because of the connection such an appointment has to foundational narratives of the nation. It is the four Okor clans who are supposed to name a new Paramount Chief, and train him in Okorhuem on what the role entails. When Nene Ada installed his own Paramount Queen Mother without consultation with the four Okor clans, it re-invoked how he has refused to go to Okorhuem to complete his own instalation. Although seemingly symbolic, these deep dismissals of foundational narratives matter and reveal how the ascension of women in traditional authority roles are being used to boost powerplays by different elements of male elite power. The Queen Mothers serve then as a cautionary tale of what symbolic gestures towards leadership versus what leadership that emerges through action and a literacy of struggle can mean. The Queen Mothers seem to suggest a new potential for women's

CHAPTER 4

empowerment, through such things as helping with the articulation of the tapestry, but are easily manipulated through phone calls, such as the Goi incident, as their positions are recent and rely on male Chiefs approval. In contrast to this, the Yihi Katsɛmɛ went from being voices within the ASAF movement, to now forming their own deeply rooted movement that is centred on women's analysis and women's willingness to act.

THE STRUGGLE OF THE SONGOR SALT PEOPLE BOOK PROJECT

The clearest concrete example of narrative restorying as an act of movement knowledge production is *The Struggle of the Songor Salt People* book project. This project began in 2011as an idea to develop a sequel to the *Who Killed Maggie* book. It quickly became something much more than a sequel to this text, however. Nonetheless, in an effort to set the stage for the restorying of the current book, it is good to briefly focus on the first book the Ada movement produced.

Who Killed Maggie (Ada Salt Cooperative, 1989) was collectively produced after the tragedy of Maggie's death in 1985. As an indication of its importance, when it was published there were several attempts to eliminate it from system: all the copies at the University of Ghana bookstore were bought up, it is assumed, by one of the companies implicated in its pages; and someone broke into the house of Father Joop Viser, a Dutch missionary living in the Ada area, and stole copies of the book that were awaiting distribution and nothing else. At the same time, since these days there has not been any attempt to reissue it. One of the first concerns of the older activists in ASAF discussions was that this book be made widely available again. While reprinting the book was beyond the scope of this research, I was able to work with the Institute of Development Studies, in Sussex, UK, to make it available, permanently archived on their website.[1]

Two features of *Who Killed Maggie* are important to share here, as they set the stage for the approach to the current book, and also speak to the long term learning of the older activists, and the Ada movement more broadly. *Who Killed Maggie*, much like The *Struggle of the Songor Salt People*, inserted into its pages an indication of the collective nature of the production of the text. Unlike the *Struggle of the Songor Salt People* text, no names were associated with the writing of the book, instead attributing it to the "Secretaries' Committee, Ada Songor Co-operative." The book identified its mission with the opening preface:

> We have been brought up in a society in which oral tradition is the major source of information. Documentation is rare, we have heard misleading stories about events that occurred within our own society. As such it is quite difficult to perceive clearly how and why certain events that are rooted in the past occur at present. This book has been written to break this cycle. The principal aim of the book is thus to enlighten the general public about the Songor Lagoon issue and to serve as a reference book for generations to come, especially for our own people, the Ada.

The book briefly discusses several issues and it deals primarily with the activities of the co-operative of salt miners.* It is, however, hoped that it contains sufficient material to serve its purpose and to ginger other Ada writers to come out with more detailed information on the Songor Lagoon. We shall welcome opinions and suggestions from all quarters.

We are most grateful to all who co-operated in diverse ways to make this work come out so well. (Ada Salt Cooperative, 1989, p. 7)

The asterisk (*) in this preface made clear to readers from the start that this text was the product of restorying, noting "* The Songor-story is an ongoing story that shows its ups and downs. This will be clear from the 'Educational Assessment' at the end of the book, which is obviously from another source" (Ada Salt Cooperative, 1989, p. 7). And yet the book does not spell out who this other "source" is. This Education Assessment section was discussed in the previous chapter, and is highly critical of the Co-operative leadership, describing how members of the Management committee made "constant unilateral decisions" that led to conflict within the co-operative, and accused these same members of furthering their "own self-interests" (Ada Salt Cooperative, 1989, pp. 122–126). From a restorying perspective, what is interesting is the acknowledgement that this section comes from another source, but there is very little else to explain its accusatory tone. The ASAF book, the *Struggle of the Songor Salt People*, addresses this conflict through its own approach to restorying, where both sides of this conflict from the past share their story – discussed further below. However, at this historical point in time, this section should likely be understood through the lens of Foley's (1999) statement that learning in struggle is often ambiguous. The *Who Killed Maggie* project itself is also critiqued by this same Educational Assessment:

> [W]hen the Songor area had returned to its present cold war peace, periodic training-for-transformation sessions were started for the secretaries of the village branches of the co-op, united in the Secretaries' Committee, in order to develop an integrated orientation towards development. It began with a long weekend – a report of which is included in this book – during which the secretaries had the opportunity to reflect in an analytical way on their recent experience of struggling for their land, and to become aware of their task ahead. The Secretaries' Committee at that time functioned as a critical structure for and next to the Management Committee, in which they were also represented. Evaluating our educational efforts now, it should be acknowledged that the animators – who came from outside and were thus not fully aware of the local situation – took too much for granted. It was, for example, not realised that people at village level were not really organised as a co-operative and were in fact merely nominal members. Instead of giving this reality the attention it deserved, a decision was made at the close of the first workshop to devote subsequent ones to the writing of the story of the struggle for the lagoon.

CHAPTER 4

> Though this was laudable as a conscientisation exercise, it was at the cost of organising a broader base to cope with the multitude of problems that were soon to be faced internally and externally. (Ada Salt Cooperative, 1989, p. 122)

Based on a Freirean model of "conscientisation," the workshops did produce this concrete product of movement knowledge production. Yet, the disconnection between the salt cooperative and community level roots still remains a problem, and is one of the reasons why Yihi Katsɛmɛ took over the main role of organizing and activism in ASAF. This is further elaborated below. However, the historical lesson was learned. Painstaking efforts were made to ensure the new book project would be collectively led by movement members, with several rounds of collective editing, and with those who had contributed to the text being named.

As previously mentioned, the new book project was first imagined as a sequel to *Who Killed Maggie*, taking off from where it reached at the end of the 1980s. In the very early stages though, it was proposed the book be a stand alone account of the history of the Songor, taken from the perspective of the people of Ada, as opposed to an account trying to establish some objective truth. This book was seen as an advocacy tool. This approach to the book project was endorsed by ASAF at a meeting on July 25–26th, 2012, and a collective timeline of events and community actions was developed by those gathered together for the two days (see Appendix A for community timeline). This meeting then sanctioned a book project steering committee to take over guiding the writing process, after which the draft of the text would be brought back for collective ASAF editing. This was to be followed by a validation in one of the most contentious Songor communities, Toflokpo. Throughout the year and a half process of developing the text, oral testimonies were taken from 28 people and inserted into the voice sections of the book. The text was divided into four eras, the pre-1980s period, the 1980s, the 1990s, and the 2000s. In each of these sections, an accessible front end of the chapter was written that aimed to offer a multi-faceted presentation of the Songor story, with several sides of the story being shared, while at the same time, making the story easy to follow for readers from many backgrounds and ages. The back section of each chapter then had voices that expanded upon, reinforced or contradicted what was shared in the front end of the chapter. This made sure people's voices were present throughout the text, and could be read in line with the storyline that was told. Through this process of combining voices and storyline a rich and accessible restorying of the Songor history rooted in the voices of those in the struggle emerged. Even the title of the book was restoried, going from *Maggie's Legacy: a People's History of Struggle in the Songor*, to its final title, *The Struggle of the Songor Salt People: None No Ko Lio No Ko Le – "What One Doesn't Know, Another Knows."* This final title was arrived at through collective deliberation by the book's steering committee, after a decision to distance the project from *Who Killed Maggie* to further allow it to stand on its own. The title takes inspiration from the Akpetiyo song quoted earlier in this book.

STORIES AND RESTORYING AS SOCIAL MOVEMENT LEARNING

Restorying, as a collective endeavour, produces not only rich narratives of social change processes, inflected with individual nuances, but also fundamentally leads to democratized movement knowledge production. Not only are stories brought forth with different versions of what happened, or different interpretations of what it meant, but the collective process itself mediates these versions to ensure powerful individuals within or outside the movement cannot silence voices of dissent. Thus the restorying process becomes a form of democratization of knowledge. The greatest example of this in this case is the origin story of the Adas, where powerful voices within the movement – as well as interests outside the movement – have insisted that it was the Tekperbiawe clan that found the Songor, and therefore they are the owners of the lagoon, whereas the other three Okor clans do not see it this way. In fact, the book documents how prominent movement members from the other clans see Korley – the one purported of having found the lagoon – as being from them. Here is the description in the book:

> Legend says the hunter in this story was the head of the Tekperbiawe clan, Korle. In some versions of this story Korle discovered the lagoon by climbing a tree – appropriate for someone whose name means eagle in Dangme. In other versions the person's name in this account is Tekper, of the Lomobiawe, who found the lagoon while looking for water. This discovery was made during an exploratory outing by representatives from the four Okor clans, Adi from the Adibiawe clan, Lomovier from the Lomobiawe clan, and Okumfo from the Dangmebiawe clan. Upon spotting the lagoon it is said Korle was accompanied by Okumfo in tracing the southern edge, while Adi and Lomovier took the northern edge. It is this based upon this division of surveying the lagoon that traditional lands have been apportioned.
>
> But there is another layer to this story, concerning the name of Korle's clan the Tekperbiawes – a clan in which no one is named Tekper. In one version of how this came to pass, the three other clans had come to settle in the Tagologo area with the other Dangme speaking people, and yet, one clan of their number was missing. In the subsequent search, it was a Lomobiawe named Tekper that found the missing people and guided them to join the other clans. This group did not have a specific leader; subsequently, they became known as Tekper's people, or Tekperbiawe. This was purported to have happened before the Songor was found. However, in another version, it was from the Okor forest by the Songor that Tekper climbed a tree and spotted an approaching group. He organized to meet them, and found them to be Dangme speaking, as well as being circumcised as they were. They thus became the fourth clan, named after the Lomobiawe man who brought them to the lagoon. Both versions of this story share a common thread that the Tekperbiawe did not carry with them a deity, as the other three clans did. Thus it made sense to make them the keepers of the Songor lagoon spirit, the Libi deity.

CHAPTER 4

> Thus it can be said that the stories agree that the four Okor clans came to settle around the lagoon together, making the Okor forest, or Okorhuem, their common meeting and spiritual hub. It is also clear that the Tekperbiawes have a special custodial and spiritual relationship with the lagoon itself – even if in some versions they may have been latecomers. (ASAF, 2016, pp. 8–9)

Presenting these multiple versions of the story at the community validation meeting in Toflokpo at the tail end of the writing process helped to increase the mutual stake over the future of the lagoon, and led directly to a community expression of deepened ownership. For instance, during this presentation, a youth in Toflokpo exclaimed,

> I never realize how we all have a stake in the Songor. I thought it was only for the Tekperbiawe, let alone solve the issues; now I see this implicating all of us. (Community Focus Group Meeting to Validate Book, August 14th, 2013)

Even children at the community outdooring of the book in Toflokpo explained how they had never heard the whole story of the Songor told to them. During the broadcast of the chapters one could hear a pin drop in the assembled crowd. "It was electrifying," said one of the Radio Ada staff. Since this outdooring, the book has been serialized, and has been broadcast on Radio Ada.

Figure 4.3. Woman in Toflokpo shares her thoughts on book draft while Radio Ada producer captures her statement for later broadcast (photo credit: Rachel Garbary)

The other major effort of restorying in *The Struggle of the Songor Salt People* picks up on the conflict within the co-operative that the Educational Assessment of *Who Killed Maggie* alluded to. Unlike this assessment, this book provided space for both sides of this conflict to share their story. This is how the ASAF book describes the conflict:

> At this time, the Cooperative – having emerged as a major revenue collector in the Songor – also faced challenges due to internal conflicts with regards to accounting for monies. This is one of the points in this text where there is an attempt to share multiple points of view regarding what happened. In essence, the conflict had to do with the leadership of the Cooperative. By this time, some breakaway cooperatives had also formed to collect tolls on salt. In addition, in late 1986, a major rift had developed within the top leadership of the Cooperative. Accusations of misuse of funds that were taken to the National Cooperative Secretariat resulted in 3 court convictions of the Vice Chairman of the Cooperative, Lawer Hushie, his brother, Dornu, and the Chairman, Lawer Agblo. Other members within this same executive, namely the Treasurer, Ofoe Blaise Mankwa, as well as Tsatsu, his brother who was Financial Secretary, initially raised these charges. Though the 3 spent several years in prison, they were able to eventually appeal and overturn the convictions in the early 1990s. In many ways, the damage had been done: Cooperative members, as well as Songor community members had serious doubts about their leadership. These doubts were related not just to the fact that these convictions had occurred, but that the leadership was so divided against itself. There are 2 versions of this falling out that are shared in the Oral Testimony section below – one from each of side of the fault line.

In the voices section of the book, Tsatsu Mankwa – brother to the one who brought the charges against Lawer Hushie – as well as Lawer Hushie each gave their account of the conflict over money. Through this, readers could make their own assessment of the situation. Rather than recapitulate this here, we will focus on what both felt had been learned through this conflict – what learning could be brought into the contemporary ASAF struggle. For Hushie the lesson had to do with being alive to attempts to destroy people's movements:

> One of the major lessons that I want us to highlight is that the attempts to kill the Cooperative, which was a major force on the side of the people, these attempts came from outside and from within and those from within were the most dangerous [...] Even for this struggle right now, there may be people within, the enemy or opposition.
>
> I would also want to mention the attack on the leadership of the Cooperative and the lesson there is that as far as possible we can have what we are trying to do now, we are all leaders, so that these single individuals are spotted as leaders of the movement, when that happens their lives are in danger because

CHAPTER 4

> people are of the opinion that if you remove them then the whole thing will collapse. Look at the intrigues that went into the arrest and the trial of the leadership of the Cooperative, 4 of them. One was acquitted and discharged by the tribunal and the 3 other persons were given very long sentences and the further attempts that happened in their absence disorganized the Cooperative [...]
>
> [A]t the time the so-called educational assessment was published, the core leadership of the Cooperative was jailed. So we immediately know the intrigues and the lesson I want to draw here. What I want to put on record, is sometimes the agents of disorganization of community advocacy that we are doing here, become most effective if they get insiders to work for them consciously or unconsciously. If insiders are bought by the enemy it is the most dangerous thing you can have because all of the pressures to get us disorganized from outside were not as effective as when people from within started working for the enemy. That is the most important lesson. (ASAF, 2016, p. 46)

For Mankwa, on the other hand, it is the way in which their conflict eroded trust in a community movement that is most important. According to Mankwa:

> [A]fter the court case the people saw that there is no trust in the leadership anymore. The villagers cannot organize themselves. It is very difficult for them to organize themselves. So once we were fighting, the leaders were fighting, who is going to organize them? So that brought the end of the Cooperative around the Songor … During that time other groups don't have confidence in the leadership any longer. They don't have confidence because of that money. They all got to know about it. So they were not happy about it so they have distrust. That is why when we come here and say we want to form cooperative, it will not work. (ASAF, 2016, pp. 48–49)

The critique of the disconnection between Songor communities and the cooperative leadership is also raised in the Educational Assessment. As part of ASAF, the revitalized cooperative (with many of the same leaders) recognized it was largely disconnected from communities, and had major trust issues to overcome. It was "during this time the Ada Songor Salt Cooperative received support from the Business Sector Advocacy Challenge fund (BUSAC), a USAID funding opportunity for business development, to help mobilize and revitalize its membership in communities throughout the Songor":

> While this funding raised the hope of many that the Cooperative could indeed return to be an important and grounded source of community ownership of Songor salt production, the follow-through by the leadership of the Cooperative has failed to produce the necessary work to actually make the funding available. This is a very unfortunate turn of events that echoes problems within the leadership of the past. (ASAF, 2016, p. 103)

In this sense, the problems of the past continued to haunt the cooperative, even though it had funding. Kofi Larweh described the growing sense that the cooperative could not be the vehicle through which ASAF could deepen its roots at the community level:

> So there should be growth in the [cooperative] system, but no growth is coming, so we have rather seen a more credible group because any time you call for a meeting, it is the same faces that you are seeing. If there is growth, you will see other people coming in, and we were thinking that within the [BUSAC] project period there would have grown other people, that other people would have emerged. And those of them who were not mining salt, they're fronting for salt-miners, would withdraw. (ASAF, 2016, p. 137)

Aside from the trust issues Mankwa identified above, it is also evident that part of the problem has to do with the mentality he articulated that without leaders, "who is going to organize" Songor communities. Kofi Larweh lays out how women's organizing in ASAF completely overturned this way of thinking. According to Kofi, the women are "a real genuine people":

> And it isn't that they were not there from the beginning; they were; it is just that they were not given opportunity to see themselves as a group that can organize itself. They were always being told "somebody else has to do it for you." That was the attitude of the cooperatives. But the women have always been there, they have suffered, they have borne the brunt of all the mismanagement activities, and Government and Assembly actions and inactions. So now that [they have] same opportunity as the so-called leaders of the cooperatives were given, you can see the women are growing, their numbers are increasing, and they know exactly what to do. So that's where we are now. (Personal communication, February 12th, 2017)

In this sense, *The Struggle of the Songor Salt People* is as much a story of the protracted fight to defend communal access to the Songor Lagoon for artisanal salt winning, as it is the restoried account of the struggle for a truly rooted movement to emerge. The complex telling is not without ambiguity, and accounts of the pitfalls of this process, but it does document how "where we are now" has emerged from a literacy of the struggle – social movement learning that has deepened over time. Wilna Quarmyne, one of the founders of Radio Ada, captures the spirit of this learning well, and why it is important to document it:

> what resonates is that all movements are human, [and] inherent in each movement is the capacity for altruism, for human glory, for overcoming, [...] the little petty petty divisions. But these are also quickly undermined by human frailty, right? [I]t can be the story of how altruism, okay, our sense of community overcomes these frailties, but we must not paper over them, because then we will forget the lessons from the Songor. I think this is the

balance, this is what I mean by balance, not he said this, and she said so, no I don't mean that kind of balance. Radio Ada has been very clear from the beginning [...] that if it is a choice between the voiceless and the voiced, the choice must always go to the voiceless. Bringing that out, that the voiceless are not always pure, and how to we bring that out, the good that is in us, even as we know there is so much that is weak in us. How do we bring that out? It will be a great book! (Book writing meeting, July 23rd, 2012)

RESTORYING STRUGGLE AS LEARNING

In the previous pages, I have endeavoured to share how the different iterations of the Ada movement defending communal access to their long standing traditional livelihood have both used stories as part of their activism, and re-worked these stories as part of a dynamic process of social movement learning over time. As such these re-worked, or restoried, narratives become new forms of movement knowledge production, forms of knowledge through which the different iterations of struggle have shaped their actions iteratively. These narratives respond to and emerge from the socio-political dynamics of the day, where during a military regime meetings to produce movement knowledge were in secret, and the knowledge production that emerged had no authors attached, to a point where today openness of documentation provides protection and an exemplar of difference to the secrecy of local and national governing authorities. The presence and active involvement of a community radio station has enabled democratic knowledge production and dissemination, and opened a space both within Ada society, and within movement organizing for women's leadership to emerge. The restorying of the movement from women's perspective has been one of the great new forms of struggle, and clearly represents a form of subjugated and subaltern knowledge destabilizing various forms of global design and truth regimes around them (Mignolo, 2000; Foucault, 1980; Gramsci, 1971). In this sense, the dynamic emergence of rooted movement knowledge has contributed to new ways of contesting the power structures the movement faces, even as the restoried narratives, such as the ASSWA Manifesto, become new strategies in and of themselves. This dynamism also reveals how the movements are adjusting over time to the new forms of dominance and power that steamrollers of truth regimes like National Development are constantly mobilizing.

At the same time, from a movement learning perspective, the collective documentation of this process of restorying, as well as the very restoried narratives that have emerged provides a crucial example of movement knowledge production and learning in action. This is why my colleague Kofi Larweh and I have described this research as "moving with the movement." It is variegated, reveals ambiguities and schisms within the struggle, but these stories also reveal, over time, how collective struggle learns, adjusts in consensus-based ways, and comes up with new knowledge to take on the forces the movement faces. Restorying in this sense is not a singular learning arc, but is divergent, complex, mostly moving in a similar direction, but also divergent and at times conflictual. The process of restorying itself helps bring these divergent voices into perspective, but without undermining the broader movement strategies that come from people deciding together on how they want to struggle for change in their world. A major mechanism that has emerged for telling the latest story of struggle is an example of the dynamism of the movement, as it has taken a far more creative approach than previous iterations of the movement. It is towards an examination of this creativity that I now turn.

NOTE

[1] See http://opendocs.ids.ac.uk/opendocs/handle/123456789/1200#.VwE4kxKLSCQ

CHAPTER 5

THE PEDAGOGY OF CREATIVE DISSENT: USING CREATIVITY TO BROADEN AND DEEPEN SOCIAL MOVEMENT LEARNING

INTRODUCTION

The sound of drums, musketry, the crowds swelling, necks straining to see the Chiefs of Ada arrive in their colourful palanquins; marching bands from Ada "diaspora" having returned from across to their motherland to display their pageantry and skills, like the soldiers returning from defending the Songor in conflicts of old. Coming at the beginning of August every year, the people of Ada, living where Ghana's Volta river estuary meets the ocean, mark the commencement of their year with the Asafotufiami Festival. This festival celebrates the historical ability of Adas to unite in the face of threats of dispossession, especially in terms of the nearby Songor salt yielding lagoon. (Langdon & Larweh, 2017, p. 231)

This chapter begins with this invocation of the Asafotufiami Festival's pageantry in order to set the scene for one of the Ada movement's most important latest victories – a victory made possible by the Yihi Katsɛmɛ's creative dissent. Since 2011, ASAF, and then Yihi Katsɛmɛ identified making an impact at the Asafotufiami Festival as a priority. Initially, being present at the Festival was a way to gain visibility, but since 2015, the mindset has shifted within the movement, as visibility was no longer enough. After the protest march and tapestry display in 2012, the women within the movement continued identifying gaining recognition at the Festival as a crucial site of struggle. When the Yihi Katsɛmɛ emerged with an independent voice in 2015, they pushed to not only be present at the Festival, but to become a legitimate part of the festival – thereby legitimating their anti-atsiakpo stance. In other words, the Yihi Katsɛmɛ movement wanted to march officially in the Festival as a way to legitimate their struggle and to gain a platform to share its message.

In August 2017, this finally occurred, with Yihi Katsɛmɛ being given an official time to march in the procession of Ada associations, and also given a time to make a statement. The brave women were also mentioned in the official program of the Festival. This alone was remarkable, but for a number of the movement leadership at the Festival grounds that day, they sensed they needed to make more of statement. Although they had a pair of local drummers with them to add a beat to their march, they wanted to increase the impact. They quickly organized and convinced other

CHAPTER 5

associations to lend them some members of their brass bands, and when they finally marched they had a huge assortment of musicians backing them. The effect was obvious to all there, as the group took the field wearing their distinctive green shirts (unlike the red shirts they wore in 2012) and traditional skirts, all eyes turned their way. So magnetic was their pull that several women from other associations ran to join them as they marched to make their statement. When returning to Radio Ada after their victorious march, they sang with pride: "Have you heard of the Yihi Katsɛmɛ, the women have come out boldly to protect the Songor, you are also invited to join the crusade and you will be happy." The Yihi Katsɛmɛ had arrived! Their songs and the brass band made this as clear as their name appearing in the official Asafotufiami Festival program (Ada Traditional Council, 2017).

This episode underscores how creativity can deepen social movement activism's impact, and illustrates how its effective use is something social movements learn to do, and learn from. It is hard to gauge what would have happened if the brass band musicians had not joined the march. Perhaps there would still have been that allure to their display, but, to some extent, what matters is that the women strategized correctly, and their adjustments on the day yielded the sense of arrival they needed. Their impact was so effective that Nene Ada himself had to respond, congratulating them for their hard work in defending the lagoon, and publicly supporting their call for the end of atsiakpo. His statement, as well as the legitimation of the Yihi Katsɛmɛ was broadcast live to all of Ada through Radio Ada's remote booth at the Festival ground.

And yet, this strategy on the day needs to be seen as building on their learning from the layered foundation of creative dissent by the movement in the years leading up to this day. This chapter, then, focuses on the cumulative use of creativity by the Ada movement on three registers. It continues the idea of restorying as a documentation of learning within the movement that was introduced in the last chapter. It also shares the pedagogy of creative dissent that the movement uses, with a specific focus on the use of song and drama in this creative-learning dynamic. And, it deepens discussion of Akpetiyo Lawer's "Nɔ nɛ nɔ ko li ɔ, nɔ ko *le*/what someone doesn't know, someone knows" (ASAF, 2016, p. ii), or the way in which the movement consistently builds the movement by building knowledge democracy by 'spreading' the knowledge production of the movement. The two main sections will focus on pedagogy of creative dissent and on knowledge democracy, while restorying will be woven throughout.

CREATIVE DISSENT AND PEDAGOGY

[S]ongs and the tapestry are how we have spread our message. (Rev. Sophia Kitcher)

Creativity is a crucial source of social movement strategy. The use of imagery, word play, movement, and puppetry all facilitate social movement communication of their causes, their campaigns (Barndt, 2015). In fact, according to Barndt (2015):

whether verbal, or non-verbal, art making that ignites people's creativity, recovers repressed histories, builds community, and strengthens social movements is in itself a holistic form of action. (p. 18)

In this sense, creative dissent can be seen not just as contributing to strategy, but a form of action itself. At the same time, Perini (2008, p. 183) points to the pedagogic potential of creativity when she argues "art creates accessible points of entry into political discussions, educating and mobilizing people in ways that may be difficult to quantify but nonetheless tangible." Fraser and Restrepo-Estrada (1998), echoing the literacy of struggle idea explored in the previous chapters as well as Reverend Sophia's statement above, underscore how activism in contexts of oral literacy often turn to creative expression to disseminate movement knowledge. With Rachel Garbary, I have laid out in the Ada example how the creation of these arts-based contributions is often an example of restoried learning in action (Langdon & Garbary, 2017). In this section, I will share how such restoried learning has emerged through the various contemporary iterations of the movement's creative expression. I begin by looking more closely at the tapestry the women in ASAF created, then focus on the emergence of song as an important learning and teaching tool, then look at how the engagement with the Asafotufiami Festival has led to creative learning and new strategies – such as the five finger approach.

Learning & the Songor Herstory Tapestry

Returning to the account of the creation of the tapestry discussed in the previous chapter, the process through which the tapestry evolved in June and July 2012, whereby Rev. Kitcher and the Queen Mothers, along with some of the women salt winners, sat together to devise the story, and then worked with the anonymous artist to produce the piece, reveals how the creation of an artistic contribution to the movement is itself a learning process. The tapestry begins with a focus on the Yomo spirit; and, it ends with a visual question-mark that Maggie's death brought – further deepened through the locked box and the image of the women forced to carry salt for wages in the top right corner. In this way, the Songor's visual history is parenthesized through a herstory. Further, the oral storyline of the tapestry created by the Songor salt winning women to share in Asafotufiami, and in events since, added another layer of learning. Not only did multiple women tell it, they learned to tell it in multiple languages, and in the face of different audiences, such as school children, tourists, visiting family, and central government politicians. This last point is a more classic pedagogic dimension of the tapestry in the sense of the learning of those who view it, and those who walk through it with Yihi Katsɛmɛ women. The tapestry was also used as an educational tool within the movement, used in both the movement strategy building retreats in Abokobi, in 2016, and Nsawam, in 2017. At the retreats, the tapestry was laid out and its story told in Dangme for new members to absorb.

CHAPTER 5

Finally, and pointing to the next section of the chapter, the manner in which the tapestry was created, the way in which moment trained to tell its herstory at the Festival and other events, and through the radio, has ensured the dissemination of this restoried account of the Songor story to a wide cross-section of the Ada community. This democratizes the knowledge the movement produces. This will be explored more in the next section. Here we will look at another example of creativity and its impact on learning in action, the creation and use of song by the Yihi Katsɛmɛ.

Learning and song has been a part of both the contemporary iterations of the Ada movement. Initially, song use came from Akpetiyo Lawer, and her incisive use of song to summarize ASAF gatherings. "Nɔ nɛ nɔ ko li ɔ, nɔ ko *le*/what someone doesn't know, someone knows" (ASAF, 2016, p. ii) is a great example of this. It also came spontaneously from communities reacting to the news in 2011 that the government was discussing relocation of the Songor communities. For instance, the traditional Priestesses of the shrine of the Yomo spirit, located near Lufenya, made it clear they would not agree to moving as they could not move their ancestors and their gods:

> if they [the government] are coming to move them from here, how are they going to move the ancestors, the Gods, to move along with them? [...] We have a lot of things, and in our moving, it will be difficult to move the things along with. So, we will not agree with this evacuation intention by the government. (Lufenya community forum, August 8th, 2011)

This led to a series of war songs sung by the Priestesses in which "they are evoking the spirits, and then they are calling on the spirits to support them to fight the common battle. [They are singing] 'Yes, come and support us to fight our enemies'" (Lufenya community forum, August 8th, 2011).

In this sense, song served as an accompaniment to the open dialogue and reflective thinking of the movement as well as the activism that emerged in reaction to the actions of those threatening communal access to the Lagoon at this time. Akpetiyo's analysis, manifest through her songs, had an impact on movement thinking, and on broader Ada discussions about the Songor, as her songs were carried by Radio Ada throughout the 2011–2013 period. As Kofi Larweh has noted, speaking of Radio Ada's contribution to the Songor struggle, "Songs and their meaning are the centre of our radio programming strategy" (Song workshop, 2016). In fact, it became clear just how much of an impact her songs were having as the organizers of the 2013 Asafotufiami Festival tried to prevent her from singing at the festival. With the benefit of time, it is clear that the organic emergence of song, and its impact on the movement began to percolate, and as the women moved into broader leadership of the movement and its activism, so too did song become a more conscious part of movement thinking and strategy. And as this chapter begins with the Asafotufiami Festival, the Festival was also central to this transition. So too was a deepened connection with the image of the thumbless hand and the missing thumb.

Learning & the Hand

The year prior to the Yihi Katsɛmɛ breakthrough at the 2017 Festival, the women were again prevented from marching officially in the procession of Ada associations. They set up a salt stand along with the tapestry in the hopes that they might catch the eye of Ghana's President at the time, John Mahama. Mahama was at the Festival as it was an election year, and Ada was a traditional stronghold of his party, the NDC. After the festival, Yihi Katsɛmɛ gathered to analyse what had happened and to strategize. According to Mary Akutey:

> [W]e tried to show our banners, our 2 banners, so as our President came and was shaking and greeting people, he will also see our banner. The police helped us, they sacked the people and drove them away and gave us room for us to also be seen. But when he was coming, I noticed he saw it, by all means he has seen the banner, by all means, but when he was coming to us, as he was supposed to stand by us and even look at what was on the banner, he never did that. After passing he went to sit down. (Song Workshop, August 11th, 2016)

This disappointment was compounded by the fact that both Nene Ada and the President made statements that day that undermined the Yihi Katsɛmɛ's call for a return to a 'Songor for all':

> What made me really unhappy, was last Saturday when we were fighting that Songor should be a resource for all, our Paramount chief of Ada, when he was going to talk or address the President John Mahama, he said that the government should come and take the Songor Lagoon. (Edith, Song Workshop, August 11th, 2016)

In response, President Mahama spoke of turning the Songor into a site of job creation that can be "integrate[d] ... downstream to the petrochemical industry" (Song Workshop, August 11th, 2016). The fact that these statements were made, and the women were ignored, was used against the movement members back in their communities:

> [W]hen I got to my community. They were asking what is the essence of we fighting for the Songor? They were calling the names of people, Radio Ada was giving live commentary and live everything, but they never heard of Songor Women speaking, and all they could hear was that the Paramount chief said that the President should use the Songor. (Mary Akutey, Song Workshop, August 11th, 2016)

Others shared how members of their community challenged the ability of the women to make a change:

> What they are asking is, can we do this? Men tried it and they couldn't, so how can women? ... Can we fight for the Songor to be for all? Because strong men

CHAPTER 5

tried to fight for it and they couldn't. (Salomey, Song Workshop, August 11th, 2016)

And yet, from this disappointment also emerged righteous indignation:

> I really got annoyed… I've gotten a mind, that if the President should come and take the Songor, and the president is using it, will [community members] benefit from the atsiakpo? (Doris, Songor Workshop, August 11th, 2016)

This failure by community members to see that they will lose their atsiakpo, as well as a general sense that Nene Ada's statement needed further explanation turned the disappointment into a growing strategy. Kofi Larweh, who was facilitating the collective deliberation summarized where they had reached:

> [W]e are saying we should educate the communities, is that not it? So that people will understand, so that people who are teasing, people who are insulting us, people who are not putting value on us, they don't regard what we are doing. (Song Workshop, August 11th, 2016)

Regina made it clear how the statements at the Festival provide an important opening:

> What happened at Asafotufiami park, it really got to places. So if we should go back again they will realize that what we are saying is the good work we are doing. (Song Workshop, August 11th, 2016)

It was in this context of recognizing the threat of the President and Nene Ada's statement, and also recognizing their own need to create space in their communities for people to hear them out, and dialogue on these threats that they began to more deeply interrogate song, its uses, and the role it could play in their new strategy. Kofi summarized this emerging analysis:

> So we say before we work, the first thing we do is that we will bring songs out to gather the people. The first thing we do is use folk songs, we bring songs to gather people. Songs we use to gather the people. After singing those songs, we have words that will back it, things that are getting missing in our culture, our tradition and cultures are getting missing. Time back, we gathered and sing those songs. But now, it's no more like that. We the Songor women won't allow that thing to beat us. That's why we are bringing out these songs. (Song Workshop, August 11th, 2016)

Based on this, the group drew out and analyzed a whole series of old, traditional songs people used to use when working together. Radio Ada shared one such song and its meaning in a broadcast developed by Yihi Katsɛmɛ:

> You have entered the room
> You are keeping long to come out,
> The community will be expecting you to give
> birth to twins! (Radio Ada Broadcast, August 2016)

THE PEDAGOGY OF CREATIVE DISSENT

Edith goes on to explain the meaning of this song in the broadcast:

> The music ... tries to refresh our minds in the olden days where the women can work on their own, and housekeeping was not a problem for the men and women. At evening the women gather and sing this song: You have entered the room and are keeping long to come out. The community will be expecting you to give birth to twins. This is a song the women used to tease each other because of the excitement they have. (Radio Ada Broadcast, August 2016)

It was therefore decided by the group that in order to open up community space to dialogue on what was being said and planned by national and local authorities for the Songor, it was necessary to draw people together with songs that conveyed the spirit of communalism and cooperation of the past. One other element was added to this connection to the past as a way to invoke the *Songor for All* manifesto, the women would go back to the original meaning of Songor, *suɔmi ngɔɔ*, it means "love is sweet." In explaining this meaning Cecilia explained:

> How it was broad and how everybody could go and win the salt shows love is really sweet. Whether Muslim or an Ada, it was broad for everybody, so that showed love was really sweet. (Song Workshop, August 11th, 2016)

Reconnecting with this powerful foundational definition of Songor as sweet "can be used as an intro," suggested Rev. Sophia (Song Workshop, August 11th, 2016), as it allows for inclusive and equitable use of the Lagoon. With the strategy taking shape, one more ingredient was added that restored this approach by connecting it to the cumulative analysis of the movement: the importance of women's leadership as the thumb that makes the movement work. Hence, the new strategy was now understood as the five finger approach:

> [T]he small finger represents the music, the music we will be using. So the songs we will use to work. The second one represents the meaning of the Songor, how the people of old were together, and unity lies in strength. The middle one is about Asafotufiami, [...] what Nene Ada said on the park [...] What the president also said [...]. The other finger is about teaching the way. The manifesto is our plan, what we want to do, and the steps we need to take so that the Songor becomes ours. The thumb we are using to call all of you, to encourage you. If it is not part, we cannot do anything. So if you don't have your thumb, it will be difficult for you to work with your finger. It represents you people and all community members to support, if you don't support, it means that we will lose our Songor. That is our [Yihi Katsɛmɛ] finger. (Mary, Song Workshop, August 11th, 2016)

In this way, the new "hand" approach built on and restored the use of the thumb by the older male ASAF activists, back in 2011, where the missing thumb was linked to missing women's leadership (cf. Langdon, Larweh, & Cameron, 2014). Zeroing

CHAPTER 5

in on the songs, Salomey rehearsed how they would use the songs to open the discussion on the Songor at the community level:

> Yihi Katsɛmɛ! Wamaasi! Brothers and sisters, we are going to sing and dance. After that, the reason why we are here, I will tell you. This kind of music that we just sang, have you realized it's been a long time since we sang this song? Which means that we are losing a lot of our customs, it's not only these old customs that we are missing, but here is a another big thing which we are losing, and that particular thing is Songor. What is the meaning of Songor? Songor means that love is good, love is sweet. The reason that we say or we call Songor love is sweet, the time our forefathers came to make Songor, Songor was open, and people from other places came to win the salt. They would go with their children to even go and win the salt. The kind of love that we have, people from other places come to win the salt. This is why we say Songor is good, and it's sweet. It is through that that we have the name Songor. (Song Workshop, August 12th, 2016)

The Yihi Katsɛmɛ gathered at this workshop acted out their interactions at the community level to deepen their learning of this new strategy. They also used it to push each other. They imagined enacting this approach in the most difficult community – the epicentre of atsiakpo, Bonikorpey. The women took it seriously, insulting and challenging their peers as they tried to walk through the five finger approach: "please, if you bring atsiakpo issue here, please don't come here," one yelled; Mary (who hails from Bonikorpey) added, "If you want to talk to us from Bonikorpey, you should be careful [...] We are the people, the Bonikorpey people, we fought" (Song Workshop, August 12th, 2016). In response to these and other challenges, the presenters used song to diffuse and redirect the growing (theatrical) tensions: "some of you are angry; I think this song will just satisfy you. Just let my sister talk to you and you will understand. Just hold on and listen" (Jane, Song Workshop, August 12th, 2016). This process of returning to song as a way to ground their activism was highlighted in the debrief of the session:

Observations:

- Song was good to refresh us.
- We intentionally made them angry but they didn't get angry.
- I realized that they were patient with us, through that, they explained a lot of things.
- The music helped a lot. (Song Workshop debrief notes, August 12th, 2016)

Learning through Song & Drama

The link between song and using drama both for learning purposes and to broaden the impact of their work can be seen to be taking shape in this workshop. In the

THE PEDAGOGY OF CREATIVE DISSENT

year that followed this workshop, this combination of song and drama became more conscious, first with the decision by Yihi Katsɛmɛ to commemorate the death of Maggie through a gathering at the site of Maggie's statue in Bonikorpey to share a re-enactment of her death. After the success of this event, discussed further below, a collective decision between the Yihi Katsɛmɛ and Radio Ada was made to use drama and song to get the Songor for All message to the national level. This led to the development of *Songor, Our Life, Atsiakpo, Our Death!*, a dance drama staged in Ada during the 2017 Asafotufiami Festival, and in Accra later that same August. The next section on knowledge democracy will share more fully the process of developing this drama and its impact, as well as the impact of the Maggie performance itself. To wrap this section up, though, a short exploration of how songs emerged in this dance drama helps describe a new facet of song use in the movement. Over the course of the months of June, July and August 2017, a self-selected group of Yihi Katsɛmɛ and Radio Ada members came together to collectively write and then perform the *Songor, Our Life, Atsiakpo, Our Death!* drama. A key part of this collective process was moving from drawing from traditional songs, to composing new songs to speak to the new challenges in the lagoon. The songs that open and close the drama literally illustrate this expansion of their process. The song that opens the drama is a traditional piece used to draw Adas together:

Hail Good News!

Okor people, hail good news!
We welcome good news!
Let it come, let it come, let it come!
Let long life come!
Let it come, let it come!
Let's conquer wickedness!
We trample wickedness!
Let's conquer our enemies! We trample them!
Welcome Peace!
Let it come, let it come, let it come!

(Songor Our Life, Atsiakpo, Our Death!, August 15th, 2017)

The song that ends the performance, on the other hand, emerged through the process of the development of the drama and was collectively composed. It invokes Yomo's spirit to speak to the destruction of the lagoon as a result of atsiakpo, reminds listeners of the original 'love is sweet' definition of Songor, and calls all the traditional authorities and community members to action:

Legendary Yomo

Our Legendary Old Lady, Yomo, has given us a wonderful legacy;
Land, Sunshine, Wind, Sea Water become Salt,

CHAPTER 5

> These four God-given resources have befriended each other to become Salt;
> The four Okor clans befriend each other to win Salt
> Adibiawe, Lomobiawe, Tekperbiawe, Dangbebiawe
> Songor says love is sweet; Atsiakpo says no more love
> Abomination on our heads; children of legendary Yomo, where are you? Chiefs, where are you? Queens, where are you? Okor Priests, where are you? Community members, where are you?
>
> (Songor Our Life, Atsiakpo, Our Death!, August 15th, 2017)

This last song echoes and restories the five finger approach developed the previous year to the original definition of the Songor, and then, yet again, reworks the thumb idea of calling all to come together to support the effort to address the conflict atsiakpo has brought to the lagoon. Holding the hand up during the performance of the song, the singers signal the four Okor clans are the four fingers, while the missing "children of Yomo," "Chiefs," "Queens," "Okor Priests," and "community members" are the thumb that is missing. This song, and its development, is a perfect illustration of the ongoing layered learning of the movement, and the role creativity has played in this learning – both internally as movement thinking and strategizing has deepened, and externally, as the ways to teach and share movement knowledge have also deepened through creativity. This second point is expanded upon in the next section.

CREATIVITY, LEARNING AND DEMOCRATIZING KNOWLEDGE

In this section, the aim is to share the interconnection between creativity and learning, and the way in which it has contributed to knowledge production and its democratization. The opening of this chapter shared the story of the Yihi Katsɛmɛ's latest victory – marching officially in the Asafotufiami festival. The debate about pulling in the brass band into this march, the aspect of their march many credit with their successful impact at the festival, had its roots in learning from the success of a demonstration in Sege in October 2016. This section shares the learning through struggle that led to this demonstration and the knowledge it helped produce and disseminate. At the same time, this section shares how the latest iteration of the movement turned to drama both as a form of knowledge production, and as a way to democratize the knowledge of the movement. The section then describes how Radio Ada, and radio programming, has played a major role in both the production of knowledge within the two contemporary iterations of the movement (ASAF & Yihi Katsɛmɛ), as well as its democratization. Finally, the section ends by sharing an analytical tool developed by the Yihi Katsɛmɛ that they first used amongst their membership, but then used in their community engagement process to at once produce a collective analysis of their struggle, and to democratize its momentum. Creativity forms part of each one of these knowledge production processes, even as the processes themselves are literal manifestations of the movement's learning.

Figure 5.1. Yihi Katsɛmɛ demonstrating in Sege (photo credit: Noah Dameh)

On October 12th, 2016, after several weeks of delays waiting for a police permit to march in reaction to the statement by the President and by Nene Ada at the Asafotufiami Festival, the Yihi Katsɛmɛ hit the streets of Sege – the largest town near the Songor Lagoon. Their goal on the march was to raise the profile of their *Songor for All* manifesto, making a visible push for it to become part of the 2016 Ghanaian election debate in Ada and to mark their displeasure in the statement of the President and Nene Ada. Radio Ada covered the entire march through remote phone transmissions while some members of the Yihi Katsɛmɛ executive simultaneously held a press conference in Accra. When the march was being planned, the leaders of the Yihi Katsɛmɛ kept returning to the idea of needing a brass band to accompany them on the march. On the day of the march, Radio Ada carried the gathering of the women with the brass band, and documented the confrontation with police that followed. After starting their march singing, the police are seen in a video of the event trying to stop them. After a brief delay, the women start singing and the brass band simply starts up again, and they march. The police look visibly uncertain what to do. Eventually, they go from trying to prevent the women's march to moving along with it – seemingly legitimating it. By the end of the march, at the final rally point, the police are shown in the livestream video post on the Yihi Katsɛmɛ Facebook site to be relaxed and even put on a display for the Yihi Katsɛmɛ on their marching techniques (https://www.facebook.com/YihiKatseme/videos/1045838252180482/). Concurrent to the march, the press conference in Accra carried this Facebook Live video coverage, so several media outlets witnessed the way the women transformed the attitude of the police. The energy of the demonstration connected with the press, as the Ghana News Agency (2016) coverage described how the Yihi Katsɛmɛ shared their views "at a media conference in Accra, while staging a demonstration

CHAPTER 5

simultaneously, at Sege, to drum home their frustrations."[1] The idea of the brass band paid off, and this success laid the foundation for the decision to draw in a brass band for the Asafotufiami march in 2017. This is the concluding part of their press statement that day:

> Thus, respectfully, but urgently, we ask, Your Excellency, our President: As a Co-Chair of the U.N. Sustainable Development Goals Champions, to support our empowerment as women and uphold inclusive and equitable development by endorsing Songor For All. As our leader on the world stage, to abide by the United Nations Declaration of the Rights of Indigenous People (UNDRIP) and work with us in developing our resource, and ensure our consent in whatever plans for it emerge.
>
> As father of the nation, to enjoin our traditional authorities to exercise their stewardship over the Songor as a communal resource and unite to eliminate atsiakpo. As the effective national manager, to ensure the coherent and consistent formation and implementation of policies relating to the Songor.
>
> As an executive President, to proactively and urgently institute policies and effect action to implement the clause in PNDC Law 287 (1992) to ensure the efficient development of the Ada-Songor Lagoon to benefit the contiguous communities and the public interest.
>
> As the main defender of our constitution, to uphold our rights as citizens by affording us an equal stake in discussions on a limited liability company and all current and future decisions on the Songor. (Ada Community Online, October 12th, 2016)[2]

It is clear from this press release that the Yihi Katsɛmɛ are producing knowledge about their struggle that blends their reaction to President Mahama's statement at the Asafotufiami Festival with their growing knowledge of the UNDRIP and the sustainable development goals, and linking them to the PNDC law 287 that guarantees "contiguous communities" should benefit from the Songor. Through this combination they assert their right to be part of the planning process for the future of the lagoon. The Yihi Katsɛmɛ ensured this press statement was carried both for the media in Accra, and over the airwaves in Ada – democratizing their call. This call was heard. This was followed by a National Forum in Ada in November 2016, where community members along with a number of senior bureaucrats from the Ministry of Natural Resources came – including the Chief Director. These bureaucrats made it clear they were ready to listen, though it should be remembered that it was an election year. Unfortunately, this readiness to listen evaporated later in the year when the Mahama government was toppled in the 2016 elections; and so a new relationship with a new government had to begin.

With a new government in place, the Yihi Katsɛmɛ came together to restrategize at a retreat in Nsawam. It was at this retreat that the Songor for All plan was restoried, based on learnings over the past year, to be Songor Livelihood for All plan – clarifying it was a return to access for all, that was the aim of the struggle and not challenging the ownership of the resource by the 4 Okor clans (a misinterpretation some in authority were using to discredit the movement). This retreat also brought in voices outside the struggle to help deepen the understanding of PNDC Law 287, and its echo of the UNDRIP, and also of the SDGs. But more than these things, the strategy of using creativity over the coming year to broaden the reach of their message was elaborated. Not only would they use song, as well as focus on marching in Asafotufiami, but they would expand beyond this to use drama to connect with audiences in Ada, and in Accra. Hopefully the audiences would include those with influence that could carry their story to the decision making table; but it was also hoped that the audience included those who didn't know, but now would – a reference to a line in Akpetiyo's famous song. The first of these forays into drama involved a re-enactment of the death of Margaret Kuwornu. Scheduled for near the anniversary of Maggie's death, the re-enactment was well attended by members of the nearby Bonikorpey and Toflokpo communities, as well as by traditional authorities. Unlike prior to the election, the Accra-based senior bureaucrats and politicians didn't attend, but the head of the local government, the District Chief Executive of one of the two Ada districts did. He issued a historic apology for the killing of Maggie that press in attendance carried.[3]

The sense of the potential of performance continued, as the Yihi Katsɛmɛ have taken advantage of the new national government's call for the end of illegal small scale mining, or Galamsey, to link atsiakpo to Galamsey. A Media Coalition Against Galamsey (MCAG) has also been pushing against the rise of illegal mining in the country, organizing Red Friday's where marches are held against the impact of illegal mining. The Yihi Katsɛmɛ joined forces with this coalition and organized one such march in both Ada district capitals, simultaneously on April 20th, 2017.[4] The enthusiasm of the Yihi Katsɛmɛ helped to convince MCAG to host one of its 2018 regional foras in Ada, which led to a historic statement by the Libi Wornor in support of the Yihi Katsɛmɛ and against Atsiakpo.[5] "Withdraw all atsiakpo agreements!" he declared to the packed crowd at the forum in Ada, speaking directly to the traditional authority figures present.

"Songor Our Life, Atsiakpo Our Death!"

The success at using a sense of drama to convey their message, much like the use of the brass band above, also convinced the Yihi Katsɛmɛ that they needed to develop a drama for the 2017 Festival, and to share in Accra – just in case they would again not be able to march in the procession. This then led to the development of a full dance drama, composed and performed by the Yihi Katsɛmɛ and members of the Radio Ada drama group. The Radio Ada drama group was central to the production of the Okor Ng Kor production, discussed last chapter. It was the combination of the sense of impact drama could have, clearly shown in the Okor Ng Kor popularity, along

CHAPTER 5

with the Yihi Katsɛmɛ seeing how enacting Maggie's death helped to connect with the audience gathered on that day, and drawing out an unsolicited apology from the District Chief Executive of the local government, that laid the ground work for the *Songor Our Life, Atsiakpo Our Death* dance drama.

Figure 5.2. Dance drama advertisement (photo credit: Liliona Quarmyne)

The dance drama was developed over 6 weeks, and was pulled together in a similar manner as the *Songor Struggles* book, with collaborative brainstorming, skit development, song composition, sequencing, and finally acting. Like the book, a self-selecting group of roughly 20 movement members and Radio Ada volunteers came together to decide the focus, shape and script of the drama. It began with a workshop in early July 2017 that built on the re-enactment of Maggie's death by the Yihi Katsɛmɛ, performed May 31st, 2017. By July 15th, the shape of the piece was emerging: it wouldn't just focus on Maggie's story, but would "upscale advocacy on Songor, and make atsiakpo a popular vocab" (Drama workshop, July 15th, 2017). Each member of the group developed skit/song ideas around this theme, and over the next two weeks intensively workshoped them – with several being folded together and some being discarded or adapted. For instance, several songs about ending atsiakpo were brought together in the finale of the drama. In addition, some new material was collectively developed to tighten scenes. The song about the four clans shared above is an example of this. Alongside this group work, some additional members of the troupe were added: two young school age poets joined the troupe, and helped add depth to the opening and closing with their dramatic traditional poetry performances in both Dangme and English. They had wowed the crowd at the Maggie commemoration, and their teacher was approached to include them in the show. A young drummer was also added to support the songs of the troupe.

The performance in Ada was watched by a large crowd – over 300 – with laughter, cheering and silence accompanying the action. For the show in Accra, on August 15th, a narration was scripted in English so that those non-Dangme speakers attending could follow along. But acting in Dangme was given pride of place as it brought out the most natural feeling amongst the troupe. At the over 100 person audience in Accra, which included chiefs, academics, the media, members of the diplomatic core, and national bureaucrats, a talk back was held at the end to draw out people's questions, and reactions. Many of the academics in the crowd didn't know about the current Ada struggle, even though they had heard of the previous iteration of the struggle in the 1980s that led to Maggie's death. Hon. Eunice Ametor-Williams, the Member of Parliament for Ada during the 1979 to 1981 government, and who brought about the cancelation of the company leases through E.I. 10, was present and spoke of how happy she was to see Songor women speaking out about the future of their resource.[6]

"We Are Spreading It!"

The key in both of these performances, beyond the entertainment value of the show, was that those who came left knowing what they previously did not know. As Akpetiyo's song states, the movement has succeeded in producing its own knowledge and "spreading it." These efforts are not going unnoticed. Jane Ocansey, for instance, described how a media outlet interested in the story of the Tapestry contacted her. She gave this account of the interaction to her peers:

> [W]hen we went to Ada ... when we went to Big Ada, the Tapestry that we used, OK FM people came; ... so they asked us what is this tapestry, what is the meaning? So I told them through the tapestry, and I told them the history of Ada; OK FM people said it's a very beautiful story. So they said they have to bring their camera to come and capture the tapestry. So they went to bring their TV Camera from UTV, and then they came to take a photograph of the whole tapestry, and they said they would like to come back to us, so they took my number that they would like to come so that we have meeting with them, and we teach them what the tapestry reflects so that they can also help us broadcast the issue of Songor. So this is what I went through at the festival. (ASAF Movement Meeting, July 3, 2013)

The Maggie performance, the Red Friday demonstration as well as the demonstration in Sege in the lead up to the 2016 election all received media attention. In the latter half of 2017, several Media outlets carried the story of the drama as well, even as Radio Ada carried the women's success at gaining legitimacy in the 2017 Asafotufiami Festival. Many of these different, and varied activist efforts by Yihi Katsεmε have helped to change the dynamics in Ada. For instance, where in 2016 Nene Ada's statement at Asafotufiami Festival did not mention atsiakpo, after the series of 2017 efforts, Nene Ada came out against atsiakpo at the Festival. Similarly, the main financial backer for the 2017 Festival, Honorable Dr. Nii Kotei Dzani – a

CHAPTER 5

member of the National Council of State representing Ada – has taken a very public stance against the atsiakpo practice.[7] He later met with Yihi Katsɛmɛ executive in December 2017 to state his support for their work.[8] As a member of the council of state, Hon. Dzani represents an important avenue into the current government. The result of all of this is that the Yihi Katsɛmɛ are transitioning to focus on updating the Master Plan, to deepen the community involvement in its framework. This became the focus for 2018.

A crucial aspect of all of this work has been for the two contemporary iterations of the movement to not only get their message across, using creativity as an opening, it has also been to open up a space of dialogue, so that planning the Songor future is not something done in secret, or in some professional or government office in Accra. As such, the alliance with Radio Ada has been crucial. Throughout the ASAF and Yihi Katsɛmɛ iterations of struggle, Radio Ada has provided air time to the movement to share their thoughts, but has also hosted phone-in segments where the listening public can call in and share their thoughts on what is happening in the Songor. For instance, from 2012 to 2015, Radio Ada provided airtime to ASAF, and one of its contributing member organizations, the Ada Songor Salt Cooperative. They joined the evening topical show, called *Gborkwe Kaanya* (Evening Bowl), for an update every few weeks. One of the programs, broadcast on April 30th, 2012, focused on:

> bringing the issues of Songor back to the centre of the [Asafotufiami] Festival as it is gradually losing its core essence as a historical ritual that should relate the issues of the past to the present. The issues that brought about the festival are still around today in various forms: issues of advocacy, defense, protecting rights, and livelihood. Instead, the festival has become ceremonial and these issues are not at the centre of it again. (*Gborkwe Kaanya* broadcast, Radio Ada, April 30th, 2012)

This program helped set the stage for the focus of both ASAF and the Yihi Katsɛmɛ on the Asafotufiami Festival as a major site for their activism. In this sense, the movement was outdooring its thinking for public discussion, not making secret plans for intervening into Ada public life. A call-in followed the rebroadcast of this show, later the same week, which gave Adas a chance to ask questions about the content of the show. This was how the show operated over the course of its airing. But Radio Ada didn't just open intentional space for these discussions; it, and its radio hosts, made time for Songor issues in shows that didn't focus on the topic directly. In fact, Kofi Larweh describes how this type of interaction was how the station even found out there was a conflict brewing in the Songor about atsiakpo in the first place:

> on Monday of this week, part of the morning program, part of the morning breakfast show was what is happening in the Songor because we have had calls, and people have been calling in […] This is a program on [Radio] Ada FM. People have called in on some other programs that we have organized in the community; people have hinted, and so they say, "well, if you are handling

THE PEDAGOGY OF CREATIVE DISSENT

this case," we were handling a case on water, "if you are talking of water, there is a more serious case of [it] if action is not taken, if people do not, if the people who are cheating us are not prevented there will be war in the Songor." Ok, so there have been various indications that this program [on Songor issues] must come on earlier, and so Monday the space was created and you see now that the people are now using their voice, community radio now as the mobilizer. (Participatory Research Group discussion, February 23rd, 2008)

This statement, made in 2008, before ASAF even emerged, shows how Radio Ada has kept a space open for community voices to report on what is happening in the Songor. This tradition of the station making room for burning issues has continued. For instance, in a legal education program aired on the station on May 18th, 2013, the original topic of the rights and responsibilities of family elders with regards to other members of the extended family was superseded by a series of callers wanting to discuss Songor issues. Here is one such call sequence:

Bosumpra
[legal resource person for the show]: Hello ... speak up; you are on air.
Oman [caller]: My name is Oman, please I am calling from Dogo.
Bosumpra: You are welcome. Go ahead.
Oman: My view is this; we have heard so much about this Songor subject and greatly appreciate your efforts but still, those engaged in atsiakpo have refused to stop the practice. Just the other day I paid a visit to the lagoon site and found people busily working on their atsiakpo plots. If it is difficult to stop, why not just allow them to continue, as it seems to have come to stay. As I said, this is my view.
Bosumpra: OK thanks. We have actually discussed so much about atsiakpo and it has taken the accolades of excuse me to say "galamsey" (illegal gold mining) because the law does not allow such practices. The law is saying salt is a mineral. Galamsey operations have been identified as a major environmental degrading practice; we heard the other day that the President has asked some ministers (put together as a committee) to stop the galamsey practices. In our case, government currently holds all the Ada lands from Sege to Obane in trust. If anyone goes to construct atsiakpo anywhere within the demarcated boundary, the programme we have been featuring is reminding them that, "Songor has regulations."
Kofi [Lawerh, host of show]: We are simply saying constructing atsiakpo amounts to breaking the law.

CHAPTER 5

Bosumpra: That's right.
Kofi: So if you want the law to deal with you, just go ahead. It could be that, there are officials who should implement this regulation who are not doing so now. It is just like galamsey. There are regulations against galamsey too but when those to implement them failed the nation, the President instituted a committee to take actions necessary. On our part, we are not waiting for any major crises over Songor, for which government will find it necessary to set up another committee, which may have to block people's access to the lagoon before we open up discussions on what should be done. We have been listening to concerns being raised by community members that atsiakpo is introducing violence and animosity hence the institution of this programme. So if listeners and observers agree that there is a problem with salt winning and are ready to use information from these programmes to find peaceful solutions so be it. That will also mean we are responsible citizens who know their rights and what to do. When the law continues to be flouted, what has happened elsewhere where people have been asked to stop work can happen here too. I think this is what our friend JK implies in his earlier contribution when he was mentioning "war." He was just cautioning us all that there are limits; when an act is considered beyond overlooking, punitive measures are employed. We can therefore extend our understanding on his contribution to this level.

Through shows like this, community opinions decrying the atsiakpo practices were shared, and linked to the law, even though this was not what the show started out to focus on. In this sense, not only was discussion of Songor issues democratized through the content of programs like this, it was also democratized through the station's responsiveness to what Ada's want to discuss – a democratization of form and content.

At the same time, Radio Ada, working with both contemporary iterations of the Ada movement, have gone to communities and built intentional broadcast space with their views. For example, when the secret Songor relocation plans by government surfaced, the station aired a show that compiled the views expressed by Songor community members about this prospect. This is one community comment from the show, aired July 23rd, 2011:

I am called Diana Sebbie. I thank Radio Ada for enlightening us on how our chiefs put price tags on us without our knowledge. Since the evacuation idea, both youth and elders have never slept and are confused. I have been selected to represent my community and to inform the movement that the evacuation will not come on today or tomorrow. The atsiakpo will not help us and therefore we should go back to the salt wining which existed since time in memoriam. (Radio Ada broadcast, July 23rd, 2011)

In this comment, the two issues the movement and Radio Ada went to discuss can be clearly seen: the atsiakpo issue and the threat of evacuation, or forced relocation. In this same program, the station also made room for one of the Members of Parliament from the area, Honorable Wallace Gborjor Abayateye, from the ruling party at the time, the NDC. Here is an extract from this part of the program where the MP decries his own government's actions, stating he:

> [...] informed the [government] delegation that [they] should go properly and that in our tradition, even if you are entering your own room through the window you will be called a thief but you should go through the door. This advice was not considered. We warned that the evacuation will not be accepted by the people especially the coastal dwellers whose main occupation is fishing and then you move them to Ada Luta, a farming community, how will they easily adapt to the new environment. We advised that they should discuss the issue of evacuation with the people and come to a mutual conclusion. (Radio Ada broadcast, July 23rd, 2011)

In this sense, the movement meetings with Songor communities were given equal importance to the elected member of government, and he was forced to respond to the concerns of these community members. This is another form of democratization of the airwaves, as the government is being held to account for its decisions, even as people present in these discussions are able to hear their views expressed on the air, and those not present updated on what is happening. These different examples reveal how Radio Ada, working with the Ada movement has contributed to democratizing the knowledge emerging from the struggle, as well as the very means of producing knowledge and action from the struggle.

In the most recent iteration of the movement, the station has continued to provide space for the movement to air its knowledge. In fact, it has worked with the Yihi Katsɛmɛ to begin producing its own program. The first one they made aired in July 2016, and in it the Yihi Katsɛmɛ used songs, such as the one about staying in your room too long, and the experience of movement members to help explain why they have decided to stand up for the resource. Victoria Kpodo for instance, shares her story in the broadcast:

> My name is Victoria Kpodo. I'm fifty years old. I'm from Sege. The Songor is there for everybody, so I also go and win the salt. When I win the salt, I use to preserve, and sell some to look after my children, pay school fees, buying their clothes, and look after the house. Because I don't have a portion there to make atsiakpo, I don't have any salt to win, so I have to go and carry salt for them [the Atsiakpo owners] before they will give me some. The distance that you carry the salt, in fact, it doesn't help me. But the money too, they will pay me is not sufficient even to pay school fees for my children ... because of this

atsiakpo problem, three [of my children] couldn't go to continue their school, because I don't have money to look after them ... this atsiakpo has made me loose a great thing. (Yihi Katsɛmɛ broadcast, July 15th, 2016)

They also used this broadcast to explain how the UN Declaration of the Rights of Indigenous People (UNDRIP) as well as the Sustainable Development Goals validate and support the movement's insistence that PNDC Law 287 should be maintained and used to underscore the centrality of Songor inhabitant-input into future planning around the Lagoon (Yihi Katsɛmɛ broadcast, July 15th, 2016). The process of Yihi Katsɛmɛ learning how to build a radio show also helped them take their story beyond the borders of Ghana. In 2016, at the launch of the Sustainable Development Goals High Level Forum in New York, the Yihi Katsɛmɛ were able to share a video message with delegates at a side event hosted by Together 2030, facilitated by the Participate group.[9] The video began with the song about keeping long in your room and was based on a radio show produced by the Yihi Katsɛmɛ as well as a speech by Rev. Sophia Kitcher. In this sense it represents a great culmination of knowledge production of the movement and its efforts to democratize this knowledge. Here I reproduce the entire speech Rev. Kitcher delivered to show this depth:

Before beginning, I would like to ask you join me in learning the catch phrase of our Brave Women just shared in our short production. I say "Yihi Katsɛmɛ," which means "brave women" and you respond "waamasi," which means "we stand firm." Let's try it – "Yihi Katsɛmɛ!!" ...

Dear Secretary general, assembled dignitaries, esteemed members of Together 2030, other Civil society members, and most pointedly any members of indigenous and marginalized groups in this hall; I am very honoured to be here with you today, as we take part in the first High Level Political Forum of the Sustainable Development Goals, but also as we mark World Youth Skills Day – more on this in a moment.

For now, let me present myself. My name is Reverend Sophia O. Kitcher, I come from Ada, Ghana, and I am here representing the Yihi Katsɛmɛ (Brave Women) of the Ada Songor lagoon who are fighting for the sustainable development and livelihood spelled out in the 17 goals of our new global SDG compact. I am the coordinator of the women's movement, and have been sent here with a clear message for not only our President and Ghanaian delegation, but for the world at large. Sustainable development must mean development for all, not for some. It must mean the improvement of livelihoods, not their sacrifice for profit making. In our case, it must mean a return to communal access and artisanal salt production in our Songor lagoon, a message we encapsulate in the shout, "Songɔ wɔ kulaa wa nɔ!!," or "Songor for All!!"

Over the past decade, the women, like Victoria Kpodo, whose voice you just heard, have lost communal access to their resource. They have become wage labourers in a lagoon that use to be the source of household security – not just for Adas, but beyond to those Ghanaians who have travelled to the Songor to win salt. The lagoon's ability to support this 400-year-old tradition was first undermined in the 1960s through changes in the natural flooding pattern caused by the Volta Dam, which was partially funded by the World Bank. These changes have put the resource under more and more pressure. In the meantime, Ghana's Government has failed to implement plans to revitalize the lagoon. For instance, a Master Plan for Songor Development that included Songor community input, has sat idle on the shelves for over 24 years. Due to this neglect, various forces within Ada, and outside it have taken advantage to turn this backbone of community well being into the epicenter of individualism and short-term greed. The traditional and elected, local and national leaders that we look to as enlightened managers of our resource have rather contributed to its diminishment: directly through sponsoring of individualized salt pans, called "atsiakpo," or indirectly by turning a blind-eye to the growing divisions in our communities, loss of independence of our women, and undermining the future of our children. It is with this growing crisis in our hearts that we turn to our leaders and call out, "Songor for All!!"

But as I stand here before you, I must be clear that I represent not only the voices of my women, and my communities, but for all those who have been part of the Participate group. The Participate initiative is a global network of participatory research organisations. It works to ensure that marginalised people have a central role in holding decision-makers to account, from local to global levels. Participate's research tells us that much like the Brave Women of the Songor, the poorest of the poor, the most marginalized are adamant that their first priority is for government and authority figures to work with them, treat them as people that count, and make decisions with them, not for or about them. Just as every person must count in sustainable development decision-making, so too must "no decision be made about us without us!"

Is this not the central tenet of SDG goal 16 that peaceful and inclusive societies are achieved through justice and participatory decision-making? Doesn't goal 5 speak of gender equality in all spheres of life? Goal 9 speaks directly to our government's need to put in-place resilient infrastructure to foster inclusive industrialization. Goal 12 speaks of responsible and sustainable production, something that a Songor for All!! can achieve – not only in terms of salt production, but also for aquaculture that emerges in the wet season when the lagoon is well maintained. We believe that a true partnership for sustainable development not only includes global governments and multilateral institutions, but also includes indigenous communities such as ours, and women within them. Together we can plan and act to achieve a sustainable resource that supports wide scale communal artisanal salt winning, as well as fishing, but also turns our lagoon into an eco-tourist destination that will help ensure the

Songor model can inspire other resource contexts, and can provide new skill building and employment opportunities for our youth, on this World Youth Skills Day.

Mr. secretary general, we were so pleased when you named our president, his Excellency John Dramani Mahama as a champion of your SDGs. We are truly excited to work within this new SDG frame, with our champion president to show the world what sustainable development can mean. And whatever steps we take, together, we will share them with all members of the Participate group family, as well as with other indigenous and marginalized communities. As the song in our opening montage playful shares, we are anxious for our Songor to return to its productive best, so that we too can return to teasing each other in the fullness of life.

Thank-you! Songor for all! Sustainable development for all!!

Yihi Katsɛmɛ! Wamaasi!!

Since the UN conference, the video has been posted to the Yihi Katsɛmɛ Facebook site and has received several hundred views. This same Facebook site has carried videos of the march in Sege, the Asafotufiami marches, the meetings and workshops of the movement, including the drama development session that led to *Songor, Our Life! Atsiakpo, Our Death!* It provides links to media stories, Radio Ada stories, and blog posts about the women, and the struggle for a Songor for all. It also carries a stark video of the environmental damage that Atsiakpo has done to the Songor, taken from the air. In and of itself, it has become a repository of movement knowledge production, and is also a mechanism for democratizing, or "spreading" it.[10] The final and most recent example of the movement working with Radio Ada to spread its knowledge was Mary Akuteye's going on air in August 2018 to raise questions about a mortuary that is being built on the edge of the Songor Lagoon. Raising this issue on air has led Yihi Katsɛmɛ to be recast as the defender of all threats to the Lagoon and has enabled them to bring together a much broader coalition of women's organizations that are campaigning against the mortuary.[11]

Learning through Creative Participatory Analysis

The last area of knowledge production and democratization by the movement involves an analytic tool developed by the Yihi Katsɛmɛ, with input from Radio Ada members, to help with their "Songor livelihood for all campaign." It emerged as part of their desire to collectively analyse their opposition and support in and outside Ada, and also as a way to learn what their support and opposition was in each community from the movement's rep from that community. It was "a visual method of analysis that would ensure women from across the 45 communities surrounding the Songor lagoon could analyze their situation, and contribute to this new [Songor

THE PEDAGOGY OF CREATIVE DISSENT

livelihood for all] strategy" (Harley & Langdon, 2018, p. 199). The tool involves a two stage process, described here:

> First, women would analyze the current situation in the Songor, focusing on whether they thought [...] [A]tsiakpo [...] should continue, or if the lagoon should return to being a resource for all, as it has been for the past 400 years. [...] These votes were a visual method in themselves, in that the vote took place with eyes closed, with arm positions showing how people felt (i.e. arm up if you wanted a return to Songor for all, down if you didn't, and in between if you weren't sure). The visual vote was also then turned into an open discussion where those who voted in different ways explained why they voted the way they did. [...] [The women] then went on to the second step, doing an analysis of allies, opponents, and those on the fence in terms of the "Songor [livelihood] for all" campaign. Using local material (leaf=ally, stick=on the fence, stone=opponent), and an approach designed by women movement leaders and [Radio Ada] researcher-allies, the women grouped those in their community who were on-side for a return to the Songor being "for all," and then whom amongst their community would be ambivalent, and who would be against it. The methodology then asked women in each of these communities to do the same analysis of those outside their community, including decision makers, as well organizations that might hinder or help their cause. (Harley & Langdon, 2018, p. 199)

The process was conducted first, on February 19th, 2016, at the movement representative level, with the Executive and 45 community representatives taking part, and developing and adjusting the tools as they went along. The first exercise allowed the women to recommit to the goals of the movement in an open way that also created room for democratic descension and dialogue. For instance, the questions used for the vote came from an update of people's thinking about the struggle, and when one of the questions about the government involvement in developing the Lagoon was asked, one of the women objected to the question, stating it needed to be further clarified. At this point it became two questions: "I want government to help us deal with the Songor problems," to which all Yihi Katsɛmɛ community reps and executive members agreed; and, "I want government to take over the Songor," to which all Yihi Katsɛmɛ disagreed. In the leaf/stick/stone process that followed this (re)confirmation of movement consensus, an in-depth analysis by community to community of support for the end of atsiakpo, and the return to the Songor being a livelihood for all, as well as a supportive rather than authoritarian role for government was laid out.

This provided the Yihi Katsɛmɛ with an internal analysis of where they felt they had support and where they faced opposition – both inside and outside the Songor. They then decided to test and deepen this analysis by gathering women at the community level in several key Songor communities throughout the month of

133

CHAPTER 5

Figure 5.3. Leaf/stick/stone analysis, done at Radio Ada (photo credit: Jonathan Langdon)

March. The result to the discussion and voting on the current state of the Lagoon and what needs to change was clear:

> Considering women have been largely excluded from the current atsiakpo practice, it is not surprising that the 345 women who participated in these focus group discussions voted overwhelmingly for Songor to return to being a resource for all. (Harley & Langdon, 2018, p. 199)

With that said, a deeper look into the notes from these meetings suggests the voting approach also enabled women to question the process, or to provide answers that deviated from the rest. Here is an excerpt from one account from the Sege meeting, held on March 21st, 2016:

> Mary [Akuteye] asked the first question: We know at first the Songor was for all, but now there has been some changes happening, so is it really necessary that the Songor should be a resource for all?
>
> 10 women said yes it should be a resource for all.
>
> Mary: One women did not raise her hand, so we will ask her why she did not raise up her hand.
>
> The woman who did not raise her hand said: Some of us here are visitors, so we don't really know anything about the Songor. That is why I did not raise my hand, but I sell the salt.

134

THE PEDAGOGY OF CREATIVE DISSENT

In this way, a clear consensus emerged across all the women's groupings in the 15 communities consulted, where the "Songor Livelihood for All" plan was supported by them, but it was far from being a rubber stamp:

> This open, transparent process meant women in communities surrounding the lagoon could delve into the complex feelings in their midst, while also building a consensus for action. (Harley & Langdon, 2018, p. 199)

Subsequent to the voting process, the women in each community provided their own analysis of the support and opposition to the Yihi Katsɛmɛ plan. This added confirmation, depth and nuance to the information that the community reps had previously inputted.

Figure 5.4. Leaf/stick/stone analysis, done at one of the Songor communities (photo credit: Erica Ofoe)

The depth of analysis that emerged was profound. In the image above, for instance, the women from that community made it clear that the stones outside the Songor were huge, and were the biggest part of the problem. In fact, "the analysis was incredibly damning for local and external decisionmakers, who were clearly identified as opponents to the efforts" (Harley & Langdon, 2018, p. 200). What was powerful to witness through this process though, was not only the emergence of this collective knowledge and analysis – likely far more robust that many scholarly studies – but also the way this knowledge became owned by women throughout the Songor. Laying it out this way helped to identify to their allies, opponents and those in-between through their own analysis who the big stones were, and led to their

CHAPTER 5

open support of the Yihi Katsɛmɛ efforts. In 2017, during Yihi Katsɛmɛ community engagements, and again in 2018, these analysis were also conducted again too as a way of documenting whether Yihi Katsɛmɛ support was growing or waining. With the exception of Bonikope – the epicentre of atsiakpo – return visits have shown the leaves growing, and the sticks, and even some stones shifting. The crucial note here is that this creative approach to knowledge generation enables people to visually absorb the information that they, themselves have produced.

OVERLAPPING REGISTERS OF "SPREADING" LEARNING AND CREATIVITY

At the outset of this chapter, I described 3 registers that the chapter would aim to speak to. These were the idea of restorying as learning, the idea that creative dissent both generates and emerges from learning, and the idea that knowledge produced and then democratized through such creative processes builds movements.

Movement creativity, such as the tapestry of herstory, the use of songs and drama, and ongoing resignification of the hand, reveals both the individual articulations of creative dissent as pedagogy, but also, over time, the restorying of the struggle that each of these articulations represents shows a deepening analysis and strategic nuance that has been learned and shared over time. The way in which the hand and the thumb are woven into different examples of creative dissent illustrates this ongoing deepening of learning and flexibility of analysis as it adds to new movement strategies. In this sense, creativity as pedagogy also overlaps with restorying as ongoing movement learning.

Parallel to this, processes of sharing knowledge production, or "spreading it" as Akpetiyo describes it also connects with creativity as pedagogy, where knowledge democracy is not just about access to information, but the active engagement with this knowledge, and contributing to it by those outside the movement. The examples from this chapter of how "Songor, Our Life! Atsiakpo, Our Death!" as well as Radio Ada dramas and call-ins, the connection to international contexts like the SDG High Level meeting, and finally, the use of participatory evaluation as a knowledge production and democratization process all reveal how this movement has been building in complex and creative ways. Building allies, building understanding, building trust, building movement knowledge, building movement numbers. On all three of these registers, the movement has been building – and people recognize this. The concluding chapter points this out by describing some of the most recent examples of government officials recognizing how the movement has been building.

NOTES

[1] http://www.ghananewsagency.org/social/ada-songhor-salt-women-s-association-want-govt-s-intervention-109006
[2] http://adacommunityonline.com/2016/10/12/songor-for-all-full-statement-of-ada-songor-women-association-petition-to-president-mahama/
[3] https://www.newsghana.com.gh/govt-renders-apology-for-the-death-of-margaret-kuwornu/

[4] https://www.graphic.com.gh/news/general-news/ada-women-go-red-friday-in-fight-against-atsiakpo.html
[5] https://noahdamehblog.wordpress.com/2018/07/31/withdraw-all-atsiakpo-agreements/
[6] https://noahdamehblog.wordpress.com/2017/08/26/making-atsiakpo-popular-drama-at-aviation-social-center-dignitaries-and-actors/
[7] http://adacommunityonline.com/2017/06/23/ada-chiefs-should-be-ashamed-of-themselves-dzani/
[8] https://noahdamehblog.wordpress.com/2017/12/31/council-of-state-members-will-be-educated-on-atsiakpo-ada-equivalent-of-galamsey/
[9] https://www.facebook.com/YihiKatseme/videos/983089715122003/
[10] https://www.facebook.com/YihiKatseme/?ref=br_rs
[11] https://noahdamehblog.wordpress.com/2018/08/26/women-of-ada-unites-for-a-common-goal/

CHAPTER 6

CONCLUSION

… and so we use the image of the dog, because the dog barks, but when you give it food, then it bows its head and eats. This is just like our leaders.
– Mary Akuteye, Popular Education Network Conference,
June 26th, 2018, Cape Town, South Africa

This book shares the (re)story of an African social movement, the Ada movement defending communal salt winning in the Songor lagoon, especially focusing on the learning within the movement, and the way in which it engages those external to the movement in an educational dialogue. The telling has aimed to both show how the movement has learned, and what knowledge it has produced, even while trying to tell the story of the movement in an accessible way. At the same time, the very way in which the movement learning has been articulated has led the telling to also argue that the Ada movement, and movements like it, are thinking, learning and producing their own analysis, theory and knowledge. The Ada movement is not some manifestation of Fanon's theories, or Nkrumah's for that matter – even as its analysis may or may not resonate with their thoughts. More than anything, to me, it is clear this movement is constantly restorying, or reworking, or retheorizing its understanding and analysis of its struggle. The quote above is a lovely instance of this dynamism in action.

In June 2018, Mary Akuteye, the Yihi Katsɛmɛ president, as well as Kofi Larweh, Erica Ofoe, and myself attended the 8th bi-annual Popular Education Network (PEN) Conference held for the first time in Cape Town, South Africa. Our group presented the social movement learning of the Ada movement, and the central voice in the presentations we made was that of Mary. The quote above comes from a great example of this, where our group was asked to share the Ada story with the PEN attendees and a wide group of popular education organizations and activist in Cape Town's Community House – a well-known anti-apartheid movement organizing space. Our group was one of three asked to share in this space, and Mary presented with Kofi translating. The quote is a reworking Mary wove of the image of the dog described in the previous chapters, and here she uses it to both invoke the chameleon and the dog. More than that, she reuses this image to bring to life the challenge the movement is currently facing with leadership that is barking at atsiakpo, but is then turning around and bowing its head to the proverbial food these interests offer. The gathered audience responded to this use of the image with energy and enthusiasm.

CHAPTER 6

In this same presentation, Mary shared the strategy tool of the hand they had developed, as well as the sticks, stones and leaves analytical tool – both discussed in Chapter 5. In fact the whole presentation was delivered as a walk-through of how the hand approach works. Based on the feedback after the presentation, no one left the plenary session with any doubt of the literacy of struggle Mary has, despite the fact that she does not read or write in either English or Dangme, nor does she speak much English. In fact, her presentation in Dangme provoked others in the space on African soil to share their thoughts in their maternal language before translating it to English – an act that at least one commentator called decolonizing, helping remind attendees of the conference that this PEN was happening in Africa.

AFRICAN SUBALTERN MOVEMENTS THINKING AND ACTING ON THEIR FUTURE

Harley (2012) makes it clear that one of the key dynamics of the Abahlali baseMjondolo movement in South Africa is its insistence on its own thinking and learning, challenging at every turn the notion that it is being run by a third force. In fact, in a recent incident where movement leadership was assassinated, Abahlali released a statement that directly addressed this issue. Part of it reads:

> The Mayor [of Durban], Zandile Gumede, said that there was a 'third hand' behind our movement. She also said that the City would not work with our movement and would, instead, work with the South African Shack Dwellers' International Alliance – the South African branch of the international NGO that used to be known as Shack Dwellers International (SDI). (abahlali@lists.riseup.net, personal communication, June 14th, 2018)

It is a special irony that the accusation that Abahlali must have some other force behind it discounts them in the eyes of the Mayor of Durban, and yet working with SDI, a clear instance of an international NGO acting as a force in local dynamics, is preferred instead. This is a stark indication of what Kapoor (2005) has described as 'taming the grass roots' through NGOization. But more importantly for this discussion, S'bu Zikode (2006), the elected President of Abahlali, has made it clear that the greatest threat his movement poses is its insistence on thinking for itself: "The state comes for us when we try to say what we think." As oppressed people, thinking and acting on their own volition is what the state is trying to repress – hence the call by state officials for shackdwellers to align themselves with a safe international NGO and not their own movement.

While the current iteration of the Ada movement, the Yihi Katsɛmɛ, have not faced similar levels of state repression, they have faced similar attempts to dismiss their thinking and analysis. As the previous chapters document, their emergence from within ASAF was in reaction to some of the patriarchal dismissal of the analysis of women salt winners within past iterations of the movement (cf. Manuh, 1992). And yet their analysis is deeply rooted in the context, and has been borne out time and

CONCLUSION

again. The songs of Akpetiyo clearly display this deep level of analysis and literacy in the struggle. Not only that, it is women within the movement who have shown the courage to take a stand and publicly call out politicians and traditional leaders for their failures, as Mary demonstrates above with her restorying of the image of the dog.

In thinking this struggle, each of the various iterations of the Ada movement have remained rooted in Ada culture, knowledge and epistemics. From earlier iterations, we have the example of insisting on the sacredness of Yomo, which led to the reduction of the company portion of the lagoon in E.I. 75. From more recent iterations, the tapestry helped to recenter the Songor story on Yomo, and her teachings; the performance of *Songor Our Life, Atsiakpo, Our Death!* made it clear how those teachings are being defied today, as the resource is put under greater and greater strain; the radio drama *Okor Ng Kor* helped to frame women's leadership through the lens of Ada traditions, rather than outside them, which contributed to opening a space for Queen Mothers to become part of the Ada traditional governance landscape; the Yihi Katsɛmɛ have used songs from the past to remind Songor community members of the way the lagoon functioned previously; and, the recent iterations of the movement have woven defence of other important Ada symbols, such as the Okor forest, or the critique of the mortuary, into their activism in order to solidify their position as defenders of Ada, rather than critics of it.

At the same time, the movement has thought up new strategies that have contributed to the deepening of its analysis and the effectiveness of its actions. In the 2011 tour of Songor communities by ASAF & Radio Ada, the combination of discussing the radio drama, the potential relocation of Songor communities by government, and the issue of atsiakpo allowed the movement, at that time to make in-roads with atsiakpo practitioners. This was when several of them admitted they had initially fought the practice, but later joined it after being arrested. Later, during the current Yihi Katsɛmɛ period, the movement developed the leaf, sticks and stones approach to analyse on an ongoing basis the effectiveness of their campaign. Through this, they have been able to document analysis from movement membership right down to the community level of the growing number of leaves supporting the return of the lagoon to communal access, rather than stones supporting atsiakpo. This accessible method of analysis, and its association with the chosen colour of the movement, green, reveals the impact of thought wedded to action. Similarly, the development of the hand as a community engagement technique, with its link to the use of songs (the pinkie finger), the recollection of Songor as love, as it used to be (the ring finger), the issue they are confronting (the middle finger), the invitation to join the action (the pointer), and finally, the reconnection with the image of the thumb as recognition of the importance of women's leadership to bind the struggle together (the thumb), also strengthened the collective work of the movement throughout the 45 Songor communities. Both of these instances deepen the literacy of struggle throughout the movement – as all members of the movement become knowledge producers, and knowledge sharers. The importance of the rootedness of this cannot

CHAPTER 6

be understated, nor can the fact that literacy does not rely on reading and writing, but rather on the effective use and understanding of information. As Kofi Larweh and I have discussed elsewhere (2014), the advent of digital technology, as well as the central place of radio and cellular phones is allowing those who deepen their oral literacy to be active voices in defining the future; the Yihi Katsɛmɛ, through such efforts as their manifesto, and their *Songor, livelihood for all* plan, as well as their radio show and marches at Asafotufiami festival are insisting on adding their voice to decisions on Ada's future.

The prefigurative future being created and fought for, however, is not of transforming Ada into something new, but rather returning to the teachings of the Yomo in a contemporary way. In articulating the importance of women's voice and analysis in the struggle, the Yihi Katsɛmɛ do not reach for outside arguments about the importance of women's voice – not that they reject these arguments – but instead point to the examples of the Yomo and Maggie as legitimating their place. For instance, in a meeting with a state official[1] who demanded to know why Yihi Katsɛmɛ should be listened to in deciding the future of the Songor, Mary Akuteye stated, "the Ada's were guided to the Songor by the Yomo, and she taught us its rules. Later, when we strayed from those teachings, and conflict came into the lagoon, it was a women who was killed. Women have played an important part in Songor's history, and we are picking up the torch" (Yihi Katsɛmɛ meeting, July 9th, 2018). They have also used their cultural knowledge and creativity to sidestep efforts at state repression, as they did in their 2016 march in Sege with a brass band and singing songs. Radio Ada's involvement has also helped root discussions of women's leadership in ways that are embedded in Ada society. Given the challenges faced by the broader women's movement in Ghana, where similarly to Abahlali the women's movement have been accused of being a Western imposition on Ghanaian society (Langdon & Anyidoho, 2017), this rootedness in Ada identity and her/history is critical. In this sense, the Yihi Katsɛmɛ have been engaged in a struggle both to regain communal access to the lagoon, and to insist on their right to think and lead the struggle as women. In many ways this leadership has flowed from the fact that it is the women of the Songor that have been ready to put thoughts into action. Harley et al. (forthcoming) connect this praxis to decolonizing struggles in Africa, noting how the independence struggles on the continent needed to be rooted in the thinking and actions of the colonized:

> [T]hese SSMs echo some of the long history of African thinkers and writers on struggle, such as Fanon, Cabral, Nkrumah, Biko. For all of these anti-colonial writers, consciousness about the reality of exploitation is necessary for struggle to even begin, and starts with the actual lived experience of those who are oppressed, and with critical reflection on this. This must be followed by action to change actual lived experience. Cabral (1979) emphasised that "We must be able to bring these two basic elements together: thought and action, and action and thought" (p. 80). They also insisted that everyone had a

role in the struggle – Nkrumah (1973), for example, always made it clear in his writing that every person, farmer, worker, student, had a crucial role to play in the transformation of society. However, current African SSMs add something new, in that they are considering a post-colonial context, a different set of hegemonic relations, a different arrangement of power and repression. Current African SSMs are also far more insistent than many anti-colonial writers that thinking the struggle (and therefore leading it) rests with the oppressed themselves.

As the chapter on African social movement learning illustrated, it is not just independence movements across the continent that have put thoughts into action, but also current subaltern social movements. It is telling that Mary's presentation at PEN provoked a similar connection to decolonization in South Africa.

AFRICAN SUBALTERN SOCIAL MOVEMENTS PRODUCING POTENTIAL

As mentioned previously, the Yihi Katsɛmɛ executive met with a state official about their suggestions for the Songor. In the meeting, one of the questions the official asked of them was why haven't they been able to stop atsiakpo. While it is ironic for an official who actually has the power to challenge the practice asked this of a movement of salt winners, this question is similar to a critique the women of Yihi Katsɛmɛ have faced numerous times in their own communities: why is atsiakpo still here? While I think it important to explore how Yihi Katsɛmɛ has taken to answering this question, I believe it is first crucial to remember Branch and Mampilly's (2015) point that protest movements should not be evaluated strictly and instrumentally on the basis of their ability to achieve their stated goals, but rather on the potential that they produce. Branch and Mampilly (2015) describe how the numerous democracy movements across Africa may not have been able to undermine neo-liberal globalization, and its insertion into the very fabric of processes of democratization, but in many cases, these movements gave birth to several other protest movements that continued these struggles and continue to challenge neoliberal logic. I, along with my colleagues in the Participatory Research Group of my doctoral research, documented this very collective realization by activists in the Ghanaian context, where the socialist movements of the 1970s contributed to the democracy movement of the late 1980s/early 1990s, and then multiplied into several key movements during the current democratic era, from the anti-neoliberal austerity movements, to the women's movement, to the anti-mining movement (Langdon, 2009). Marfleet (2016), as well as Amin (2012) have argued along similar lines in the context of Egypt, and what Amin calls the "people's spring." The Tahrir square revolution that toppled Mubarak was only one moment in a series of protest movements that may have culminated in the 18 days in January, but have continued in different forms since, and most importantly, according to Marfleet (2016), have embedded themselves in people's consciousness as to what is potentially possible.

CHAPTER 6

In the case of the Ada movement, the historical legacy of what is possible deeply informs the contemporary iterations of the movement. One need only think of the image of the thumbless hand to see this reflective learning: the movement of the 1980s, with its cooperatives, and its legal and political manoeuvring did succeed in ending company ownership in the Songor lagoon, and yet it wasn't managed well (the thumb was missing) and so confusion, selfishness and greed have crept back into the resource. They also did not manage to get the Master Plan implemented. The more recent reflection upon the thumbless hand, and what the missing thumb was, led to the realization that women's leadership had been missing in this iteration of struggle. In this sense, the movement of the 1980s created a belief that Adas can stand up to power, and at the same time, this potential has been informed by reflective learning along the lines of Foley's (1999) notion that reflecting on the ambiguities of struggle helps movements to learn new strategies.

All the same, the question raised in the recent meeting with a state official about the Yihi Katsɛmɛ's effectiveness in ending atsiakpo must be addressed. Their answer to this official is telling. First they emphasized all the problems atsiakpo is causing in the Songor, and in the Songor communities, and then they said, essentially, we are fighting these things because they are wrong and because no one else is doing it, what are you doing? Here, again, they emphasise the way in which male leadership as well as state/official leadership has failed in addressing these issues, forcing them to come to the fore. This type of questioning is clearly having an impact, and is part of the reason the state official came to consult with them to begin with. In another, more public example, the current District Chief Executive of the Ada West district came to the commemoration of Maggie's death the Yihi Katsɛmɛ organized in 2017, and was asked at the time to state his position on atsiakpo by the women. After officially apologising for Maggie's death, he begged for patience on the question of atsiakpo as he had just assumed his post, but promised he would study the situation and give them his position publicly in the future. True to his word, at a forum at Nakomkope organized by Yihi Katsɛmɛ on April 19th, 2018, he gave his position live on Radio Ada: "The atsiakpo menace will belong to the past!" The ongoing efforts of the Yihi Katsɛmɛ are clearly beginning to turn the tide on atsiakpo in the Songor, as their community outreach and dialogue efforts are making an impact. As one of the Queenmothers at the event noted on Radio Ada, while demanding to know where the Tekperbiawe chiefs were, "never mind, together with Yihi Katsɛmɛ, there were enough of them to make a difference and ensure the right thing is done" (Nakumkope Forum, April 19th, 2018). In this way, the Queenmother points to another area of potential the Yihi Katsɛmɛ are contributing to. And yet it needs to be recognized that the Yihi Katsɛmɛ cannot be expected to end atsiakpo alone.

As elaborated in the last chapter, one of the major areas in which the Ada movement, especially the Yihi Katsɛmɛ – its most recent iteration – is contributing to popular education is in the area of women's leadership in Ada society. Not only has the movement publicly taken on the fight of the Songor after men failed to do so, they have also inspired other areas of women's organizing to stand up to be counted. At the 2017 Asafotufiami Festival, not only were the Yihi Katsɛmɛ outdoored as official associations in the festival, but the Market Women's association was also marching in the festivities for the first time. Later in the fall of 2017, Ada celebrated its first Ada women's day, and the two women honoured on the day were one of the Queen Mothers, Nana Adede I, and Mary Akuteye, the President of Yihi Katsɛmɛ. Over 600 women marched in the women's day march on that day. This acknowledgement in such a significant event was a public endorsement of Yihi Katsɛmɛ and the good work they have been doing. And yet other aspects of the movement work also contributed to this growing potential of women's voice in leadership contexts – such as the recent work on a mortuary in the lagoon, discussed below. As mentioned earlier, the radio drama, *Okor Ng Kor*, publicly asked the question, why can't we have women leaders? at the very moment clans throughout Ada were beginning to think about installing Queen Mothers. This was a question at the heart of the thumbless hand learning from the movement's past. While the Queen Mothers have yet to demonstrate direct leadership of the struggle, their support of Yihi Katsɛmɛ's work, and their involvement in the Women's Day festivities supports the idea that there is greater potential of women impacting decisions in Ada today than any time in the past. The fact that a state official came to speak directly to Yihi Katsɛmɛ to solicit their opinion on the Songor's future is indication enough of this potential.

Finally, the movement's attention to openness, Akpetiyo's notion of "what someone doesn't know, someone knows," or call to share knowledge, and the general popular education approach of the movement has deeply added to the potential of a future that will benefit all, and not just some. While the movement of the 1980s did not exhibit this openness, and paid the price for it, there is clear learning from that time that it is crucial the movement be rooted in Songor communities, and in the realities of their lived experience. This was learned the hard way through the tensions that arose in the leadership of the salt cooperative at the end of the 1980s. The contemporary iteration of the Ada movement exhibited this openness from the start, led by the example of Radio Ada, which has consistently created a platform for people-led, and community-led change since it first went on the air in 1998. Not only have movement meetings remained open learning spaces, they have also been moved on several occasions from the open air studio at Radio Ada to several communities in the Songor. This is as true today as it was in 2010. Similarly, the movement has made its deliberations and ideas known on radio. In fact, in a recent instance while on air, Mary Akuteye even used some of the Yihi Katsɛmɛ time on air to speak to other pressing community issues such as the lack of water flow to Songor communities, and plans to build a mortuary on the edge of the lagoon – with its potential water contamination. Much like the Okor forest issue before, these efforts by the movement to contribute to the general well-being of Songor life contribute directly to the movement's open agenda of positive change for all those living around the lagoon. Finally, there is the clear, open contributions of the popular education efforts of the current iteration of the movement, with its creation of a popular education tapestry to share the herstory of the Songor, its use of songs from the past to remind people of the way communal life use to cater for one and all, its use of song-composition to convey the challenges facing the Songor today, its creation of a dance-drama and books to deepen and disseminate knowledge about the struggle around the lagoon for different audiences, and its work with Radio Ada to convey these creations, songs and ideas over the airwaves in an open fashion that allows callers to respond to what they hear and ask for more information. All of these efforts provide an ever richer backdrop of potential, a potential reached for by Rev. Sophia Kitcher when she asked, "what do we need to do to unlock the locked box of the Songor for the benefit of all Adas?," as well as the invitation to join the thumb contained in the hand strategy.

In this sense, the issue of atsiakpo remains unresolved, but the movement has remained undaunted. The enormity of the task, with its deep links to various levels of authority, has led to movement realizations that in order to overcome a phenomenon that has literally divided families, there is a need to build wide-spread support, and to build the legitimacy of the movement. Movement members has also realized that it is not up to them alone to stop atsiakpo – that they must draw out those in positions of authority that are prepared to act. In this sense, building the potential of others to contribute to this change is at the heart of the movement learning and strategy in the current iteration. This is echoed in the hand, with the pointer finger calling on others to take action along with the thumb, the Yihi Katsɛmɛ on this issue. It is also echoed in the dance-drama, where the story of the lagoon and its struggle was taken to those in positions of authority to appeal to their conscience. It is echoed in the taking-up of other issues by the movement in order to deepen its legitimacy throughout the Songor. It is echoed in each year's series of community meetings, where collective, deliberative dialogue on the issues confronting the Songor informs where the movement is, and where it is going. It is echoed in the tapestry's locked box used to draw those hearing and seeing the (her)story into an active dialogue on what can be done to change the situation in the lagoon. And finally, it is echoed in the moment, when confronted by a state official about why atsiakpo still exists, when the movement executive turned the tables and asked, but what have you done to end this scourge? Why not come and join us as we work on it every day.

CREATIVITY AND NON-VIOLENT ACTIVISM

As was discussed in Chapter 2, African social movements need to be assessed based on their own realities, rather than seen through the prism of other contexts. Nkrumah's contribution to thinking about change in Africa is therefore particularly relevant considering the context of the Ada movements. His push for and use of non-violent direct action created a legacy in Ghana, where widespread violence has not surfaced, despite the numerous coups and heavily contentious partisan politics of the country. In fact, this may be one of his greatest legacies. As Fanon notes, though, struggle is intrinsically linked to the adversary faced, and the violence they are prepared to use to suppress movements for change. In this sense, one must not

CONCLUSION

fall into the simplistic analysis of Fanon's work, and interpret him as saying violence must be used for real change to happen, but rather, understand him to be reinforcing the idea of context as being the dominant mechanism to determine the nature of struggle that must emerge to make a change.

With this said, the context of the Ada movements shifted over the course of the forty years of their activism. As such, the nature of their organizing has changed. During the early stages of the company presence, there was a lot of legal organizing, and resistance, as well as efforts to influence government policy. Victories included getting the Yomo section added to the consolidation of the company consignment in EI 75, as well as the repeal of the total consignment through EI 10 in 1981. Nonetheless, this type of activism changed when the nature of governance changed on December 31st, 1981, with the PNDC revolution. As was shared in some depth in Chapter 3, the different forces present within the PNDC fold kept oscillating between supporting the people of Ada and the interest of company ownership. An illustrative example of this is the radio announcement both renewing the company concession and calling for the formation of a community salt coop. The killing of Maggie Kuwunor shifted the balance dramatically in favour of the people of Ada, but even up until the signing into law of PNDC law 287, this shift was not complete. Nonetheless, it is important to recognize how the state violence used against the cooperative at that time, as well as citizens of Ada in general contributed to the secrecy of resistance organizing. In the current era of democratic dispensation, and with a community radio at the heart of Ada daily life, the nature of struggle has again changed, where the role of public perception, and partisan politics are much more at play. Hence, according to one of the older activists, it makes sense to now have movement meetings in the open and let everyone know about movement campaigns as it contrasts government secrecy so effectively.

But at the same time, to place too much emphasis on context determining struggle is to ignore people's agency – their ability to be active agents in their own futures and lives. Nkrumah, Fanon, and Cabral all agreed that it was through active involvement in the struggle that change would come about, yes through the actions taken, but also through the change in mindset that emerged through the realization that change is possible. This learning shouldn't be minimized. The long term learning that led to the realization that women's leadership was missing in the last iteration of the movement was a crucial opening for the Yihi Katsɛmɛ to emerge. But what must also be seen is the decision to act on these ideas that is crucial in making change. The image of the missing thumb did not automatically mean the Yihi Katsɛmɛ would emerge. In fact, the same older men that came up with this image were initially resistant to having women from the Songor communities who speak little English, and didn't attend school, to be leaders of the movement. But the Yihi Katsɛmɛ didn't ask permission; they acted when no one else would. And they have continued to act in ways that defy traditional context-driven realities to deepen the impact they are making. By using creative approaches, the women have broadened the contextual norms for women in Ada society, and have sometimes used those norms to enhance their work, and other

CHAPTER 6

times defied them to insist on their right to voice in decision-making. This echoes Kapoor's (2008) description of how subaltern social movements used different approaches, and draw on different discourses to further their struggle – refusing to be contained by the interpretations of them by others.

In this sense, I think it bears reemphasising that ASAF did not by-in-large use creativity in its messaging – even as Radio Ada did contribute things like the *Okor Ng Kor* radio drama; and yet, the Yihi Katsɛmɛ, emerging in largely the same context as ASAF, but being led by a different set of people, has consistently used songs, dance, creative use of music, poetry, theatre and the tapestry to defy the efforts of all those around them to define what it is they are fighting for, and who they are. The example of the use of the brass band in the confrontation with police reveals how the movement has done this. Similarly, Jane Ocansey, Treasurer of the Yihi Katsɛmɛ, noted in their meeting with the state official that they also used a different approach than the youth who tried to fight atsiakpo at its start:

> Some people try to combat atsiakpo but they could not succeed. But when we came, because we are women and non-violent, we have been championing the stop atsiakpo advocacy. No death was recorded so we are of the people, so that is why we say if something must be done then the women should not be left out. (Yihi Katsɛmɛ meeting, July 9th, 2018)

From Jane's perspective, the approach the women are using partly justifies why they should be part of decision-making. In this way, context does play a large part in defining the nature of struggle, but so do the choices of those involved in the struggle, and the consequent results. Learning is at the centre of how these choices are informed by movement experience over time. Again, the decision to gather a brass band in the Asafotufiami March in 2017 shows how the previous police experience informed the movement what they needed to do to deepen their impact on the monumental day when their movement was legitimated.

WHERE THE MOVEMENT IS HEADED NOW, OR THE LATEST AREA OF LEARNING

With a new government in place in Ghana after the 2016 election, the Yihi Katsɛmɛ are beginning to make inroads with their activism. The statement made by the DCE mentioned above, as well as the fact that a high ranking state official sought them out for a discussion on the future of the Songor both reflect this. With that said, atsiakpo remains firmly in place, and there is the potential the new government could use atsiakpo's presence to justify expropriation of the lagoon. This is, after all, the cornerstone idea of the Land Use Plan, produced by the currently governing NPP when last in power in 2007. As such, and emerging out of the Nakumkope meeting in April 2018, the movement has made it clear the three planks of their Songor, livelihood for all plan remain in place. In fact, Mary Akuteye captured it well in the recent meeting with this state official:

the Songor Lagoon should be a livelihood for everybody and this means that the atsiakpo must stop in the Songor Lagoon. The second resolution is that the PNDC law should remain. The third is that if someone wants to develop or maintain the Songor Lagoon, we as Yihi Katsɛmɛ should not be left out. Thank you.

In strategizing on how to ensure PNDC law 287 remains, the movement is exploring legal options in collaboration with a legal NGO, called Law and Development Associates (LADA). At the centre of this discussion is whether or not to collaborate with government in trying to implement 287, or whether or not to take the government to court for its negligence of the fiduciary duty to the people of Ada, and the Songor's traditional title owners, and its contiguous communities. Bolstering their sense of the law being on their side is the UN Declaration of the Rights of Indigenous People (UNDRIP), which clearly echoes PNDC Law 287's placing Songor contiguous communities at the center of any development made in the lagoon. In fact, this declaration was referenced by the Yihi Katsɛmɛ in their recent discussions with the state official, to obvious affect.

Along with the continuation of their *Songor, Livelihood For All* plan, the Yihi Katsɛmɛ also continue to foster connections with a national and global audience. As mentioned at the outset of this concluding chapter, visiting South Africa enabled Mary Akuteye to share the story and approaches of the Ada movement with an international audience. It also allowed her to meet with prominent South African movements, such as the Abahlali, and those fighting against mining related evictions, as well as the effects of fracking near Newcastle, South Africa. It was also clear that the video of *Songor Our Life, Atsiakpo, Our Death!* dance-drama was meaningful to many of the activist audiences that saw it in South Africa. This further reinforced the current effort of the movement to put together different types of digital media for those outside Ada, and outside Ghana to connect with the movement's story. This includes a short film that will dramatize the situation in the lagoon, emerging from the dance-drama piece.

LEARNING IN, THROUGH AND TO STRUGGLE

From the 1970s and 80s, through relative peace of the 1990s, and into multiple levels of organizing in the 2000s, the various Ada movements to defend communal access to the Songor Lagoon have learned on the moved. They learned to play the political and legal game, they learned to form cooperatives, they learned to mourn for the victims of police violence, they learned to speak truth to power at a government commission, they learned to ask questions about the wait for government to fulfil its promise of development, they learned to contest when individualism crept in as a result of government inaction, they learned to use information and its spread as a weapon to battle secret government plans, they learned to take stock of the past and ensure women were part of the leadership of the movement, they learned that

CHAPTER 6

women from Songor communities must be the leaders of this fight, they learned that creativity and doing the unexpected keeps authorities off balance and provides room for their message to get out, and their support to grow, and they are re-learning how to deal in politics and use the law to guarantee the Lagoon will be developed in a way that secures a "livelihood for all." This is the accumulation of several decades of learning in, through and to struggle, and it is dynamic. The term 'social movement' is apt for this struggle, as the challenges the people of the Songor face have moved and changed dramatically over the last 40 years. And yet, through it all, there has been dynamic action, and reflection, that has moved to meet these challenges. In documenting the important moment of transition in the Ada iterations of struggle when women's leadership really emerged, Kofi Larweh and myself (2015) described our research as "moving with the movement." It warrants a moment to recognize just what it has meant to be able to document and be in the midst of a movement, moving. Through this work, the research team in the Ada movements, as well as in Radio Ada, and with the involvement of St Francis Xavier University students and myself, has documented countless hours of movement meetings, learning sessions, community engagements, radio programs, demonstrations, and meetings with political and traditional authority. Throughout this time of documentation, the subtle and monumental shifts within the movement have taught me so much about organizing, and about learning in struggle. In truth, I can say my literacy of the struggle has grown, even while I still need translation of Dangme. Watching, and being part of these shifts though has taught me so much about the ineffable quality of activism, the magical way in which people build the collective tools they need to meet the challenges they face.

As a human endeavour, movements are constantly in motion, as their inner dynamics constantly change – even as the challenges they face evolve. Understanding this dynamic, I think, highlights the importance of what Foley (1999) pointed out in his work on learning in social action. Social movement learning can have ambiguous results if it does not happen in a conscious, reflective fashion that is linked to the evolution of movement strategy. It is easy, in the midst of struggle, to get caught up in dealing with the challenges the movement faces, but maintaining space and time for collective reflective analysis has been crucial to the Ada movement in being able to shift with the changing nature of the struggle without losing momentum. In fact, this learning space has been a crucial aspect of the movement itself. In preparing for the presentations Mary Akuteye, Kofi Larweh, Erica Ofoe and myself did in South Africa, we brainstormed in Dangme and in English while sitting around the breakfast and then lunch and then dinner table. We unpacked years of accumulated learning to string together the long term learning of the movement, its learning *in* struggle; we then thought about the moments of intense learning, or learning *through* struggle, that came as a result of a major event or conflict – such as the death of Maggie; finally, we discussed the way in which the literacy of the struggle, or learning *to* struggle, has emerged in the movement over time (cf. Langdon, 2009a, for learning *in*, *through* and *to* struggle). This reflective space helped us see just how far the movement has come, especially its latest iteration, the Yihi Katsɛmɛ, and also see how the latest iteration is connected to Radio Ada, its community radio station. The previous pages of this book have contained this learning and need not be recapitulated here. Nonetheless, it warrants some examples of what we discussed at the table in South Africa. We talked of the learning *in* struggle that led to the emergence of women's leadership in the movement, where the image of the thumbless hand helped to illustrate the women's leadership as the missing piece, and where the thumb itself has now come to symbolize the women, and their importance in leading the struggle. We also talked of the intensity of learning that emerged *through* the demonstrations the movement has held at the Asafotufiami festival, and on the streets of Sege, where who was with the movement and who was against it became crystal clear – much as the rock and leaf can easily be identified by women at the community level. This learning has helped the movement in disconnecting with those who betray it, as well as understanding who might be unlikely allies like the current District Chief Executive of Ada West District, if approached well. Finally, we spoke of the way in which the movement has deepened the literacy of struggle throughout Ada, and not just in its movement, over the last few years. The popular education heuristic of the tapestry has played an important role, as have the radio shows, the songs, and the community dialogue sessions. These concerted efforts have meant the Yihi Katsɛmɛ have the support at the community level to ensure they are taken seriously by government – a point noted by a Queenmother in Nakumkope this year, and made even clearer by the recent meeting with a state official to sound out the movement as to what it wants to see happen in the Lagoon. This effort to ensure those who don't know, now know is at the heart of this iteration of the movement, and has meant it is not just the Yihi Katsɛmɛ, but all of the Songor communities that are learning *to* struggle. The Adas have been called difficult by central government officials, because they resist Development being imposed on them. The truth is, though, that they have learned *through* struggle what this type of development means – where their livelihoods were dramatically undermined by a dam project, and then taken away by a company concession. They see through this mirage; however, when the government planned on implementing the Master plan, which was written in consultation with community, Songor communities were on side – so much so that they began construction in impatience for it to start. This is the kind of ambiguous learning that can happen *through* struggle without a reflective space to strategize collectively. Though perhaps well intentioned, this impatient construction has led to atsiakpo today. Unfortunately, the intentional neglect of central government, and the emergence of atsiakpo, may have created the impetus for Ghana's government to now step in to the Lagoon in force. Fortunately, the movement has anticipated this, and the songs of Akpetiyo have predicted this potential for some time: "Look behind us, there comes Government after us Okor People," she sang in 2011, "Government could not help but to step in. They told our Elders, they are going to take over Songor, to quell conflicts" (ASAF, 2016, p. iii). And so the movement is ready for this move, with a clear message that is contained in their hand approach, work with

CHAPTER 6

us, and we can do something really positive for the people of Ada in the lagoon, work against us and you will have every community around the Lagoon against you. The greatest chapter of this movement's struggle is perhaps yet to unfold.

With this idea in mind, it was especially heartening to witness the President of Yihi Katsɛmɛ, standing before an audience on an international stage, display the dynamism of this movement. The Restorying of the image of the dog she shared showed movement thinking and movement learning at work. The literacy of struggle of this movement is an oral one. It takes the oral account of Yomo's teachings as its foundations, and imagines and prefigures a future where these teachings are respected again. It is a living effort that defies being contained by simple written accounts. With that said, it has been my honour and privilege to work with, and witness the depth of both the Ada Songor Advocacy Forum, and the Yihi Katsɛmɛ. I am not sure there is a more meaningful role for an activist-scholar than this. Nonetheless, as this book ends, I must acknowledge its limitations, and its hubris in believing what I have written can truly capture the energy, momentum, and deepening of thinking and strategy of this struggle. All of us involved in the research have done our best to move with the movement. I hope sharing its story, even as the story is already changing will convey some of this dynamism and creativity. As Akpetiyo concludes in her song, mentioned above, "we are spreading it." Please consider this my contribution to "spreading it."

NOTE

[1] This meeting is sensitive in nature, and therefore the state official's identity is not being shared here.

APPENDIX A

Timeline of Events Surrounding Songor

(As generated in ASAF book writing process, pre-Independence to 2013)

Date/Year	Actions/Reactions of Ada people	Actions/Reaction of government (SMP&LUP), institutions, companies or outsiders	Lessons learned/Points of emphasis or questions to keep in mind
Before independence	• Regulation by Okor clan heads • Priests and priestesses go to Yomo • Harvesting in the main lagoon (Yomo) • Oaths of war • Rivalry in salt tolls/revenue	• Wars fought to defend Songor • Colonial court cases (internal fighting amongst chiefs, officials and traditional priests about rituals concerning Songor salt winning; who controls proceed) • All salt winners pay salt tax (calabash) • Local control	• Lack of colonial policy on salt
After independence (1960–1966)	• Ada starts to lease lands	• Government introduces mining laws • Akosombo dam affects Songor • VRA mitigation on paper of Halcrow report • HALCROW report • Tsobi chemicals formed (MP of Ada and minister)	

(cont.)

APPENDIX A

Date/Year	Actions/Reactions of Ada people	Actions/Reaction of government (SMP&LUP), institutions, companies or outsiders	Lessons learned/Points of emphasis or questions to keep in mind
1969–1979	• Western portion leased • Eastern leased to star chemical • Citizens resist (stones) • COC Amartey imprisoned • Assisted by WG Nartey protests/petition to gov't to exclude Yomo (worship) • MP Lawyer Olaga as Traditional Lawyer and shareholder in Vacuum • Company time leads to less access so struggle started/tension	• Lease to Wuddah and Apenteng Company rivalry • 2 Coys • Start operations • Watchman killed (January 1974) • Coy rivalries • Lots of arrests • Nene Djagbletey and Lindquist died • 16 people detained • Exec invest EI30 by Acheampong – 1974 while lagoon acquisitions by government • Yomo excluded from government acquisition EI 57 • Govt leased Songor to Star Ch. and Vacuum	• ACO – aliens sacked lots of take-over by Ghanaians • Use of locals for acquisition • Military Government listens to people
1980–1989	• Ada MP – Mrs Ametor-Williams and community petition government • 3 sources of salt for Kasseh • PDCs report to INCC stops soldiers from coming to Ada • 14/10/82 – massive demonstration by chiefs and citizens take over vacuum. • Citizens formed IMC (youth) • Youth mismanaged	• Star chemicals salt for community and Coy winning 2:1 ratio • 1981 – govt cancel leases granted • Apenteng brings soldiers to Songor – private monopoly (1982) • Beating of females and seizure of salt It Ewa • Soldiers used to harass citizens • Burning of preserved salt • Chewing of salt and beatings • Govt sacks citizens from Vacuum (Dec. '83) • January 1984 – government care-take Mgt committee	

(cont.)

154

APPENDIX A

Date/Year	Actions/Reactions of Ada people	Actions/Reaction of government (SMP&LUP), institutions, companies or outsiders	Lessons learned/Points of emphasis or questions to keep in mind
	• Hushie and others formed coops –06/84 • 1985 – April 13, "white flag" order by citizens to win salt • Death of Maggie – massive mobilization of support (in and outside Ada) • Lawyer Akler Ocansey in Government helps the cause of Adas • ATAF formed • Co-ops and Ada Traditional council united to work at the 1986 probe – pd lawyers • Lomobiawe ceded role to traditional council	• January 1984 – government directs Adas to form co-ops • Customs duty on salt duty introduced in 1989 • Co-ops gain tax books and invoice to collect tax for govt • Police harassments continues ('85) • February 1985 – leases re-granted to coys • Maggie shot and killed 1985 • 1986 – salt as mineral by law • Fr. Viser as intermediary with Rawlings. • District assembly started tax collection • Later Probe by Amissah Commission 1986 • 1988 – leases re-granted to Coys	
1990–1999	• Advocacy by Coop for designate winning site • Coop worked with Cuban Team • Tekpebiawe takeover IMC • Lomobiawe takeover from Tekpebiawe • Ada citizens appointed members of IMC (Govt) thru agitations	• PNDC white paper • Dr. Abilio and Cuban Team invited by GNPC – Tsikata • Cuban team present Songor Master Plan (SMP) 1991 • 4 sites "allocated" for Coop winning salt • PNDC law 287 enacted, supporting SML • GNPC Coy on Songor ASSL created but no work	• Difficult funding of community interest in salt (alongside Coy) • Could SMP have started in small way? • PNDC Law 287 is based on SMP implementation

(*cont.*)

155

APPENDIX A

Date/Year	Actions/Reactions of Ada people	Actions/Reaction of government (SMP&LUP), institutions, companies or outsiders	Lessons learned/Points of emphasis or questions to keep in mind
		• Ada Reps appted without consultations • GNPC counld not fund Master Plan • 5 yr trg for Local Salt Techno (Consultants) • Salt and Crude Oil – GNPC butter trade • Conflict of cristalization site	
2000–2009	• Assembly frustrate new bill against PNDC law 287 • Adas demonstrate outside parliament against LI 1716 – Bill withdrawn • Local activists disagree with LUP • Press conference to defuse plans to bring in South African investors (mortgage disguised) • Salom Adas or Adjumanikope started atsiakpo (some chiefs and some individuals involved) • Two types of atsiakpo – inside and outside (DESPA outside)	• District assembly and minerals commission in agreement over LUP • Tagoe and Associates – inconsistent consultations • Land use plan (LUP) initiated • Salt Bill and LI 1716 • PEF "colluded" with some chiefs – $160 million from South Africa • 750,000 metric tonnes potential • 2009 – PEF – Ghana Salt Strategy (LUP) • 2009 – Draft Salt Bill (didn't go through)	• LUP needs a new law to operate • Any scholarship scheme for Adas? (Songor) • LUP – private/individuals interests • SMP – collective interests • Lack of local knowledge and support have prevented actions from happening

(cont.)

APPENDIX A

Date/Year	Actions/Reactions of Ada people	Actions/Reaction of government (SMP&LUP), institutions, companies or outsiders	Lessons learned/Points of emphasis or questions to keep in mind
2010 – 2013	• Atsiakpo instensified • Mobilization and education of communities • ASAF – Ada Salt Advocacy Forum • Salt Cooperative revival • Akpetiyo songs crusade • 2011 Salt Coop and DESPA demonstration at Asafotu • 4 Okor Clans unite to respond to minister • 2 MPs – review of visit (Radio Ada) • Drama/Prog on air (Radio Ada) • Ada Reps on NCOM (National Coalition on Mining) • TC Adhoc Committee on Songor • Chiefs protest involvement of Dr. Buer Ocansey • ASAF Media Forum meeting establishes collective tasks around Songor issue • At 2012 Asafotufiami Festival, women leaders from salt communities and nearby towns march and appeal to government and local leaders to include them in Songor planning • Thousands of Asafotufiami festival attendees are guided through visual history of Songor on canvas produced by women leaders	• Visit of ministerial delegation to meet Ada four clans separately instead of as a team • DEDA – secretly signed memo to minister/ government supporting change of PNDC Law 287 • Some Ada chiefs sign attestation in support of change of law • Minister's memo to cabinet • News in media that Ada Songor Salt Project to become limited liability company • Who Killed Maggie digitalized by StFX Research team • "Those deprived should get lion's share of the national cake" Pres. Mills • Media friends/allies and stakeholders of Ada: Radio Ada, Joy FM, Public Agenda and The Sun • Advocacy for SMP by Coop (funded by BUSAC) • Advocacy Community Forums (July) • Songor bed destruction on increase • Apenteng lease ends 2018	

157

APPENDIX A

QUESTIONS THAT INFORMED THE ABOVE TIMELINE

1. What have been the policies and plans around Songor?
2. What has been the community contribution, reaction, etc., to these policies and plans?
3. What lessons have we learnt from the policies and plans?
4. How do these lessons inform our future actions?

REFERENCES

Abrahamsen, R. (2000). *Disciplining democracy: Development discourse and good governance in Africa*. London: Zed Books Ltd.

Ada Community Online. (2016). *Songor for all: Full statement of Ada Songor Women Association petition to President Mahama*. Retrieved October 12, 2016, from http://adacommunityonline.com/2016/10/12/songor-for-all-full-statement-of-ada-songor-women-association-petition-to-president-mahama/

Ada Salt Cooperative. (1989). *Who killed Maggie? The story of the Songor Lagoon*. Accra, Ghana: Ada Salt Cooperative Committee/Africa Centre. Retrieved from http://opendocs.ids.ac.uk/opendocs/handle/123456789/1200

Ada Songor Advocacy Forum. (2016). *The struggle of the Songor salt people: Nɔnɛ Nɔ Kɔ Lio, Nɔ Kɔ Lɛ*. Sogakope, Ghana: Comboni Press.

Ada Traditional Council. (2017) *Asafotufiami festival programme, 2017*. Big Ada, Ghana: Ada Traditional Council.

Amate, C. O. C. (1999). *The making of Ada*. Accra, Ghana: Woeli Publishing Services.

Amin, S. (2012). The Arab revolutions: A year after. *Interface, 4*, 33–42.

Anyidoho, N. A., & Gariba, S. (2016). *An analytical paper on monitoring, evaluation and learning from collective action movements in Africa*. Tamale, Ghana: Rockefeller Foundation with the Institute for Policy Alternatives.

Ayine, D. (2001). The human rights dimension to corporate mining in Ghana: The case of Tarkwa district. *Mining, Development and Social Conflicts in Africa*, 85–101.

Barndt, D. (Ed.). (2006). *Wild fire: Art as activism*. Toronto, CA: Sumach Press.

Berry, L. B. (1995). *Ghana: a country study*. Washington, DC: Federal Research Division, Library of Congress.

Blaser, M., Fiet, H., & McRae, G. (2004). Indigenous peoples and development processes: New terrain of struggle. In M. Blaser, H. Fiet, & G. McRae (Eds.), *In the way of development* (pp. 1–25). Ottawa: Zed Books and IDRC.

Branch, A., & Mampilly, Z. (2015). *Africa uprising: Popular protest and political change*. London: Zed Books Ltd.

Bratton, M., & Van de Walle, N. (1997). *Democratic experiments in Africa: Regime transitions in comparative perspective*. Cambridge: Cambridge University Press.

Carroll, W. K. (Ed.). (1997). *Organizing dissent: Contemporary social movements in theory and practice: Studies in the politics of counter-hegemony*. Toronto: University of Toronto Press.

Chamberlin, J. E. (2003). *If this is your land, where are your stories? Finding common ground*. Toronto: Knopf Canada.

Chilcote, R. H. (1991). *Am'ilcar Cabral's revolutionary theory and practice: A critical guide*. Boulder, CO: L. Rienner Publishers.

Chovanec, D. M., & González, H. M. (2009). A participatory research approach to exploring social movement learning in the Chilean Women's Movement. In D. Kapoor & S. Jordan (Eds.), *Education, participatory action research, and social change* (pp. 223–237). New York, NY: Palgrave Macmillan.

Choudry, A. (2010). Global justice? Contesting NGOization: Knowledge politics and containment in antiglobalization networks. In A. Choudry & D. Kapoor (Eds.), *Learning from the ground up* (pp. 17–34). New York, NY: Palgrave Macmillan.

Choudry, A., & Kapoor, D. (2010). Learning from the ground up: Global perspectives on social movements and knowledge production. In A. Choudry & D. Kapoor (Eds.), *Learning from the ground up: Global perspectives on social movements and knowledge production* (pp. 1–13). New York, NY: Palgrave Macmillan.

Dickson, K. B. (1969). *A historical geography of Ghana*. Cambridge: University of Cambridge Press.

REFERENCES

Dixon, C. (2017). Sticking around in struggle: Lessons from and for the long haul. In A. Khasnabish & M. Haiven (Eds.), *What moves us: The lives and times of the radical imagination* (pp. 33–44). Halifax, NS: Fernwood Publishing.

El-Hamalawy, H. (2012). *Al-mahmul fi muwagiha Maspero (1)* [The mobile against Maspero: Part 1]. Revolutionary Socialists. Retrieved from http://www.e-socialists.net/node/8297

El-Meehy, A. (2012) Egypt's popular committees. *Middle East Report*, 265.

English, L. M., & Mayo, P. (2012). *Learning with adults: A critical pedagogical introduction*. Rotterdam, The Netherlands: Sense Publishers.

Fals-Borda, O. (2006). The north-south convergence: A 30 year personal assessment of PAR. *Action Research, 4*(3), 351–358.

Fanon, F. (1959). *A dying colonialism*. New York, NY: Grove Press.

Fanon, F. (1963). *The wretched of the earth* (C. Farrington, Trans.). New York, NY: Grove Weidenfeld. (Original work published in 1961)

Fanon, F. (1967). *Black skin, White masks* (C. L. Markmann, Trans.). New York, NY: Grove Press Inc. (Original work published in 1952)

Ferguson, J. (2006). *Global shadows: Africa in the neoliberal world order*. Durham: Duke University Press.

Ferguson, J., & Gupta, A. (2002). Spatializatiing states: Toward an ethnography of neoliberal governmentality. *American Ethnologist, 29*(4), 981–1002.

Fine, M. (2007). *In the PARticulars: Critical dilemmas and radical possibilities of participatory action research*. Paper presented at The American Education Research Association conference, Chicago, IL.

Fine, M., Torre, M. E, Boudin, K., Bowen, I., Clark, J., Hylton, D., & Rosemarie, A. (2004). Participatory action research: From within and beyond prison bars. In L. Weis & M. Fine (Eds.), *Working method: Research and social justice*. New York, NY: Routledge.

Finger, M. (1989). New social movements and the implications for adult education. *Adult Education Quarterly, 40*(1), 15–22.

Fitzclarence, L., & Hickey, C. (2001). *Pedagogical narrative methods*. Retrieved July 2007, from http://www.deakin.edu.au/edu/crt_pe/activities/narrative_idea.htm

Foley, G. (1999). *Learning in social action: A contribution to understanding informal education*. London: Zed Books.

Foucault, M. (1980). *Power/knowledge: Selected interviews & other writing*. New York, NY: Pantheon Books.

Foucault, M. (1991). Governmentality. In G. Burchell, C. Gordon, & P. Miller (Eds.), *The Foucault effect: Studies in governmentality* (pp. 87–104). Chicago, IL: University of Chicago Press.

Garbary, R. (2016). *Okor Songor Yihi Akpe: Songor for all, sustainability forever* [Video]. Ada: Yihi Katseme. Retrieved from https://www.facebook.com/YihiKatseme/videos/983089715122003/

Gariba, S., & Langdon, J. (2005). *Community voices: A civil society assessment of the pro-poor policies and programmes of Ghana's Poverty Reduction Strategy (GPRS) from 2004–2005*. Accra, Ghana: Institute for Policy Alternatives.

Gellner, D. N. (Ed.). (2010). Varieties of activist experience: Civil society in South Asia. In *Governance, conflict, and civic action* (Vol. 3). New Delhi: Sage Publications.

Geschiere, P. (1993). Chiefs and colonial rule in Cameroon: Inventing chieftaincy, French and British style. *Africa, 63*(2), 151–170.

Ghana News Agency. (2016). *Ada Songhor salt women's association want government's intervention*. Retrieved from http://www.ghananewsagency.org/social/ada-songhor-salt-women-s-association-want-govt-s-intervention-109006)

Government of Ghana. (1986). *The Amissah commission report*. Accra: Assembly Press.

Government of Ghana. (1991). *Master plan for salt development in Ghana*. Accra: Assembly Press.

Government of Ghana. (1992). *PNDC law 287*. Accra: Assembly Press.

Government of Ghana. (2003). *Minerals and mining act*. Accra: Assembly Press.

Gramsci, A. (1971). *Selections from the prison notebooks* (Q. Hoare & G. Smith, Eds. & Trans.), New York, NY: International Publishing Company.

REFERENCES

Guha, R. (1983). *Elementary aspects of peasant insurgency in colonial India*. New Delhi: Oxford University Press.
Gunn, L. (2014). *From dogs to wolves: A look at the role of learning and organizing processes in women's empowerment in Ada, Ghana* (Honours dissertation). St. Francis Xavier University, Antigonish.
Gyau-Boake, P. (2001). Environmental impacts of the Akosombo Dam and effects of climate change on the lake levels. *Environment, Development and Sustainability, 3*, 17–29.
Hall, B. L. (2005). In from the cold? Reflections on participatory research from 1970–2005. *Convergence, 38*(1), 5–24.
Hall, B. L. (2012). 'Giant human hashtag': Learning and the #Occupy movement. In B. Hall, D. E. Clover, J. Crowther, & E. Scandrett (Eds.), *Learning and education for a better world: The role of social movements* (pp. 127–140). Rotterdam, The Netherlands: Sense Publishers.
Hall, B. L., Clover, D. E., Crowther, J., & Scandrett, E. (Eds.). (2012). *Learning and education for a better world: The role of social movements*. Rotterdam, The Netherlands: Sense Publishers.
Hall, B. L., & Turray, T. (2006). *A review of the state of the field of adult learning: Social movement learning*. Ottawa, CA: Canadian Council of Learning.
Harley, A. (2012). "We are poor, not stupid": learning from autonomous grassroots social movements in South Africa. In B. L. Hall, D. E. Clover, J. Crowther, & E. Scandrett (Eds.), *Learning and education for a better world: The role of social movements* (pp. 3–22). Rotterdam, The Netherlands: Sense Publishers.
Harley, A. (2014). The pedagogy of road blockades. *Interface, 6*(1), 266–296.
Harley, A., Langdon, J., Larweh, K., & Sikode, S. (forthcoming). Subaltern social movement learning in two African contexts. In P. Rule & J. Preece (Eds.), *Adult learning in Africa*. Leiden, The Netherlands: Brill Sense.
Harvey, D. (2004). The new imperialism: Accumulation by dispossession. *Socialist Register, 40*, 63–84.
Hilson, G. M. (2004). Structural adjustment in Ghana: Assessing the impact of mining-sector reform. *Africa Today, 51*(2), 53–77.
Hilson, G. M. (2012). Poverty traps in small-scale mining communities of Sub-Saharan Africa. *Canadian Journal of Development Studies, 33*(2), 180–197.
Holford, J. (1995). Why social movements matter: Adult education theory, cognitive praxis and the creation of knowledge. *Adult Education Quarterly, 45*(2), 95–111.
Holloway, J. (2010). *Crack capitalism*. New York, NY: Pluto Press.
Höller, C., & Mbembe, A. (2002). Africa in motion: An interview with the post-colonialism theoretician Achille Mbembe. *Cosmopolitics, Springerin, 3*(2). Retrieved from http://www.springerin.at/dyn/heft.php?id=32&pos=o&textid=o&lang=en
Holst, J. D. (2002). *Social movements, civil society, and radical adult education*. London: Bergin & Garvey.
Hutchful, E. (2002). *Ghana's adjustment experience: The paradox of reform*. Geneva: UNRI.
James, C. L. R. (1977). *Nkrumah and the Ghana revolution*. Westport, CT: Lawrence Hill & Co.
Kane, L. (2001). Popular education and social change in Latin America. London: Latin American Bureau.
Kapoor, D. (2008). Subaltern social movement learning and the decolonization of space in India. *International Education, 37*(1), 10–41.
Kapoor, D. (2009). Participatory academic research (par) and people's Participatory Action Research (PAR): Research, politicization, and subaltern social movements in India. In D. Kapoor & S. Jordan (Eds.), *Education, participatory action research, and social change* (pp. 29–44). New York, NY: Palgrave Macmillan.
Karpiak, I. (2000). Writing our life: Adult learning and teaching through autobiography. *Canadian Journal of University Continuing Education, 26*(1), 31–50.
Kelley, R. D. G. (2002). *Freedom dreams: The Black radical imagination*. Boston, MA: Beacon Press.
Kenyon, G. M., & W. L. Randall. (1997). *Restorying our lives: Personal growth through autobiographical reflection*. Westport, CT: Praeger.
Kilgore, D. W. (1999). Understanding learning in social movements: A theory of collective learning. *International Journal of Lifelong Education, 18*(3), 191–202.

REFERENCES

Kluttz, J., & Walter, P. (2018). Conceptualizing learning in the climate justice movement. *Adult Education Quarterly, 68*(2), 91–107.

LADA. (2018). *Legal opinion on Songor Lagoon.* Accra: Law and Development Associates (LADA).

Langdon, J. (2009a). *Democracy and social movement learning in Ghana: Reflections on 15 years of learning in the democratic terrain by Ghanaian activist-educators* (PhD thesis). McGill University, Montreal.

Langdon, J. (2009b). Learning to sleep without perching: Reflections of activist-educators on learning in Ghanaian social movements. *McGill Journal of Education, 44*(1), 79–105.

Langdon, J. (2010). Contesting globalization in Ghana: Communal resource defense and social movement learning. *Journal of Alternative Perspectives in the Social Sciences, 2*(1), 309–339.

Langdon, J. (2011a). Social movement learning in Ghana: Communal defense of resources. In D. Kapoor (Ed.), *Critical perspectives on neoliberal globalization, development and education in Africa and Asia*/Pacific (pp. 153–170). Rotterdam, The Netherlands: Sense Publishers.

Langdon, J. (2011b). Democracy re-examined: Ghanaian social movement learning and the re-articulation of learning in struggle. *Studies in the Education of Adults, 43*(2), 147–163.

Langdon, J. (2015). Democratic hopes, transnational government (re)ality: Grounded social movements and the defense of communal natural resources in Ghana. In D. Kapoor & D. Caouette (Eds.), *Beyond colonialism, development and globalization* (pp. 49–66). London: Zed Books.

Langdon, J., & Anyidoho, N. A. (2016). Ghana: vitalité du militantisme en démocratie. In F. Polet (Ed.), *État des Résistances dans le Sud d'Afrique.* Louvain-la-Neuve, Belgium: CETRI.

Langdon, J., Cameron, S., Quarmyne, W., & Larweh, K. (2013) *Community radio and social activism: A case study of the tension between neutrality and activism in Ada, Ghana.* Paper presented at the Canadian Communication Association conference, Victoria.

Langdon, J., & Garbary, R. (2017). Retor(y)ing hope: Stories as social movement learning in Ada Songor salt movement. *Education as Change, 21*(3), 1–18.

Langdon, J., & Larweh, K. (2014). Seeing the synergy in the signals: Reflections on weaving projects into social movement mobilizing through community radio. In H. Pleasants & D. Salter (Eds.), *Community-based multiliteracies and digital media projects: Questioning assumptions and exploring realities.* New York, NY: Peter Lang.

Langdon, J., & Larweh, K. (2015). Moving with the movement: Collaboratively building a Participatory Action Research (PAR) study of social movement learning in Ada, Ghana. *Action Research, 13*(3), 281–297. doi:10.1177/1476750315572447

Langdon, J., & Larweh, K. (2017). Guided by the Yomo spirit: Resistance to accumulation by dispossession of the Songor salt lagoon in Ada, Ghana. In D. Kapoor (Ed.), *Against colonization and rural dispossession: Local resistance in South/East Asia-Pacific and Africa.* London: Zed Books.

Langdon, J., Larweh, K., & Cameron, S. (2014). The Thumbless hand, the dog and the chameleon: Enriching social movement learning theory through epistemically grounded narratives emerging from a participatory action research case study in Ghana. *Interface, 6*(1), 27–44.

Larzilliere, P. (2016). *Activism in Jordan.* Chicago, IL: University of Chicago Press.

LeBon, G. (1896). *The crowd: A study of the popular mind.* New York, NY: T. Fischer Unwin.

Mamdani, M. (1996). *Citizen and subject: Contemporary Africa and the legacy of late colonialism.* Princeton, NJ: Princeton University Press.

Mamdani, M. (1998). Africa: Democratic theory and democratic struggles. In M. Mohanty, P. N. Mukherji, & O. Tornquist (Eds.), *People's rights: Social movements and the state in the third world* (pp. 83–98). New Delhi: Sage Publications.

Mamdani, M., & Wamba-dia-wamba, E. (Eds.). (1995). *African studies in social movements and democracy.* Dakar: CODESRIA.

Manuh, T. (1991). Women and their organisation during the convention people's party period. In K. Arhin (Ed.), *The life and work of Kwame Nkrumah* (pp. 108–134). Accra: Sedco Publishing.

Manuh, T. (1992). Survival in rural Africa: The salt co-operatives in Ada District, Ghana. In D. R. F. Taylor & F. Mackenzie (Eds.), *Development from within: Survival in rural Africa* (pp. 102–104). New York, NY: Routledge.

Marfleet, P. (2016). The political subject in the 'Arab Spring.' *Contemporary Levant, 1*(1), 4–11.

REFERENCES

Mattingly, C. (1991). Narrative reflections on practical actions: Two learning experiments in reflective storytelling. In D. A. Schön (Ed.), *The reflective turn: Case studies in and on educational practice*. New York, NY: Teachers College Press.
McMichael, P. (2009). *Development and social change* (4th ed.). New York, NY: Sage.
McTaggart, R. (1991). Principles of participatory research. *Adult Education Quarterly, 41*(3), 168–187.
Melucci, A. (1980). The new social movements: A theoretical approach. *Theory and Methods, 19*(2), 199–226.
Mentinis, M. (2006). *Zapatistas: The Chiapas revolt and what it means for radical politics*. London: Pluto Press.
Mignolo, W. (2000). *Local histories/global designs: Coloniality, subaltern knowledges and border thinking*. Princeton, NJ: Princeton University Press.
Mulholland, J., & Wallace, J. (2003). Strength, Sharing and Service: Restorying and the legitimation of research texts. *British Educational Research Journal, 29*(1).
Neocosmos, M. (2006). *From 'Foreign Natives' to 'Native Foreigners': Explaining Xenophobia in Post-apartheid South Africa*. Dakar, Senegal: Council for the development of social science research in Africa.
Newman, M. (1994). *Defining the enemy: Adult education in social action*. Paddington: Stewart Victor Publishing.
Newman, M. (2006). *Teaching defiance: Stories and strategies for activist eduators*. San Francisco, CA: Jossey-Bass.
Ninsin, K. A. (2007). Markets and liberal democracy. In K. Boafo-Arthur (Ed.), *Ghana: One decade of the liberal state* (pp. 86–105). London: Zed Books & CODESRIA.
Nkrumah, K. (1957). *First independence day speech*. Retrieved from https://www.myjoyonline.com/news/2017/March-6th/full-text-first-independence-speech-by-kwame-nkrumah.php
Nkrumah, K. (1973). *Revolutionary path*. London: International Publishers.
Patel, R. (2006). A short course in politics at the University of Abahlali baseMjondolo. In A. Alexander & R. Pithouse (Eds.), *Yonk'indawo umzabalazo uyasivumela: new work from Durban* (pp. 81–99). Durban: Centre for Civil Society.
Perini, J. (2008). Art as intervention: A guide to today's radical art practices. In K. Van Meter, C. Hughes, & S. Peace (Eds.), *Uses of a Whirlwind: Movement, movements, and contemporary radical currents in the United States* (pp. 183–197). Oakland, CA: AK Press.
Prah, M. (2007). *Ghana's feminist movement: aspirations, challenges, achievements*. Accra: Institute of Democratic Governance.
Pithouse, R. (2006). 'Our struggle is thought, on the ground, running': The University of Abahlali baseMjondolo. In A. Alexander & R. Pithouse (Eds.), *Yonk'indawo umzabalazo uyasivumela: New work from Durban* (pp. 5–47). Durban: Centre for Civil Society.
Radio Ada. (2002). *Radio Ada Oral Testimony Documentary: Resource Conflict – The Songor Lagoon*. Ada, Ghana: Radio Ada.
Rancière, J. (1999). *Disagreement: Politics and philosophy* (J. Rose, Trans.). Minneapolis, MN: University of Minnesota Press. (Original work published in 1995)
Randall, W. (1996). Restorying a life: Adult education and transformative learning. In J. E. Birren (Ed.), *Aging and biography: Explorations in adult development*. New York, NY: Springer.
Rodney, W. (1973). *How Europe underdeveloped Africa*. Dar-Es-Salam, Tanzania: Bogle-L'Ouverture Publications.
Rossiter, M. (2002). *Narrative and stories in adult teaching and learning*. Columbus, OH: ERIC Clearinghouse on Adult, Career, and Vocational Education.
Shillington, K. (1992). *Ghana and the Rawlings factor*. New York, NY: St. Martin's Press.
Spencer, B. (1995). Old and new social movements as learning sites: Greening labor unions and unionizing the greens. *Adult Education Quarterly, 46*(1), 31–42.
Sutton, I. (1981). The volta river salt trade: The survival of an indigenous industry. *The Journal of African History, 22*(1), 43–61. doi:10.1017/S0021853700019009
Third World Network-Africa. (2017). *Towards optimal exploitation of salt from the Keta Lagoon Basin in Ghana*. Accra, Ghana: Third World Network – Africa.

REFERENCES

Tilly, C. (1998). *Durable inequality*. Oakland, CA: University of California Press.
Tuck, E., & Yang, K. W. (2012). Decolonization is not a metaphor. *Decolonization: Indigeneity, Education & Society, 1*(1), 1–40.
UN General Assembly. (2007, October 2). *United Nations declaration on the rights of indigenous peoples: Resolution adopted by the general assembly* (A/RES/61/295).
United Nations. (2015). *Sustainable development goals report 2016*. UN.
Vincent, S. (2012). *Dimensions of development: History, community and change in Allpachico, Peru*. Toronto: University of Toronto Press.
Walter, P. (2007). Adult learning in new social movements: Environmental protest and the struggle for the clayoquot sound rainforest. *Adult Education Quarterly, 57*(3), 248–263.
Walters, S. (2005). Social movements, class, and adult education. *New Directions for Adult & Continuing Education, 106*, 53–62.
Welton, M. (1993). .Social revolutionary learning: The new social movements as learning sites. *Adult Education Quarterly, 43*(3), 152–164.
Welton, M. (1995). In defense of the lifeworld: A Habermasian approach to adult Learning. In M. Welton (Ed.), *In defense of the lifeworld: Critical perspectives on adult learning* (pp. 1–10). Albany, NY: State University of New York Press.
Welton, M. (2001). Civil society and the public sphere: Habermas's recent learning theory. *Studies in the Education of Adults, 33*(1), 20–34.
Yeebo, Z. (2007). *Ghana: 1957–2007, a brief political overview*. Retrieved Febraury, 2009, from http://ghanaianoracle.wordpress.com/the-history-of-ghana/
Yihi Katsemɛ. (2017, August 15). *Songor our life, Atsiakpo, our death!* [Theatre performance]. Accra, Ghana.
Zikode, S. (2006). The third force. In A. Alexander & R. Pithouse (Eds.), *Yonk'indawo umzabalazo uyasivumela: new work from Durban* (pp. 1–4). Durban: Centre for Civil Society.
Zikode, S. (2014, October 20–21). *Twenty years of hell in shacks*. Paper presented at the DDP Conference on 'Twenty Years of Local Democracy in South Africa,' Durban. Retrieved from http://abahlali.org/node/14413/

INDEX

A

Abahlali baseMjondolo movement, (South African shackdwellers movement), 19, 24, 37–38, 140, 142, 149
Accumulation by Dispossession, 6, 7, 43
Activism, 3, 6, 7, 24, 32, 33, 36, 38, 46, 68, 70, 72, 75, 94, 97, 102, 108, 112–114, 118, 126, 141, 146–148, 150
  digital activism, 36
Ada
  history of, 6, 14, 82, 125
Ada communities
  Adzomanikorpey, 66
  Agbedrafor, 53
  Anyamam, 70
  Bonikope, 41, 56, 136
  Koluedor, 53, 55
  Lolonya, 67
  Lufenya, 70, 114
  Luhuor, 70
  Okorngmleku, 58
  Sege, 47, 57, 120–122, 125, 127, 129, 132, 134, 142, 151
  Toflokpo-Kpalamkorpey, 53
  Dawa, 56, 59
  Goi, 70, 81–83, 89, 94, 95, 100
Ada Songor Advocacy Forum (ASAF), 7, 10, 11, 69, 70, 72, 78, 79–89, 91, 94–102, 105–107, 111, 113, 114, 117, 126, 127, 140, 141, 148, 153, 157
Ada Salt Cooperative, 55
Adibiawe, 45, 103, 120
Adivasi movements (India), 24
Amattey, C.O.C., 51

Ametor-Williams, Eunice, 52, 125, 154
Amissah Commission, 50, 59, 60–63, 73, 86, 87, 155
  White Paper, 62
Adams, Alhassan, 3, 5, 71
Agyeyomah, Coleman, 3, 5
Akosombo dam, 49, 153
Akuse, 50
Akuteye, Mary (President, Yihi Katsɛmɛ), 69, 97, 132, 134, 139, 142, 145, 148–150
Algeria, 18, 27
  liberation struggles, 29, 30
Algerian National Liberation Front (FLN), 29
Amate, C.O.C, 45, 48, 51
Amin, Samir, 35, 143
Anyidoho, Nana Akua, 34
Apetorgbor, Albert Adinortey, 46, 60
Arab Spring, 34, 35
Asafotufiami festival, 46, 70, 71, 90, 92, 95, 99, 111–114, 119–123, 125, 126, 132, 142, 145, 148, 151, 157
Ashanti, 46, 48
Asiedu, Michael, 56
ASSWA (Ada Songor Salt Women's Association), 79, 84, 108. *See also* Yihi Katsɛmɛ
Atsiakpo, 7, 12, 64, 65, 67, 68, 70, 78, 87, 88, 90, 119, 120, 123, 124, 129, 132, 136, 141, 149, 157
Ayine, Dominic, 62

B

Barndt, Deborah, 24, 112
Battle of Dodowa of 1866, 46

INDEX

Branch, Adam, 17, 18, 20, 27, 30–32, 34, 35, 143
Bratton, Michael, 32

C
Cabral, Amilcar, 19–21, 25, 31, 38, 142, 147
Carroll, William K., 20
Chamberlin, J. E., 77
Choudry, Aziz, 8, 9, 24, 25, 77
Chovanec, Donna, 24
Colonialism, 1, 19, 21, 30, 48
Committees for Defence of the Revolution (CDRs), 32, 52
Community radio, 5, 11, 14, 18, 65, 72, 108, 127, 147, 151
Cudjoe, Hanna, 31
Cross-fader, 20, 22

D
Dangme, 6, 10, 44, 45, 64, 65, 78, 80, 89, 92, 97, 103, 113, 124, 125, 140, 150
Dangbebiawe, 45, 120
Democratization, 3, 4, 27, 31, 32, 34, 38, 41, 42, 79, 103, 120, 128, 129, 132, 136, 143
Dialogue-based movements, 4
Dixon, Chris, 21
Djah, Gifty, 3
Doku, Sohia, 31

E
Egypt, 19, 35, 36, 143
El-Hamalawy, Hossam, 36
English, Leona M., 24, 25, 78, 92, 97, 124, 125, 140, 147, 150
Ewe, 46

F
Fanon, Frantz, 29–31, 38, 139, 142, 146, 147

Foley, Griff, 4, 8, 22, 23, 28, 30, 101, 144, 150
Foucault, Michel, 43, 83

G
Gariba, Sulley, 34
Gerschiere, Peter, 47, 48
Gellner, David N., 24
Ghana Economic Recovery Program (ERP), 54, 61
Galamsey, 123, 127, 128, 137
Gramsci, Antonio, 2, 20, 21, 83
Guha, Ranajit, 21, 83
Guinea-Bissau, 19, 21, 31

H
Hall, Budd L., 8
Harley, Anne, 24, 25, 37, 38, 140, 142
Hilson, Gavin, 72
Holloway, John, 26
Holst, John D., 20, 23
Hushie, Lawer, 54, 63, 72, 105, 155

I
Ibrahim, Tanko, 3
India, 21, 24

J
James, C. L. R., 27

K
Kane, Liam, 8, 25
Kantamanso war of 1826, 46
Kapoor, Dip, 8, 9, 21, 24, 25, 72, 77, 140, 148
Kelley, Robin, 20, 21
Kitcher, Rev. Sophia, 83, 91, 92, 95, 113, 130, 146
Kume Preko, 33
Kuwornu, Maggie, 6, 41, 50, 56, 57, 59, 123

L

Land Use Plan, 61, 65, 66, 70, 148, 156
Langdon, Jonathan, ix–xi, 25
Lanuer, Thomas Ocloo, 41
Larweh, Kofi, ix, 3, 5, 10, 25, 46, 64, 68, 77, 83, 84, 86, 107, 108, 114, 116, 126, 139, 142, 150
Larzilliere, Penelope, 24
Lawer, Akpetiyo, 65, 68, 69, 78, 112, 114
Liberation movements, ix, 18, 19, 25, 27, 30, 31
Libi Wornor, 44, 45, 47, 48, 67, 123
Lomobiawe, 45, 103, 120, 155
Le Bon, Gustav, 20
Luxemburg, Rosa, 1, 21

M

Mahama, John, 115, 122, 132
Mamdani, Mahmood, 1, 13, 17, 22, 25, 32, 37, 38
Mampilly, Zachariah, 17, 18, 20, 27, 30–32, 34, 35, 143
Manuh, Takyiwaa, 44, 47, 64, 74, 85, 87
Marfleet, Philip, 35–37, 143
Marxism, 21
Master Plan, Songor, 7, 60, 61, 63–66, 68, 71, 72–75, 93, 94, 126, 131, 144, 151, 155, 156
Mayo, Peter, 24, 25
Mbembe, Achille, 56
McMichael, Philip, 56
Mekporgbey Lawerteh, 56
Melucci, Alberto, 21
Mining Act, Ghana (Act 703), 61, 66, 75
"Moving with the movement", 5, 108, 150
Movement for Freedom and Justice (MJF) (Ghana), 33

N

Nene Ada, 46, 47, 50, 81–83, 89, 93, 99, 112, 115–117, 121, 125
Nene Akwada, 47
Nene Kabu Abram Akuaku III (current Nene Ada), 53
Nene Korley II, 51, 77
Nene Pediator, 49, 81
Neocosmos, Michael, x, xi, 37
Newman, Michael, 4, 24
New Social Movements (NSMs), 2, 21
Ninsin, Kwame A., 33
Nkrumah, Kwame, 17, 27–29, 31, 33, 38, 49, 51, 139, 142, 143, 146, 147
NƆ NƐ NƆ KO LI Ɔ, NƆ KO LE, 122, 114
Nyerere, Julius Kambarage, 31

O

Okor clans, 45, 46, 61, 66, 69, 81, 99, 103, 104, 120, 123, 157
Ocansey, Doris, 56, 59
Ocansey, Jane (Treasurer, Yihi Katsɛmɛ), 69, 89, 92, 125, 148
Occupy Ghana, 34
Osabutey, Edith (Secretary, Yihi Katsɛmɛ), 117

P

Patel, Raj, 37
Patriotic Front liberation movement/army (Zimbabwe), 30
Pedagogy of creative dissent, 111, 112
People's Defence Committee, 32, 56
People's National Defence Council (PNDC), 7, 32, 33, 42, 52, 54, 55, 61–63, 73, 75, 86, 122, 123, 130, 147, 149, 155–157
PNDC Mining law 153, 61, 62
PNDC Songor law 287, 7, 42, 61, 62, 73, 75, 86, 122, 123, 130, 147, 149, 155–157

INDEX

Post-colonialism, 2, 20, 25, 43, 143
Protests, ix, x, 17–20, 23, 27, 31–36, 111, 143, 154, 157

Q

Quake, Leticia, 31
Queen Mothers, 91, 99, 113, 141, 144, 145, 151

R

Radio Ada, 5, 7, 10, 11, 14, 29, 52, 64, 65, 67–70, 78–83, 88–90, 92, 95, 97, 104, 107, 108, 112, 114–116, 119, 120–129, 132, 134, 136, 141, 142, 144–146, 148, 150, 151, 157
Rancière, Jacques, 26
Rawlings, Jerry John, 33, 52, 53, 56, 59, 63, 65, 155

S

Salt winning, 6, 7, 12, 45, 47, 48, 52, 56, 64, 68–71, 73, 88, 90, 91, 95, 107, 113, 128, 131, 139, 153, 155
Social Movement Learning (SML)
  incidental and informal processes of learning, 22
  knowledge production, 1, 6, 14, 22, 24, 39, 65, 72, 73, 77, 100, 102, 108, 112, 120, 130, 132
  learning *in* struggle, x, 4, 22, 23, 28, 30, 31, 81, 84, 101, 150, 151
  learning *through* struggle, x, 4, 23, 120, 150
  learning *to* struggle, x, 4, 23, 150, 151
Socialist movement, Ghana, 4, 33, 143
Songor Lagoon, 1, 3, 5–7, 10, 13, 39, 41, 44–46, 48, 50–53, 60–62, 90, 92, 100, 101, 103, 107, 115, 121, 122, 130, 132, 139, 144, 149
Songor, Our Life, Atsiakpo, Our Death!, 78, 119, 123, 124, 141, 149

South Africa
  Abahlali baseMjondolo movement, 19, 37, 140
  apartheid, 35, 37, 139
  post-apartheid, 37
Struggle of the Songor Salt People, The, 44, 50, 54, 59, 61, 63, 69, 73, 75, 87, 100–102, 105, 107
Subaltern, 2, 14, 18, 19, 21, 25, 26, 35, 41–43, 83, 84, 108, 140
Subaltern social movements, ix, x, 13, 19, 21, 25, 38, 72, 143, 148
Structural Adjustment Programs (SAPs), 32

T

Tahrir Square, Egypt, 19, 35, 143
Tamale, 3, 5, 46
Tanzania, 31
Tekperbiawe, 44, 45, 48, 50, 51, 53, 77, 93, 103, 104, 120, 144
Turray, Thomas, 8

U

United Nations Sustainable Development Goals, 75, 122, 130, 131
  SDGs High Level Forum, 14, 130
United Nations Declaration of the Rights of the Indigenous (UNDRIP), 75, 122, 123, 130, 149

V

Vacuum Salt Products Limited, 50, 51, 53, 54, 56, 58
Van de Walle, Nicolas, 32
Veranda boys, 17, 27, 28

W

Walter, Shirley, 8, 24, 25
Wamba Dia Wamba, Ernest, 32
Who Killed Maggie, 50, 54, 56, 63, 73, 100–102, 105, 157

INDEX

Women's Movement, Ghana, 3, 130, 142
World Bank, 8, 32, 49, 52, 54, 131

Y
Yeebo, Zaya, 52
Yihi Katsɛmɛ (Brave Women!), 7, 11, 12, 14, 72, 74, 75, 77, 84, 87, 89, 96, 97, 99, 100, 102, 111–116, 118–126, 129, 130, 132, 133, 135, 136, 139–149, 151, 152

Nsawam, 113, 122
Manifesto "Songɔ wɔ kulaa wa nɔ!!" ("Songor for All!!), 74, 77, 87, 117, 121, 142
Yomo, 44–47, 49, 51, 52, 67, 70, 81, 93, 94, 113, 114, 119, 120, 141, 142, 147, 152–154

Z
Zikode, S'bu, ix, 25, 37, 140

Printed in the United States
By Bookmasters